D0938932

Declaring Disaster

DECLARING DISASTER

Buffalo's Blizzard of '77
and the Creation of FEMA

Timothy W. Kneeland

Syracuse University Press

ST. JOHN THE BAPTIST PARISH LIBRARY
2920 NEW HIGHWAY 51
LAPLACE, LOUISIANA 70068

Copyright © 2021 by Syracuse University Press
Syracuse, New York 13244-5290

All Rights Reserved

First Edition 2021

21 22 23 24 25 26   6 5 4 3 2 1

∞ The paper used in this publication meets the minimum requirements
of the American National Standard for Information Sciences—Permanence
of Paper for Printed Library Materials, ANSI Z39.48-1992.

For a listing of books published and distributed by Syracuse University Press,
visit https://press.syr.edu.

ISBN: 978-0-8156-3699-1 (hardcover)
      978-0-8156-1127-1 (paperback)
      978-0-8156-5511-4 (e-book)

Library of Congress Cataloging-in-Publication Data
Names: Kneeland, Timothy W., 1962– author.
Title: Declaring disaster : Buffalo's blizzard of '77 and the creation of FEMA /
    Timothy W. Kneeland.
Description: First edition. | Syracuse : Syracuse University Press, 2021. | Includes
    bibliographical references and index. | Summary: "Buffalo's 1977 blizzard was
    the first snowstorm to be declared a disaster in US history and, in "Declaring
    Disaster," Kneeland offers a compelling examination of whether the 1977 storm
    was an anomaly or the inevitable outcome of years of city planning. From the
    local to the state and federal levels, Kneeland discusses governmental response
    and disaster relief, showing how this regional event had national implications
    for environmental policy and how its effects have resounded through the
    complexities of disaster politics long after the snow fell"— Provided by publisher.
Identifiers: LCCN 2020027498 (print) | LCCN 2020027499 (ebook) |
    ISBN 9780815636991 (hardcover) | ISBN 9780815611271 (paperback) |
    ISBN 9780815655114 (ebook)
Subjects: LCSH: Blizzards—New York (State)—Buffalo. | Disaster relief—New York
    (State) | United States. Federal Emergency Management Agency—History.
Classification: LCC HV636 1977.B84 K54 2020 (print) | LCC HV636 1977.B84 (ebook) |
    DDC 363.34/925097479709047—dc23
LC record available at https://lccn.loc.gov/2020027498
LC ebook record available at https://lccn.loc.gov/2020027499

Manufactured in the United States of America

*Dedicated to my wife Laura
and with gratitude to all of those
who work in the often thankless
job of keeping the roads open
and dry in the winter.*

Announced by all the trumpets of the sky,
Arrives the snow, and driving o'er the fields,
Seems nowhere to alight: the whited air
Hides hills and woods, the river, and the heaven,
And veils the farmhouse at the garden's end.
The sled and traveler stopped, the courier's feet delayed
All friends shut out, the housemates sit
Around the radiant fireplace,
Enclosed in a tumultuous privacy of storm.

—Ralph Waldo Emerson

Contents

Illustrations

Acknowledgments

Although writing a book is oftentimes a solitary affair, making a book is a community effort. This study draws on the ideas of scholars from diverse fields of research, such as natural disaster policy, automobility, and New York State politics. Access to their ideas came through dozens of books and articles obtained from libraries, which I could not have accessed without the assistance of the fine interlibrary loan staff at Nazareth College.

The primary material for this work is drawn from archives in locations ranging from Washington, DC, to Kansas City. My thanks to the archivists and staff at the National Archives in College Park, Maryland; the New York State Archives in Albany, New York; librarians and staff at the Central Library in downtown Buffalo, New York; and the archives of the State University of New York at Buffalo. A special thanks is due to staff at the Missouri Historical Society in Kansas City, Missouri, which holds the American Public Works Association records. I spent several days visiting this archive during the summer of 2013, and the staff was as warm and gracious as the weather. Similarly, the staff and archivists at the Jimmy Carter Presidential Library and Museum in Atlanta, Georgia, made me feel very welcome in December 2012.

I wish to thank those people who agreed to be interviewed, including the late Ned Regan, who was an Erie County executive at the time of the Blizzard; corporation council Les Foschio; and countless others who shared personal stories of their experience in the Blizzard of '77. Although their stories may not have been included here, I have kept them in mind when constructing the book.

This work also benefited from the insights and wisdom of my colleagues in the Rochester US Historians (RUSH) group. Their encouragement and suggestions have been greatly appreciated during the years I worked on this project.

Finally, I should acknowledge the many hours my wife Laura dedicated to this work; her editorial insights vastly improved the book.

Abbreviations

APWA	American Public Works Association
FDAA	Federal Disaster Assistance Administration
FEMA	Federal Emergency Management Agency
HUD	Housing and Urban Development
JCPL	Jimmy Carter Presidential Library
OEP	Office of Emergency Preparedness
OMB	Office of Management and Budget
SEMO	State Emergency Management Office

Declaring Disaster

Introduction

Snow Control, Public Policy,
and the Environment

When it first aired on December 9, 1965, the TV special *A Charlie Brown Christmas* perfectly encapsulated a romantic image of snow, which is depicted in the background of the animated program as soft curves. Snow is something the children play in and play with, and even something for them to eat as the Peanuts characters catch snowflakes on their tongues. Vince Guaraldi's delightful musical score plays as the snow falls heavily, reinforcing this idealized version of snow as friendly and fun. Throughout the story, the white snow stands in opposition to the garish artificial colors and commercialized spirit that threatens the meaning of Christmas.[1]

In stark contrast to this idealized view of snow were warnings from those charged with keeping snow and ice off American roads and highways during the same era. They imagined snow as an existential threat to mobility, and G. E. Taylor warned attendees at the annual American Public Works Conference in 1958 that snow was a danger to modern society. He reminded his audience that "almost all essential services vital to health, safety, and welfare of our citizens are now motorized." Still, Taylor said, a snowstorm could stop traffic and shut down travel: "Imagine how disastrous it would be if milk, food, or fuel deliveries were held up for even a short time, or the chaos that would result if the movements of official equipment, police cars, ambulances or emergency repair trucks were seriously interrupted and hampered by impassible streets."[2]

Throughout the mid-1960s, academics and public works employees raised the idea that snow was a threat to urban mobility. Sociologists working at the Disaster Research Center at Ohio State University expressed concern that a snowstorm could trigger an urban disaster.[3] Moreover, with some amazement, urban historian Blake McKelvey recognized that even a moderate-sized snowstorm could cause significant disruption to American cities. Meanwhile, geographer John F. Rooney Jr. created a scale to measure the adverse effects of snow on cities. Thus, by the 1960s, experts from many fields were increasingly aware of how snow was a potentially deadly foe that needed to be controlled.[4]

At first, this threat was only viewed as a potential disaster and existed mainly in the imagination of public works personnel, urban historians, and geographers. Their work had little impact beyond their professions, and the public did not feel threatened by the hazards of winter. However, the threat became a reality on Friday, January 28, 1977, when a blizzard struck Buffalo, New York, bringing subzero wind chills and whiteout conditions that lasted for days. The blizzard killed twenty-nine people, stranded tens of thousands more, disabled public utilities, paralyzed regional transportation, and caused millions of dollars in economic losses and property damage.

A million people lived in the Buffalo metropolitan region when the blizzard hit, and for a week they faced grave challenges. Snowdrifts twenty to thirty feet high buried houses, inundated highways, and stalled air and rail travel. The immobilized residents found it nearly impossible to meet their essential needs, and it took the combined resources of local, state, and federal governments to rescue Buffalo and its environs. Moved by the plight of the people of western New York, President Jimmy Carter issued the first disaster declaration on account of snow.

Policymaking

This book examines the Blizzard of 1977 as a pivotal point in American policymaking. Buffalo, the first city to be designated a major disaster area due to snow, became the tipping point for how the long-term policy of preferential treatment of private automobiles over rail-driven public transport created conditions for a disaster. The blizzard exposed the vanity of officials across the United States who had constructed a system of transportation that necessitated bare, dry pavements in winter so that travel to and from the suburbs and cities for work, school, and shopping would remain unimpeded. This policy could be managed only through the increased use of technology and deicing with road salt, which allowed plows to clear pavements. Salt became popular after World War II, and its growth was stimulated by the Salt Institute, which represented firms that mined and processed salt. However, the reliance on salt came with an environmental price tag that experts are only now beginning to calculate.

The dependency on rubber tires, the suburbanization of the population, and the natural conditions of lake-effect snow and blizzards in western New York combined to create the disaster known as the Blizzard of 1977. It moved President Jimmy Carter to declare the first major disaster for snow. Carter's decision resulted from intense political pressure by the New York State congressional delegation and the influence of the powerful Democrat Joseph Crangle Jr. These circumstances point to an essential factor in understanding disasters—that is, the role of public officials in the United States, who rarely separate political considerations from public policy. In this case, the political decision was a response not only to the snowstorm but also to the perilous economic situation in Buffalo.

Impoverished and nearly bankrupt, the city of Buffalo had few resources to draw upon when the blizzard struck, and it was driven further into debt by the feeble attempt to manage the crisis. Hugh Carey, the governor of New York, had the resources to assist in immediate snow removal but did not have the financial wherewithal to aid Buffalo. Carey had already overextended the state by tying its fortunes to New York City in 1975, and doing the same with Buffalo in 1977 was politically out of the question. A federal disaster declaration allowed the entire cost of snow removal to fall on the federal government rather than come out of the city's coffers. Desperate to keep Buffalo solvent, Jimmy Carter made a disaster declaration but spent the rest of his presidency rejecting similar requests from other regions. To strengthen his hand over disaster policy, President Carter created the Federal Emergency Management Agency (FEMA).

The blizzard provoked a series of changes in public policy, which are explored in some depth in the following chapters. During the remainder of Carter's presidency, the federal government refused to issue another disaster declaration for a snowstorm. Ronald Reagan and George H. W. Bush followed suit during what some have called the "no dough for snow" era of federal policy. Their successors in the White House have not been so scrupulous with public funding and happily mix politics with policy when it comes to making winter-weather declarations even for limited amounts of snow.

Federal policy formulated the outlines of what constituted a winter disaster while Buffalo and the state of New York developed plans that created more effective snow-fighting procedures, enhanced planning and coordination, and a willingness to impose driving bans to keep populations safe. Driving bans were unpopular and politically toxic for politicians in the twentieth century, but in the last decade or so, they have been imposed even before a storm hits. This shift happened because of the changing definition of mobility in the twenty-first century. Whereas the car culture defined twentieth-century mobility, in the twenty-first century mobility arises from the internet and has reduced the dependency on rubber-tired motor vehicles.

Public Policy and the Rise of Automobility

The Buffalo disaster resulted from decades of public policy that led Americans to become entirely dependent on rubber-tired vehicles to move goods, services, and people in and out of cities. Rubber-tired vehicles that run on asphalt roadways are hindered by snow and ice in a way that trains, trams, and even horse-drawn sleighs are not. Once Americans abandoned older forms of transportation, it was only a matter of time before a storm of the magnitude that struck Buffalo would lead to near economic collapse.

In the pages that follow, readers will learn how changes in modes of transportation made Americans more vulnerable to snow and ice in the twentieth century. Blizzards and heavy snowfall are relatively frequent in the history of Buffalo, a city prone to lake-effect snow and receiving an average of ninety-four inches of snow a year. Despite its geographical location in the Snowbelt, Buffalo managed to survive storms and blizzards for a century and a half before being imperiled by the Blizzard of 1977. This book explores the public policy that encouraged the private automobile and made this disaster inevitable.

To describe the hegemonic rise of the automobile in American society, social scientists have coined the term "automobility." This term emphasizes the central role that cars play in modern political, economic, and cultural life. The term is a play on words and connects the ideal of individual autonomy, or *auto*, with the freedom and liberty to choose when and how to move, or *mobility*, a hallmark of modern society. Government policy in the early twentieth century created conditions favorable to the automobile and allowed it to replace other means of transport.[5]

The rise of the private automobile created a society that perpetuated the myth of Americans as an independent, autonomous, and individualistic people. Automobility brought new social, political, and economic costs that are not always evident to private car owners. These costs include pollution that adds to global climate change, the creation of a US foreign policy set on securing and maintaining control of global oil deposits irrespective of the cost, and as many as 37,000 people killed and 2.3 million injured annually in road accidents in the United States alone.[6]

Automobility came about as interest groups lobbied the government to pass legislation supporting cars. The Good Roads League and the American Automobile Association advocated on behalf of automobile owners. They urged elected officials in cities, counties, states, and the federal government to build new roads, revamp existing streets, and provide other support for automobiles. Lobbying efforts by the Lincoln Highway Association led to a gravel highway running from New York City to San Francisco, a forerunner to the interstate highway system. Efforts by groups like this led to the Dixie Highway, completed in 1915; it runs from Chicago to Miami, and it was funded by the federal government. These and future toll-free roads were paid for by US tax dollars and became available to anyone owning an automobile.[7]

As motorcars replaced preexisting transportation systems, cities became dependent on cars and buses to move goods, services, and people. City planners responded by reshaping the cityscape. They built municipal parking lots, mandated that businesses allow on-street parking in front of their stores and shops, adopted road regulations that required new signage and traffic lights, and paved roads and maintained them to encourage automotive travel. In addition to changes brought about by the government, private enterprises added service stations, car washes, automobile dealerships, and garages to maintain the automobile.

By the end of the twentieth century, the combination of roads, streets, parking lots, automotive service stations, car dealerships, signs and traffic lights, and other elements accommodating automobiles made up nearly half of the physical area of any American city. As cities ceded more space to the car, they removed space from other modes of conveyance, narrowed or removed pedestrian sidewalks, tore up and paved over streetcar lines, and closed subway systems.[8] Roads became the lifeblood of urban areas, so much so that public servants labeled main thoroughfares in cities "arterials" after the blood vessels in the human body. David Williams, a public works manager, once compared traffic congestion to the blockage of arteries in the human body because they both threatened vitality. Williams evoked this image at the American Public Works Association (APWA) North American Snow Conference of 1987. Comparing the city to a creature, Williams said, "the creature regards any interruption of its life-giving flow of people and material as a threat to its existence."[9]

To keep urban arterials clear, federal, state, and local governments have invested heavily in massive infrastructure projects meant to reduce congestion and enhance the flow of cars and trucks into and out of urban areas. In 1920, officials began work on the New York City Vehicular Tunnel, a one-and-one-sixth-mile-long roadway built beneath the Hudson River that opened in 1927 as the Holland Tunnel, the first ventilated roadway in US history.[10]

To maintain traffic flow in Boston, city leaders built the central arterial, a six-lane roadway that opened in the 1950s. After completion, the road allowed more traffic but at the expense of isolating Boston's North End from the rest of the city. The arterial removed entire neighborhoods, which were replaced with the new roadway. By the 1970s, congestion once again threatened Boston. Public officials, bankrolled by the federal government, spent twenty years and $16 billion on the single most expensive public works project in history, the "Big Dig," which revamped traffic flow in and out of Boston. Reflecting on the massive public works projects created to serve the automobile, postmodernist Roland Barthes compared them to the Gothic cathedrals erected in Medieval Europe to serve God.[11]

In modern times the great builders have been men such as Robert Moses, who remade New York State through his vision and ruthless drive for power. Moses single-mindedly reshaped the entirety of the five boroughs of New York City by creating a dozen expressways and many parkways that spread out to the suburbs. Moses wove together and tore apart New York State by creating roadways to the northernmost parts of New York State and across the Niagara frontier to Buffalo.[12]

While Moses remade New York, President Eisenhower remade America. Eisenhower oversaw the building of the most significant public works project in modern history—the 41,000-mile interstate highway system. At the cost of $30 billion, the federal government built four-lane roads running from the East Coast to the West Coast. The interstate system is a project as of yet unfinished as every year sees a new spur, entrance, or exit ramp to accommodate traffic flow.[13]

Although the federal government had a transportation department within the Department of Commerce from the early twentieth century onward, in 1967 President Lyndon Johnson elevated the Department of Transportation (DOT) to cabinet status. The DOT protects the highway systems, feeds the demands for roads, and works with private corporations in promoting US highways.

The importance of the automobile in US policy and the preferential treatment given to it extends well beyond the DOT. The US government used its resources to supply Americans with oil necessary for producing gasoline and asphalt for roads; the US Department of Energy seeks to protect oil resources domestically and overseas; the US Department of State has used diplomacy; and the Department of Defense uses the US military to control and safeguard oil imports from the Middle East.[14]

Government protection of the automobile is not surprising given that, by the 1920s, the car was already synonymous with the American economy and modernity. Henry Ford's mass production of the Model-T spurred individual ownership of automobiles but also signified the modern use of the assembly line, as "Fordism," became the standard for manufacturing and production of all goods in the United States.

Throughout the twentieth century, the automotive industry dominated the national economy, spurred by the manufacture, sales, and service of hundreds of millions of cars built in the United States during the twentieth century along with millions of Americans employed by this industry. At one time, General Motors was not only the largest company in the United States but also the largest corporation in the entire world.

Every car manufactured created forward and backward linkages to the oil, steel, rubber, aluminum, platinum, and concrete industries. Garages, gas stations, and car washes developed to service the automobile. Automobile dealerships and financial institutions such as banks, credit unions, and savings and loan companies benefited from the consumer market for automotive loans. Organizations such as the American Automobile Association (AAA) provided assistance and service to millions of members and promoted driving as a means of tourism.[15] Moreover, highway experts fixated on economic productivity began to track the amount of time lost by Americans in their daily commute.

An automotive fetish accompanied the economic dominance of the car culture and is reflected in the social and intellectual course of American life. To sell automobiles, networks of dealerships spent millions of dollars in advertisements. In order to achieve this, they conceptualized the car as more than a tangible and material object; instead it was portrayed as an ideal of American life. Advertising campaigns featured images of gratification and reinforced gender stereotypes of masculinity and femininity. Through advertising, automobiles became synonymous with an image of Americans as mobile, independent, and individualistic—an image reinforced in literature, television, and movies. Stories of the open road, drag racing, and car chases dominate twentieth-century fiction and entertainment.

Americans enshrined the auto as part of their entertainment. Automotive-inspired song lyrics have inhabited popular music, from the Beach Boys' "Little Deuce Coupe" to Prince's "Little Red Corvette." Most major newspapers, including the *New York Times*, devoted weekly columns to news about the automobile. Cars inspired new forms of competition and sports through racing. NASCAR, the National Association for Stock Car Auto Racing, could boast by the end of the twentieth century that it had more fans than the combined number of fans of all other US sports.[16]

For much of the twentieth century, young adults saw earning a learner's permit or driver's license as a critical rite-of-passage to adulthood. The journey from home to work adapted to the car by creating new rituals such as "drive time," which referred to the time Americans spent in their cars going to and from work. Radio stations added traffic reports and hosted shows built around the idea that listeners were likely to be listening in their vehicles rather than at home. Cars became a mobile living room. Later, automakers added cup holders to allow commuters a space for their morning coffee. The automobile is also a space where many Americans consumed meals. In the 1950s, McDonald's had no indoor seating because people ate in their car. Although indoor seating appeared, so too did the later addition of drive-thru windows, turning the vehicle once again into a substitute dining room.[17]

From the middle of the twentieth century onward, federally sub-sidized highways made it easier for vehicle owners to relocate to the suburbs and own their own homes. Publicly financed roads allowed individuals with cars to live further from the core of American cities and engendered urban sprawl and suburbanization. This spurred the postwar economy by enhancing industries tied to the car, such as steel, the automotive industry, and the construction industry, which built highways and homes. By 1970, half of the residents in any given metropolitan area lived in the suburbs. In Boston, this figure rose to 80 percent of the residential population. As populations relocated, so did businesses. By the early twenty-first century, 60 percent of all urban office space lay along the suburban fringe of freeways and highways.[18]

This is the first study of how automobility functioned to create a new category for a major disaster. Automobility reshaped the US transportation system so that by midcentury modern cities could not exist without cars, buses, and trucks. To maintain the vital services of a city, even in winter, it became imperative to keep traffic flowing. To ensure this flow, public works officials adopted the "bare pave-ment policy," the practice of removing all snow and ice on urban thoroughfares down to the dry pavement to allow drivers to move freely without the impediment of snow and ice. This policy created conditions that were ripe for the disaster that occurred in 1977.

Environmental History

The Buffalo experience is also a case study on how humans have reshaped and adapted to an environment of snow and ice. Although geographers and meteorologists have examined this intersection, environmental historians have done far less.[19] This book suggests a new area of environmental study on how snow patterns shaped the political and social response to winter in the Great Lakes region and created a mythic sense of identity for the people of Buffalo.[20]

The book demonstrates that technologies deployed to combat threats to human mobility were themselves an environmental threat.

This has been especially true of the use of road salt, which became the sine qua non for ensuring winter travel for cars and buses. Snow control policies subsidized and allowed for more significant postwar suburbanization, which was spurred by private automobiles. Rural areas that once had seasonal roads that closed in winter months became part of a suburb or exurb, resulting in an increase in the number of road miles that governments maintained and the amount of salt utilized. Without salt, winter travel in the Snowbelt would be almost impossible.

This book highlights the importance of the Salt Institute, a trade organization that played a critical role in making road salt the deicing standard for the entire United States. Salt altered the dynamic of wintertime travel by making it possible to scrape snow and ice down to the bare pavement. However, salt damages roads, bridges, and cars. More importantly, it is inimical to the environment, and the Canadian government declared road salt a toxic substance in need of regulation.

The book also shows how the Buffalo region has been indelibly shaped by its snowy environment. It has shaped social institutions, technology and identity. At the local level, blizzards and snowstorms have reshaped politics in Buffalo, forced the city to develop new techniques to deal with snow, and created a public image of the town as a frozen wasteland that the people of Western New York continue to struggle against to this day.[21]

Although the Northeast is today better prepared to deal with snow events like the Blizzard of '77, in an era of climate change lessons from this disaster ought to be applied to regions outside of the Northeast that are experiencing stochastic weather patterns, as occurred in December of 2018 when more snow fell on Lubbock, Texas, and Ashville, North Carolina than Anchorage, Alaska.[22]

1

Buffalo and Snow Control

From the Age of Mass Transit
to the Rise of the Automobile

Founded on the eastern shore of Lake Erie, Buffalo, New York, had a few hundred inhabitants until the Erie Canal transformed the small village into a city by 1832. Ultimately, Buffalo's position as the western terminus of the Erie Canal led it to become the "Queen City of the Lakes," serving as the primary hub between New York City and the Midwestern markets via Lake Erie. The addition of multiple railroads through the city furthered trade links among the East Coast, the Great Lakes, and Canada. By its centennial, Buffalo boasted of being the "fourth greatest port of entry and clearance" in the civilized world and the "greatest railroad center in the United States."[1]

Geography provided Buffalo with the ability to become a hub of trade and transport, but the city's location also positioned it to be one of the snowiest places in the eastern part of the United States. Buffalo lies in the Snowbelt, a series of cities that receive six to nine feet of snow every year.[2] Buffalo sits on the eastern shore of Lake Erie, an area prone to lake-effect snowfall. Lake-effect snow occurs when cold air sweeps over Lake Erie and picks up moisture from the lake, which turns into snow once it rides above the more frigid land adjacent to the lake. Although snow falls on Buffalo anytime from October through May, it is most prone to lake-effect storms in December and March when Lake Erie is unfrozen and cold air blowing across the lake picks up moisture and dumps it on the city and its environs. Large-scale lake-effect storms are less frequent after

December because Lake Erie, the shallowest of the Great Lakes, usually freezes by January, thereby reducing the moisture available to make snow. In March, as the ice breaks up, moisture from the lake can fuel late winter and early spring snowstorms.[3]

Snow Control until 1940

Nineteenth-century Americans had a different view of weather than their twenty-first-century descendants. In the era before creation of the National Weather Bureau, forecasting was more art than science, left to publications such as the *Old Farmer's Almanac*, which has been published since 1792. Furthermore, most people saw weather as an act of God, outside of the control of mere humans. Thus, calamities and disasters such as severe snowstorms and blizzards were beyond human control and had to be accepted rather than managed.[4]

Before the twentieth century, falling snow was a hindrance but it was not always considered a disastrous impediment to travel,[5] mainly because Buffalo, like most American cities, remained densely compact.[6] For much of the eighteenth and nineteenth centuries, the average American commuted only one to two miles to and from work, a walking distance of a half-hour or less. People adapted to icy conditions and snow by changing their footwear or converting horse carts to sleighs and sleds. After it snowed, men with shovels cleared streets, leaving just enough snow on the roads to abet sleigh traffic.[7]

The advent of railroads in the 1840s allowed both for a faster means of travel between cities and for people to move farther away from the central city, thereby doubling their commuting radius. In Buffalo, the first railroad ran to Attica, and from there to Rochester and then beyond to Albany and Boston. In 1852 the Erie Railroad connected Buffalo to Hornell and from there to New York City.[8] Travel remained easiest in the summer and hardest in the winter because snow and ice on the tracks slowed mobility and caused trains to derail. To battle snow and ice on roads, railroads initially employed gangs of men to shovel and clear the snow. After a storm in February 1845, the *Commercial Advertiser*, a Buffalo newspaper that began publishing in 1842, noted that the Rochester and Canandaigua Railroad hired 300 men to clear the tracks between those cities.[9]

Frustrated by the delays caused by snow and ice, railroads invented the first snowplows. Designed as large rectangles, these straight plows attached to the engine car and pushed the snow off the tracks. Despite this innovation, heavy snow continued to impede travel. "It sometimes took three days to get from Boston to Portland," a writer in the *Boston Globe* complained.[10] In the 1860s, railways perfected the plow by fashioning it into a wedge shape that pushed the snow to the sides and away from the tracks rather than forward on the tracks. In the 1880s, railroads adopted another innovation in their battle against snow: the rotary blade plow attached to the front engine. Much like a modern snowblower, this device cut into the snow and sent it flying a hundred feet away from the tracks. The Leslie Rotary Snowplow became the industry standard, and with only minor alterations it remains in use today.[11]

Travel within cities improved in the mid-nineteenth century with the invention of horse-drawn streetcars used for interurban travel. Sometimes called omnibuses, these intracity transportation systems expanded the effective commuting distance of residents and allowed for creation of new suburbs. The first horse-car line opened in Buffalo in 1860.[12] Trams and trolleys moved commuters around the commercial center and in and out of the streetcar suburbs. Streetcars, like railroads, ran on tracks requiring only limited amounts of roadspace and could run in nearly all kinds of weather. When snow and ice impeded the tracks, streetcar companies used snowplows to clear the tracks or specially prepared cars to lay down sand. In a heavy snowfall or blizzard, the companies hired gangs of men to shovel the rails manually. In Rochester, New York, this method allowed companies to clear tracks within a day of a significant snowfall or blizzard.[13] In Boston, the streetcar company replaced horse-drawn plows with a "monster rotary plow" that ran along the trolley lines. The *Boston Globe* reported that the machine effectively destroyed any snowdrift.[14]

1. Snowplows were first invented by railroads to help clear the snow from the tracks. This image from 1866 shows an early plow being used in the Midwest. (Photo courtesy of the Library of Congress.)

The advent of urban electrification in the 1880s allowed streetcar lines to replace horse-drawn cars with electric trolleys. Unlike horses that became ill or injured by the weather, electric cars operated faster and more efficiently in nearly all weather. They, too, adopted trolley-driven plows that swept over the tracks quickly and efficiently during typical storms, but even when heavy snow fell, the equipment allowed the car lines to reopen within a day.[15]

Trolley lines did have one weakness—their dependency on electricity, which was carried by wires over city streets, using the same network that competed for space with telegraph and telephone wires.[16] When an early October storm swept across Buffalo in 1906 the winds downed the wires, creating a massive tangle that electrocuted passersby and crippled nearly all communication and transportation, thus forcing citizens to walk to work.[17] The paralysis was only temporary, and within a day the services and communication networks had been patched up and returned to working order.[18] By 1900 Buffalo had grown to a population of 350,000 and was the eighth-largest city in the United States. Residents spread out from the central city to suburbs such as Kenmore and Tonawanda.

Before the advent of municipal street departments, the responsibility for dealing with snow removal fell on the railroads, streetcar lines, and businesspeople who were responsible for keeping their storefronts free of snow. This system often pitted the groups against one another. For example, after eighteen inches of snow fell on Buffalo in January 1865, railroad workers tossed the snow from the tracks and onto the nearby street, thereby blocking roadways and access to local businesses. Angered by this, locals organized into a battalion and began shoveling the snow back onto the tracks, thereby blocking the trains. In response, the directors of the railway ordered their men out to shovel snow off the rails, yet they were unable to compete, and the Main Street railway was stalled.[19]

Despite this incident, the city took no action, and tension continued to simmer between shopkeepers and railroad men until it boiled over again following a massive snowfall in March 1875. According to local papers, "people turned out en masse and began shoveling the snow on the tracks," but snowplows merely swept it back off.[20] Realizing they could not win by merely shoveling the snow onto the tracks, the businessmen and their paid allies began packing snow down into the rails and forced the cars to stop running on Exchange Street. One newspaper, the *Daily Courier*, was appalled by the behavior of the shopkeepers and cited a municipal law that favored the rails.[21]

Conflict returned after heavy snow in January 1877, which saw snowplows sending snow into the front of stores along Genesee Street, thereby blocking trade. This time, to stop the cars, gangs of

2. Interurban trolley lines adopted plows to their cars, and after a snow-storm they could quickly remove snow from the line. In severe snowstorms there might be a need to hire workers to manually remove snow. (Photo courtesy of the Library of Congress.)

men resorted to not only packing down the snow but also adding water, which turned the track into ice. The *Daily Courier* again sided with the railroads: "Filling up the railroad is no laughing matter . . . railroads are the principal means by which people patronize the various mercantile establishments . . . and are near to being an absolute necessity." The article dismissed the idea that sleighs could ever replace railroad cars, which carried considerably more people.[22] Following this incident, the city of Buffalo addressed the responsibility of clearing the streets.

To remove snow from the streets, municipalities adopted the snowplow first used by the railroads. In Buffalo, the first snowplow appeared in the streets on February 3, 1855, and consisted of two boards attached in a wedge shape to a cart, which was pulled by a team of four horses that leveled the snow for sleigh and sled travel.[23] Plows initiated a long history of snow control efforts by private citizens and government authorities in the Northeast.

By the Progressive Era, all municipal governments had reorganized and accepted street cleaning as a corporate responsibility to maintain health and sanitation. Across the United States, municipalities added departments of public works to their municipal structure and either elected or appointed streets commissioners to direct them. From the outset of this new profession, road supervisors complained about the difficulties of snow removal, which was especially true in cities like Boston and Buffalo where narrow, crooked streets made it impossible to employ large snow-removal equipment.[24]

Although nearly half of all urban streets in the United States were unpaved in 1880, the newly organized public works departments began to pave roads as part of their effort to modernize and sanitize their streets. Initially, urban officials laid down cobblestone or macadam roads. In heavily trafficked areas, where horses needed traction, municipal authorities laid cobblestone. The more inexpensive macadam was paved in areas beyond the center city.[25] This practice changed in the 1890s when a series of pamphlets and lectures by civil engineers and health experts sounded the alarm about health risks posed by the unsanitary amount of horse dung dropped on city streets. Health officials in Rochester, New York, suggested that, if gathered together, the total amount of horse manure produced annually in that city alone would fill an acre of ground 175 feet high and provide breeding grounds for sixteen billion flies.[26]

Officials in Buffalo responded to the perceived crisis by paving their streets with asphalt, considered easier to clean and, therefore, healthier for residents.[27] In 1894, Buffalo boasted of being the "best paved" city in the world with 200 miles of "clean, durable, and noiseless" asphalt.[28]

Horses remained on the streets through the opening of the twentieth century, but asphalt allowed new kinds of vehicles to operate and compete for space on city streets. Bicycling enthusiasts found asphalt much more comfortable to negotiate than cobblestone and macadam. Officials in Buffalo claimed their city was a bicyclist's paradise due to the 200 miles of asphalt and 19 miles of parkways. In 1896 an estimated 60,000 bicycles were used in Buffalo, which led the way in manufacturers of bicycles and bike repair shops.[29]

In the first decade of the twentieth century, bicyclists were joined by automobile enthusiasts. Automobiles found smooth travel on asphalt, and their presence accelerated the repaving of streets with asphalt because automobile tires tore up the lighter gravel and macadam road surfaces.[30] Motorcars grafted themselves onto existing systems of transport created for horse-drawn carriages and streetcars. Automobile and bicycle owners called for replacing gravel and dirt streets with "good roads." They pressured governments to replace older roads with concrete covered by a layer of asphalt, which better accommodated rubber-tired vehicles and encouraged more people to adopt bikes and cars.[31]

Many writers make the implicit assumption that the coming of automobiles was an inevitable byproduct of technology and progress. However, several factors led to rubber-tired vehicles dominating transportation systems in the United States. Cars were nurtured by the existing asphalt roads, adopted by wealthy advocates who influenced local and state politics, and they did not initially pose a threat to existing transportation systems such as interurban railways or railroads.

Buffalo: A Study in Automobility

Buffalo, New York, is a microcosm of automobility, or the privileging of the private car in US politics and society. A city of grain mills and steel mills, the Queen City of the Lakes served as the site of a burgeoning American automobile industry. Although Detroit won the title of "motor city," many cities vied for that title in the early twentieth century, including Buffalo.[32] Although Buffalo was home to thirty different models before 1950, the most famous automobile produced in Buffalo was the Pierce-Arrow, made by George N.

Pierce, who went from manufacturing bicycles to making motor cars at the turn of the twentieth century.[33]

The Pierce-Arrow motor car had a four-cylinder engine, making it one of the most potent vehicles of its time. The car was popular with presidents from William Howard Taft to Franklin Roosevelt, and it was beloved by film stars and America's elite. Made in Buffalo from 1901 until 1937, initially handmade, the Pierce-Arrow Motor Car Company built a new factory on Elmwood Avenue in 1906. The 1,500,000-square-foot plant may have been the first factory solely focused on manufacturing automobiles. The company peaked under the leadership of Charles Clifton, who had been president of the National Automobile Manufacturers Association. Still, the company declined with the onset of the Great Depression, which gutted the market for expensive luxury items. In decline, the company was sold to Studebaker, but that company went bankrupt in 1933. Private equity bought the company, which lingered for a few more years before going out of existence in the late 1930s.[34]

Lesser-known companies such as Stewart Motor Trucks and Atterbury Motors also created cars and trucks in Buffalo until 1940.[35] Atterbury Motors produced electric and gas-powered vehicles designed for sightseeing, trucking, and light duties. The Great Depression, which sounded the death knell for many motor companies, was responsible for the demise of both Stewart and Atterbury, which produced their last lines in 1931.

Although Pierce-Arrow, Stewart, and Atterbury folded, Buffalo remained a center for automotive manufacturing. The Ford Motor Company and General Motors built cars in the Buffalo area. Ford opened its first plant in 1913, and by 1960 General Motors operated seven factories in the Buffalo area. In addition to companies that made cars, other Buffalo manufacturers produced auto parts. Buffalo Tool and Die, American Radiator, American Brass, Dunlop Tire, and Trico, a maker of windshield wipers, were all headquartered in Buffalo. Bethlehem Steel, which provided the raw material for making cars, built the largest steel plant in the United States just south of Buffalo, thereby single-handedly creating the suburb of Lackawanna.[36]

The automotive industry employed tens of thousands of workers, making them both an economic and political force in the region. Many of these workers were union members who favored the Democratic Party, which made Erie County a powerful ally of downstate Democrats. The automotive industry was a favorite of the Buffalo Chamber of Commerce, which used its publication *Buffalo Live Wire* to display ads for the industry and promote local auto shows. Editorials argued for an expanded system of roads and highways to accommodate car traffic into and out of Buffalo, but they often condemned the railroad industry.[37]

The Automobile Club of Buffalo, at one time the largest auto club in the world, provided critical support for automobiles in Buffalo and throughout the state of New York. Led by an elite group of men—lawyers, judges, physicians, and businesspeople—the group fought against antimotoring laws, pressured local and state officials to build roads suitable for cars, and began wresting control of the streets from pedestrians and giving them to car owners.[38]

The Buffalo Police Department created a traffic squad to regulate roadways and pedestrians. At first, officers were stationed at main points around the city to direct traffic, but they were replaced by mechanized signs that told drivers when to stop and when to go. The city passed legislation banning "jay-walking," a term that meant indiscriminately crossing streets outside of defined crosswalks. Buffalo was one of the first cities to adopt laws controlling pedestrians and signaling that the road belonged to the driver and not the walker. Buffalo was also one of the first cities to adopt traffic lights after Henry Osborn, city traffic engineer, persuaded the Common Council to replace the old green-and-red traffic signs with new stoplights that included a third yellow caution light.[39]

Mass transit in the region followed the pattern set in other metropolitan areas, in which a government-run bus system replaced private streetcars. Across the United States, public transportation shifted from trolley lines and streetcars to buses. The decline of streetcars came about for a variety of reasons. During the progressive era, these companies became the perfect foil for politicians and muckrakers looking to arouse public sentiment for more government regulation, taxation, and other policies related to progressivism. Journalists and politicians depicted streetcar line owners as greedy capitalists whose monopolistic grip on cities exploited the working class. Politicians saw a benefit in creating municipal bus lines controlled by city authorities rather than privately owned companies.[40]

At the turn of the twentieth century, the seven interurban railways operating in the Buffalo metropolitan region merged to form the International Railway Company (IRC), which ran all the public transit systems within the Niagara Frontier and into Canada. The company, which also managed the transit lines in Philadelphia, operated under the Milburn Agreement that required riders to pay only a nickel, and this included the right to transfer to any other line.[41] Streetcars peaked in 1920: "In that year, the competition of private automobiles began to be felt," lamented the IRC.[42]

In the decade of the 1920s, as the mass transit system faced increasing competition from private automobiles, it met with outright hostility from Buffalo City mayor Francis "Frank" X. Schwab, who served from 1922 to 1929. Schwab was an outspoken critic of the IRC and a proponent of buses. Schwab waited just one day into the 1922 strike by IRC workers before he issued five thousand jitney licenses.[43] A jitney was an early taxi service, and vehicles operating as jitneys could be anything from a standard automobile to a flatbed truck with some rope strung along the sides to keep people from falling out.[44] Even after the strike was resolved, Schwab allowed the jitneys to operate, which led to a series of court battles that the corporation won.[45]

Schwab attempted to use the strike to wrest control of public transportation away from the IRC and create a municipal bus line.[46] He offered a public referendum on this shift in November 1922.[47] Although he failed to get bus lines in 1922, for the next seven years he used annual reports to the Common Council as a basis for arguing against the "inadequate" streetcar system and calling for a bus line.[48] Throughout his tenure in office, Mayor Schwab undermined the private company. He proposed that the IRC accept the "Cleveland Plan" and set rates at five cents.[49] When the Common Council proposed a traffic study in 1929 to alleviate congestion, the mayor rejected the idea and instead suggested they "remove streetcar tracks from busy streets."[50]

As the mayor rhetorically condemned the IRC, public policy privileged the private automobile over mass transit. In 1920 a group of leading businessmen formed the City Planning Association. The association called for a radical redesign of the city to accommodate the automobile according to the belief that the future of the city was tied to the rise of cars. Before the plan was implemented, cars were hindered in the city by the lack of on-street parking and narrow city streets that caused traffic congestion. The association planned on widening all the main roads by three feet, reducing sidewalks, and cutting down trees. As they remade the city, they also encouraged the rise of inner-ring suburbs such as Kenmore, Tonawanda, and Lackawanna that extended the commuting distance for Erie County residents.[51]

While political figures railed against the monopolists, the advent of private automobiles undercut the economic viability of streetcar lines, which experienced declining revenue and ridership. Municipal laws made it impossible for many of these lines to increase their fares to make up for the decline in revenue, which slowly bankrupted private companies. Those companies that continued to provide service remained underfunded, and their lines were unable to make new repairs or to add new lines to meet public needs. In the public mind, travel by streetcar became synonymous with delay, overcrowding, or shabby and out-of-date modes of travel. Public sentiment supported bus lines, which replaced most existing interurban transportation by the end of World War II.[52]

Buffalo's mass transit system lacked the subsidies offered to private car owners and struggled to remain profitable. The system was beset by labor unrest in 1913 and 1922, unable to raise fares, and required to conduct their own snow-removal services and repair their own track lines. When buses replaced trolleys, they had to pay to repave the roadways, which cost the IRC an estimated $605,000 between 1930 and 1940.[53]

By 1941 the company no longer ran a transit line to Canada. It had abandoned its Niagara Falls and Lewiston routes and converted the entirety of Buffalo's Westside to buses only. Ridership went up during World War II, but in 1947 the company went bankrupt. After a period of government receivership, the county government took over the line and created the Niagara Frontier Transit System (NFTS). The NFTS ceased all trolley lines in the summer of 1950, and after that, only government bus lines operated in Buffalo and Niagara counties. In 1974 the NFTS acquired Grand Island Rapid Transit and changed the name from NFTS to the Niagara Frontier Transit Authority (NFTA).[54]

Snow and Ice Control in the Age of Automobility

The city of Buffalo and much of the country largely abandoned railways for roads, trolleys, and trains for cars and buses. They were now dependent on cars and buses for transportation to keep people and things moving, something one could not always guarantee in Snowbelt cities.

At the dawn of the twentieth century, the postmaster of Buffalo, Dr. Samuel G. Dorr, falsely predicted the automobile would be more effective in snow than other forms of transportation. Frustrated when a March 1900 storm hindered postal delivery, Dorr told one local newspaper, "I wish I had some automobiles to try on this storm. They would run all right. Where a Trolley can run an automobile can go."[55] Dorr was correct in thinking that an automobile could follow the cleared tracks of a trolley line to move people and goods but only because the road was kept clear by the private company running the interurban line. Cars were more of a nuisance for those using public transportation because they fouled up the transit lines by packing down the snow into the tracks, making it difficult or impossible for transit plows to remove it.[56] At other times, cars traveling on the tracks stalled and then were abandoned, thereby blocking the trolley lines.[57] Even when cars managed to drive along the tracks, they slowed the interurban lines and caused delays in service, which angered the public. "Failure of service on the International system practically halted all industry," the *Evening News* declared after a snowstorm in November 1920, but the article also revealed that the delays were caused by stalled cars in the center of streetcar tracks.[58]

To accommodate rubber-tired vehicles, the snow had to be removed entirely from the road because even a small amount of snow caused tires to lose traction and skid. As more and more of the vital services in a city depended on the free flow of automotive traffic, city managers adopted the "bare pavement" program, whereby cities and counties invested in the personnel and technology necessary to keep roads bare and dry throughout the winter.

A study of Rochester, New York, in 1917 found that the majority of the 15,000 registered motor cars operated all winter long. This created a dilemma because motor cars and horse sleighs needed access to city streets in the winter. Sleighs needed snow on the ground to travel, but automobiles required all the snow to be cleared from the streets. Rochester leaders decided that the future lay with cars, and the city council banned sleighs from the downtown business district and main thoroughfares.[59]

In the days before mechanized snow removal, the work of clearing streets of snow and ice was done manually. The larger the city, the more personnel were required. New York City's Department of Street Cleaning planned well in advance for winter, "just as the General Staff of an army develops its strategy and plans campaigns long before the war is declared." In 1914, New York City spent $2.5 million dealing with snow, but this amount fell short of was what was needed when a strong storm struck the city. When the business community complained that snow-blocked streets cost them $60 million in economic transactions, the city doubled the street commissioner's budget to $5 million, but even that proved insufficient.[60]

After World War I caused a labor shortage, urban officials switched to the mechanical snowplow. Boston bought its first motorized snowplow in 1914, a modified Model-T that rolled on harrow wheels. New snowplows pushed the snow into piles where it was and then shoveled it into the sewers or onto trucks for dumping in canals, rivers, or fields. This process, known as "snow panning," usually left some snow on the roads and streets.[61]

Having pressured local governments in the quest to clear snow and ice from streets, organizations such as the Good Roads League and the Automobile Club of Buffalo lobbied the New York state government to assume responsibility for snow removal on roads such as New York 5, which runs from Buffalo to Albany, and the Transit Road that runs from Buffalo to Lockport. State officials had been content to leave snow removal to local and county governments. During World War I, the demands for war materials and the slower pace of trains led many states, including New York, to add snow removal to their remit.[62]

In the age of automobility, winter storms became much more of a threat to the Buffalo metropolitan region than they had been during the era of mass transit. By 1920, with 40,000 motor vehicles registered in Erie County, the snow became more dangerous for commuters. During the decade of the 1920s, snowstorms caused traffic jams that clogged roadways between towns and cities for days on end because of the need to tow abandoned cars to open up narrow roads.[63]

A December 1927 storm trapped hundreds of motorists in their cars when heavy and blowing snow created drifts of five to seven feet on the roads, which had to be closed for the better part of the week. Unable to open the roads, authorities sent out bobsled teams to feed the motorists who had found shelter in farmhouses, government offices, and public buildings. The storm did not cripple the region entirely because train tracks were open within less than twenty-four hours, allowing goods and people to get into and out of the city. An early-season snowstorm on October 17, 1930, dropped four feet of heavy wet snow on the area and stranded thousands of motorists, stalling automobile travel in the regions outside of Buffalo for a week. Travel within the city remained largely unimpeded because it did not take long to clear the IRC tracks and restore the rail system to service.[64]

The most devastating storm to hit Buffalo in the first half of the twentieth century was a late winter storm on Saint Patrick's Day in 1936, which dropped twenty inches of snow on the area in less than twenty-four hours. By 1930 there were 160,000 private automobiles in Erie County, and the process of dismantling the IRC had already begun. Although the trolley still existed in the city, several lines had already closed and public transportation was shifting to buses, which could not travel on snow-filled streets. Due to a budget dispute between Mayor Zimmerman and the Common Council, the mayor did not order the street department to begin snow clearing until long after effective snow-fighting should have started. The streets department made only a feeble attempt to respond to the storm because it had expended all of its winter budget by January and could not afford to hire additional workers to help shovel the snow.[65]

For three days, the city was immobilized. Desperate, the newly elected mayor turned to state and federal authorities for assistance. Governor Herbert H. Lehman sent in National Guard units. President Roosevelt sent the city money from the Works Progress Administration (WPA), which allowed the city to hire 25,000 temporary snow fighters. The increased personnel along with seventy-five pieces of snow removal equipment lent to other towns in Erie County resolved the crisis. However, just as the city was on the cusp of removing the snow, conditions worsened when more snow fell on the region on March 21, stranding buses, cars, and commuters. It was not until Monday, March 23, that all major roads reopened.[66]

Although the snowstorm of 1936 was the most challenging storm the city faced in the era of the car,[67] it was not nearly as threatening as the Blizzard of 1977. The Saint Patrick's Day storm in 1936 shut down many services within the city for seventy-two hours, but because the people of the city had not yet become entirely dependent on rubber-tired vehicles, some services remained. Movement within the city did not come to a complete standstill because car owner-ship had not become so prevalent that every family owned a car. Commuter and freight trains were still in operation in the 1930s, and along with the remaining interurban railway lines they quickly reopened. The population density of the city was higher and allowed people to move around their neighborhoods on foot. The overall population of Erie County was more concentrated, which also facili-tated the restoration of roads and services, especially in comparison to the urban sprawl and suburbanization that happened in the 1950s and 1960s.

Suburbanization, combined with the end of interurban and local passenger train travel, expanded the need for families in the towns outside of Buffalo to own at least one or even two cars to remain mobile. The population shift to outlying villages and towns created hundreds of new road miles and major arteries that needed to be maintained and cleared of snow after the 1960s. Although the ingre-dients for a disaster were on hand in 1936, it would be another forty years before the recipe for disaster was written.

2

Buffalo and Snow Control
in the Age of the Automobile

When snow falls on a dry asphalt roadway with a surface temperature above freezing, it melts into water but will refreeze into ice once the air temperature falls below thirty-two degrees Fahrenheit. This ice forms a chemical bond with the asphalt. If the temperature of the asphalt is already below thirty-two degrees Fahrenheit, falling snow will remain on top of the asphalt, but once a car or truck drives over the roadway the friction of rubber tires on the snow will melt it into water. When temperatures are already below freezing, this meltwater turns into ice, which forms a chemical bond with the asphalt. As more snow falls on the ice, it creates a blanket and insulates the ice from the friction of automobile tires so that the ice remains frozen.

Any combination of snow and ice denies automobiles traction on the road and causes vehicles to slip and slide over the roadway, usually leading to accidents. Snowplows can scrape the snow off but cannot break the adhesion formed between the ice and the road, which is so strong that the plows are more likely to tear up the asphalt than the ice, which is what causes potholes. If a plow only removes the snow and leaves the ice untouched, the roads remain too slick and slippery for safe driving.[1] From the beginning of the twentieth century, street commissioners knew that "the most difficult problem of the street cleaning department is the removal of snow and ice from the roadways."[2]

Even a small amount of snow can cause accidents and snarl traffic. Blizzards and ice storms may shut down transportation for days.

By the 1960s, snow- and ice-related traffic problems were more than mere economic disruptions and travel inconveniences. A Midwestern blizzard in 1966 killed twenty-seven people who died in their cars after being trapped on a highway for over a day. To keep roads open and travelers safe, governments annually spend hundreds of millions of dollars for snow-fighting operations that require highly technical logistics, thousands of workforce hours, and chemical deicers such as road salt.[3]

Public works engineer Robert Lockwood, writing in the 1960s, was struck by the paradox that the "highly mobile, mechanized society" of his day was "more vulnerable to winter storms" than earlier and less technologically advanced forebears, "who found a little snow on the ground no disadvantage."[4] Travel became riskier in the 1960s, especially in the Snowbelt, the region of heavy snowfall that runs along the southern border of the Great Lakes into New England and includes the cities of Milwaukee, Chicago, Cleveland, Buffalo, Rochester, Syracuse, Boston, and Philadelphia. Urban sprawl and suburbanization had extended commuting distances for people traveling to work, home, and stores.

A revolution in public transportation occurred when buses displaced trolley lines and streetcars in America between 1924 and 1946. Many cities now look back and lament the decline of interurban rail lines. Once they were removed, public transportation was untethered from rails, and more rubber-tired vehicles joined the growing traffic flow of cities. All of these developments created new problems for daily commuters and another headache for public works employees. It also led cities to become less compact and less pedestrian-friendly and encouraged urban sprawl and suburbanization.[5]

By the early 1960s, most commuters no longer had trains or interurban streetcars to rely on; instead, they drove themselves or rode in buses and taxis, all of which depended on rubber-tired vehicles. These automobiles worked fine in the summer, but they were inhibited by the snow and ice that were endemic to the northern part of the United States. In the first two decades of the twentieth century, automobiles replaced most other forms of transportation and re-shaped the contours of American cities.

This was certainly the case in Buffalo, New York, which had grand visions for connecting to the New York State Thruway in 1949. The 570-mile-long thruway, like the Erie Canal a century earlier, connected New York City to Buffalo. At a cost of $600 million, the Thruway inspired a call for new roads into and across the Buffalo metropolitan area. The consensus of the time was that unimpeded traffic was critical to the continued growth and success of the city.[6]

In 1950, the year the city abandoned rail transit throughout the Buffalo metropolitan region, officials began work on the Scajaquada Expressway, also known as the New York State Route 198 (NYS 198 or "the 198"). Contained wholly in the city of Buffalo, the 198 connected Buffalo to the New York State Thruway and ran from Buffalo's Black Rock neighborhood to the Kensington Expressway. This expressway took just a few years to build, but it continued the process of cannibalizing greenspace and neighborhoods. The city appropriated parkland from Delaware Park and took more housing from residential neighborhoods located along the old Humboldt Parkway. Engineers placed the road below ground level, further divorcing drivers from the neighborhoods they passed.[7]

One of the defining elements of the Buffalo cityscape in the second half of the twentieth century is the Skyway, opened in 1955 and hailed at the time of its construction as an emblem of modernism. Many locals saw it as a barrier to the shores of Lake Erie and a dangerous road in bad weather. Built to connect Lackawanna, Hamburg, and South Buffalo to the city of Buffalo, the elevated narrow road, located on the lakefront, is vulnerable to lake-effect snow. More often than not, it is the first road closed when a winter snowstorm hits the city.[8]

In 1960 the region launched the $45 million Kensington Expressway, running from the Buffalo Airport in Cheektowaga through the city of Buffalo. Proposed in 1946, the Kensington was not completed until 1971. The roadway was justified by civil defense authorities who testified that it would facilitate the evacuation of the city should there ever be an atomic attack. Known to locals as "the 33," the Kensington was built over part of the original Humboldt Parkway, a road designed by Frederick Law Olmsted. The 200-foot-wide Humboldt Parkway was one of the first parkways in the United States, and it was designed to connect a series of urban parks by a tree-lined thoroughfare. Replacing this green jewel was the expressway consisting of a six-lane canyon that divided entire neighborhoods, further segregated the African American community, and displaced hundreds of families, many of whom moved to the suburbs. The expressway did not alleviate traffic congestion and went on to become the site of the highest number of traffic fatalities in the region.[9]

City officials eagerly built thruways, highways, and expressways, believing them to be conduits for newcomers to come into the city. However, they also served as the path out of the region for people fleeing poor schools, high crime rates, and other social problems associated with urbanization, real or imagined. Racialized suburbanization, or "secessionist automobility," saw mobile white residents leave cities rather than stay and integrate with nonwhite urban residents. As the second Great Migration (ca. 1940–70) brought African Americans north, "white flight" or the movement of whites to the suburbs accelerated. The city of Buffalo lost eighty thousand white residents, or 15 percent of its population, to the suburbs between 1950 and 1960.[10]

In a vain attempt to bring shoppers back, downtown urban planners created more space for parking. Parking had always been a concern to city planners in Buffalo. Private enterprise, especially during the Great Depression, supplied parking by tearing down buildings and paving them over for parking lots. By the 1950s, the need for parking plagued the city, so rather than wait for private investors to create parking spaces, the city council voted to clear two blocks of lower Main Street to build a parking garage.[11]

Urban planners accommodated the automobile for the city, but other factors pulled people to the suburbs and innovations kept them there. By the 1960s, towns and villages outside of Buffalo were dotted with supermarkets and shopping plazas that took away the need for a shopping trip into the city. For example, the aptly named Thruway Plaza opened in the eastern suburb of Cheektowaga in 1952. Located about ten miles from downtown Buffalo on sixty-nine acres of land, the Thruway Plaza was the largest in the state of New York and the second largest in the entire United States. Symbolizing the shift of population to the suburbs, the $7 million shopping center attracted 100,000 people for its grand opening.[12]

The first indoor shopping center in the Buffalo area was the Boulevard Mall, which opened in 1962 in the northern suburbs of Buffalo, about thirteen miles from downtown. In response to the rise of the mall, the Thruway Plaza remodeled and reopened as the Thruway Mall in 1974. Other malls were planned and opened throughout the 1970s.[13]

Automobiles and Snow Control after 1950

Once Buffalo abandoned track-driven public transportation for a government-run bus system, the people of Buffalo became less prepared for the annual battle with snow and ice, forcing street commissioners to develop technology to battle the elements and expending an ever-increasing amount of tax dollars in keeping the roads open.

An early spring storm hit the Buffalo area on March 29 and 30 in 1954 and caused, according to local newspapers, "the most complete traffic paralysis in the region's history." Ten people died, five hundred cars were stalled in Buffalo, and the transit system nearly failed as it took buses three to five hours to crawl a few miles downtown. A similar crisis played out in 1958 when a storm that covered the Eastern Seaboard struck Buffalo. Across the nation, 142 people died, while locally drifts of over twelve feet trapped thousands at home or work, shut down travel, and busted regional snow removal budgets. As just one example, the city of Buffalo ran a deficit of $200,000 that year.[14]

A weekend storm that struck the region on January 22–23, 1966, shut down the local transit system when more than thirty public buses were stalled in the heavy snow and blocked roadways. When the Niagara Frontier Transit System sent out wreckers to remove the buses, these too became stuck in the snow, causing even more traffic congestion. Angry residents blamed Buffalo mayor Frank Sedita for failing to anticipate the storm, for failing to get plows onto streets early enough, and for not clearing side streets once the storm had passed. Sedita, who had taken office on January 1 of that year, placed the blame on his predecessor Chester Kowal for failing to maintain the snow-fighting equipment adequately. The mayor did get the city reopened in a matter of days. Since no significant storms struck the region for the remainder of his tenure in office, the public either forgot or forgave Mayor Sedita for his initial fumble.[15]

The anger aimed at Sedita made it clear to everyone that in order to meet the challenges of a highly mobile suburbanized population living in the Snowbelt, armaments of equipment and a large snow-fighting war chest were required to keep roads and streets open during the inevitable snowstorms.

Before World War II, municipalities had begun using motorized snowplows. However, these plows did not fully replace manual snow shoveling until the 1950s when the development of specialized vehicles and V-shaped snowplows made them unnecessary. The V-shaped plow sent snow flying out of roadways and was useful on highways but not on narrow city streets. City streets were treacherous for snowplows, which often hit parked or moving cars and caused other property damage. As protection against lawsuits, cities granted themselves immunity from tort action.[16]

Another technology adopted at midcentury was the snow loader. Used first in Chicago, the snow loader consisted of a giant scoop that fed snow onto an inclined conveyor belt, which was then dumped into a waiting cart or dump truck and eliminated the need for gangs of men who once shoveled snow off the streets. For much of the first half of the twentieth century, cities dumped snow into freshwater streams, ponds, or nearby rivers, but this created unintended problems, such as freezing of the water or ice dams that spawned flooding.

To avoid problems caused by dumping frozen snow into waterways, cities tried first melting the snow before dumping it, an idea first tried out in Canada in the 1930s when the city of Scarborough mixed snow with hot water to melt it. Melting the snow solved another problem—that of space. Frank Lucia, New York City street commissioner, commented that urban growth in the postwar era made it more difficult to find vacant lots where workers might dump snow. In contrast, construction along the East and Hudson rivers made access to these rivers a challenge. Melting the snow and dumping it in the sewers obviated both problems.[17]

Rodney Fleming, who led the American Public Works Association (APWA) in the 1960s, predicted that snow melters were the wave of the future for snow removal and promoted their use at the APWA-sponsored North American Snow Conference. Boston's public works commissioner, James W. Haley, returned from the 1961 North American Snow Conference inspired by a snow-melting machine he saw there. Initially skeptical, Haley became convinced that the machine could increase snow removal from Boston's narrow roadways and save labor costs from trucking it to the harbor. Boston acquired several snow melters in the 1960s, including the massive "SNOWTRON," which cost the city $100,000 in 1965. The Snowtron melted 150 tons of snow an hour. These machines meant that rather than piling snow in parking lots or on roadsides where it remained a nuisance, street department personnel dumped the snow into the melter, which emptied the melted snow into a nearby sewer.[18]

Dumping snowmelt into sewers alarmed environmentalists whose concerns led state and federal officials to ban the practice of dumping snow and melted snow into creeks, streams, rivers, and sewers that emptied into freshwater streams and rivers. Regulations passed in the 1970s and 1980s forbade dumping melted snow into sewers. In addition to the burdens imposed by environmental regulations, the rising cost of fuel to run snow melters made them economically inefficient. Boston, Philadelphia, and Washington, DC, abandoned these devices.

For a short period in the 1960s, some cities tried infrared snow-melting methods. Affixed to a building or built beneath sidewalks, infrared machines immediately melted snow and ice. City crews quickly realized the folly of this scheme. Three to five inches of packed snow melts into one inch of water, which floods streets and then refreezes into ice, making for dangerous and slippery walkways. Many hailed these heating machines as the way of the future, but they proved no panacea for snow removal.[19]

The Salt Solution

Before the dominion of road salt, snowplows could not remove all the snow and ice from roadways. To allow cars the necessary traction on snow or ice, public works personnel covered roads with thin layers of sand, cinders, or fine gravel to create an abrasive surface for rubber tires to grip until the sun melted the snow and underlying coating of ice.

The use of ash cinders as abrasives was standard in all Northeastern cities until after World War II when they became less available because railroads and industry converted from coal to gas and electricity. Sand was used and is still used today in some Midwestern cities, but it can cause as well as deter accidents. Once they become wet, sand particles lose their sharp edges and with it their abrasive quality. Rather than supply traction, wet sand becomes slick and eliminates traction. Sand adds other problems—it clogs modern sewers and it can also destroy machinery at sewage treatment facilities. Fine gravel contributed problems of its own. After the snow melts, the gravel becomes a hindrance to travel and requires a work crew to clean it off the road, a cumbersome and time-consuming process that became cost-prohibitive when labor costs rose following the start of World War II.[20]

In the second half of the twentieth century, the preferred method of combating the adhesion of ice and snow on roadways is road salt, a chemical made from sodium chloride, the same elements as table salt used in food. Road salt is also referred to as deicing salt.[21] Adding salt to water lowers the freezing point of water until the temperature reaches six degrees below zero, when it reaches the eutectic point or temperature at which the freezing point of water cannot be lowered further. Theoretically salt works in temperatures below zero, but it is virtually useless once the outdoor temperature reaches about ten degrees Fahrenheit, after which road crews have to combine salt with other chemicals and abrasives to combat the hazardous conditions.[22] According to the most recent data available, Americans annually use just over 22 million tons of deicing salt on roads in the winter, which equates to 137 pounds of salt for every American.[23]

Salt is the most ubiquitous chemical on earth. As a food additive, salt is consumed by all seven billion people on the planet, and it is added to pharmaceuticals and industrial chemicals, health and beauty products, water softeners, and swimming pools. It is also used as a deicer by consumers, commercial businesses, and public works authorities. The salt industry is controlled by a small number of multinational corporations with salt-producing operations on every continent except Antarctica.

In the United States, most individuals are familiar with Morton Salt, which is a wholly owned subsidiary of the German fertilizer firm K+S Aktiengesellschaft, the largest salt manufacturer in the world. Cargill, which dominates the global food industry with earnings in 2015 of $1.58 billion, is another manufacturer. Sterling Salt, owned by the International Salt Company, once operated the largest rock salt mine in North America, located at Restof, between Buffalo and Rochester, New York. The mine was closed after it flooded in 1994, and a new mine opened in nearby Mount Morris, New York, as a means to get at the vast underground salt deposit.[24]

In the nineteenth century, streetcar companies experimented with salt to melt snow from their rails. However, city residents and business owners complained that it thwarted sleigh traffic once the snow melted. Melted snow turned into slush or ice and made walking difficult for horses and pedestrians.[25] Public works authorities disliked salt because it discolored brick pavement, but this objection faded once brick pavement gave way to asphalt.[26]

Public works departments found that salt was more expensive than cinders, sand, or gravel. Salt was used sparingly before World War II, mostly as an additive to sand and cinder piles to keep them from freezing together in the winter. A few cities, like Rochester, New York, experimented by adding salt with cinders to remove ice from intersections, but it was not until the winter of 1940–41 that Americans crossed the Rubicon. During that winter, New Hampshire and Massachusetts adopted the use of road salt statewide, arguing it was a labor- and tire-saving device necessitated by wartime. One layer of salt could alleviate the problem of ice on a road that might take three or four layers of sand to cover. Following this, there was no turning back, and road salt laid the ground for the adoption of the bare pavement policy, which could have only come about due to the use of salt.[27]

The rise of road salt was carefully guided by the Salt Institute, which used its charm, cash, and research to bolster the use of salt on roadways.[28] Founded in 1914 as the Salt Producers Association, the association was renamed in 1963 as the Salt Institute. It is not coincidental that salt use increased at a time that the trade group promoted it as a useful tool against winter. The ascendency of road salt owes a great deal to William Dickinson, who presided over the Calcium Chloride Institute in the 1950s and then presided over the Salt Institute from 1966 until 1987.[29] During his three decades promoting salt, Dickinson allied with the American Public Works Association (APWA), and the two organizations had a close and symbiotic relationship.

The Salt Institute

The Salt Institute, headquartered in Alexandria, Virginia, represented the interest of salt-producing companies, including mining companies and salt manufacturers. The Salt Institute has enormous influence and is on the front line battling attempts to reduce salt in food or ban it from roadways. When Mayor Michael Bloomberg of New York City demanded that salt be removed from the tables of restaurants, the Salt Institute fought back by contributing to politicians who opposed this idea. They then worked to discredit the idea that sodium added to food causes hypertension and were successful in their attempt to defeat guidelines proposed by the Food and Drug Administration that would have regulated salt intake.

Besides, political contributions, the Salt Institute has used the courts to battle policies they consider inimical to their association. In their work to shape public opinion, they have employed the "Salt Guru," Mort Satin, who appeared on social media such as Twitter and Facebook, featured in newspapers, and hosted his own YouTube Channel to challenge what he and the Salt Institute claim are myths about salt. Satin, who holds a degree in biology, often appeared in a white lab coat and decried "bureaucrats" who seek to impose their will on the general public.[30]

Deicing salt accounts for nearly 40 percent of the total sale of salt in the United States and accounts for a significant part of the $1.5 billion annually spent on snow and ice control. The widespread acceptance of deicing salt for snow and ice control came about due to a series of educational campaigns by the Salt Institute that led public works personnel to embrace the bare pavement policy. The Salt Institute sponsored research that demonstrated the value of deicing salts and shared this in pamphlets provided to libraries and public works officials. In other cases, sponsored research appeared in publications issued by the National Research Council and the National Academy of Sciences. Dickinson either wrote or was cited in many studies while presiding over the Salt Institute.

Data supporting the use of road salt appeared in trade journals aimed at public works and city managers, such as *American City*, *Public Works*, and *Rural and Urban Roads*, as well as in pamphlets prepared by the APWA or organizations concerned with highway safety. In addition to the benefits of reaching public works managers and others interested in issues of road deicing, the research wing of the trade group legitimized its position as an authority on the subject of road clearance. Thus, when the media covered winter snow fighting, they inevitably turned to the Salt Institute for information.

When the National Transportation Research Board of the National Research Council worked on a study of issues related to highway maintenance, they drew on information provided by the Salt Institute, which reported that for every dollar spent on road salt, $6.40 was saved in costs of accidents.[31]

The Salt Institute was a vital underwriter of the American Public Works Association's annual North American Snow Conference, which began in 1961. These conferences, which continues to this day, bring thousands of public works personnel to sessions devoted to dealing with winter hazards. The American Public Works Association, with membership in the tens of thousands, hosts the springtime meetings, which feature demonstrations of the latest equipment for snow removal and panels of experts to share their knowledge and insight into how to cope with winter problems on streets and highways. Not surprisingly, these experts include representatives from the Salt Institute.[32]

The institute issued multiple editions of the *Snow Fighter's Handbook*, which urged public works personnel to remove all snow and ice from the pavement as soon as possible after storms. These brochures contained statistics showing the importance of bare pavement in winter. Eighty-two percent of commuters used an automobile; 92 percent of all intercity travel was by motor vehicle; while "access to retailers, service establishments and other businesses are often wholly dependent on auto or truck transportation." Readers of the pamphlet were admonished to adopt bare pavement maintenance to keep traffic flowing; allow commerce and industry to go on at a near-normal pace; and reduce accidents, injuries, and death while facilitating the movement of emergency vehicles in the wintertime.[33]

The increased use of road salt changed the behavior of drivers who began to expect bare pavement and dry roads in winter months and therefore abandoned the precautions of an earlier generation. In the first part of the twentieth century, drivers in rural areas wrapped their tires in chains to give them traction in the snow. This practice continued until after World War II.[34] In the Snowbelt suburbs, to reduce their risk of accident, most motorists owned two sets of tires, one they kept on their car from April until November, and snow tires, which have broader and deeper grooves to ensure maximum traction in winter. Sales of snow tires rose throughout the 1950s and peaked in 1963, just as urban sprawl and suburbanization were making wintertime commutes more challenging.

The decline of snow tires occurred for two reasons. One was the redesign of automobiles in the 1970s, which moved from rear-wheel drive to front-wheel drive. Front-wheel drive provided better traction due to the heavy engine in the front of the vehicle. In addition to front-wheel drive, all-season radial tires became standard issue on new cars, making snow tires less necessary. One tire salesman lamented the change: "It's tough when a guy comes in and says he's gotten along fine without snow tires." Today, snow tires account for less than one percent of all tire sales in the United States.[35]

Corrosive, Expensive, and Environmentally Hazardous

Road salt has more side effects. Initially, the chief complaint against road salt was its corrosive effects on automobiles, metal bridges, and roadway infrastructure. The Salt Institute rejected the idea that salt was to blame and suggested that water, the electrolytic action, and pollution were at the root of corrosion. General Motors rebutted this by pointing out that while corrosion was common in Detroit, which used road salt, it was uncommon in Miami, which did not.[36]

Consolidated Edison claimed that the brine created by road salt caused short circuits in their electrical grid. A 1972 EPA report cited that in addition to vehicle corrosion, salt damaged concrete decks on bridges and weakened the reinforced steel rods in roads and on bridges. One cost estimate of the damage left by road salt placed it at $3.5 to $7 billion a year. That included $2 billion a year for vehicle damage; $500 million a year or more in various repairs to bridges; a similar cost for repairing highway pavements, concrete, and steel reinforcement underneath highways; hundreds of millions more for parking garages and snow removal equipment corroded by deicing salt; and other miscellaneous costs.

Rather than abandon the use of salt, the Salt Institute called for changes in the manufacturing of cars and bridge supports. They suggested that automobile manufacturers provide special undercoating to protect cars and trucks from salt and to improve the steel used in auto production. To enhance bridge supports, they urged transportation authorities to coat bridges with protective material to reduce corrosion and advised that construction teams use epoxy resin and waterproof membranes under asphalt to protect streets.[37] In response, automobile manufacturers and shoe and boot makers began to build into their ads claims about their products' resistance to road salt.[38]

Regulating Drivers

As more resources poured into fighting snow and ice to keep the roads open, more and more drivers used these roads. Exasperated street commissioners could not keep up with the demand for bare pavement and called on city councils to regulate the use of automobiles. In the 1960s, elected officials finally recognized the benefits and efficiency that resulted from modifying the behavior of drivers and began to regulate the use of automobiles by legislating parking and emergency driving bans during heavy snowstorms.[39]

City streets become snow-clogged when plows cannot travel through them due to parked cars. Parking regulations written to assist in snow removal became common in the 1960s. Some of these regulations are seasonal, with most cities defining winter as running from October 15 through April 15 and writing ordinances regulating on-street parking during these months. In Buffalo, parking regulations require alternate street parking on every day but Sunday, which is considered a free day.

Cities experimented with a variety of regulations. Some laws gave the city the right to post no-parking signs when required; other cities have tried alternate street parking; and others, such as Stamford, Connecticut, passed a general law fining anyone who parked a car in such a way as to impede snow removal. Many cities created

Snow Emergency Routes that banned all parking on designated streets when heavy snowfall was expected. In many suburban and rural areas along country roads, officials banned overnight parking on streets from November through April. Another means of regulating behavior is a total driving ban. When drivers fail to follow any of these regulations, cities can ticket and tow the vehicles to an impoundment lot, thus removing them as obstacles to snowplows.

None of these laws are popular, and residents in a variety of cities have challenged these regulations in court. Moreover, whenever a city official undertakes a massive towing operation, residents take their wrath out on the elected mayor and council members.[40] Driving bans are the most unpopular regulations. Workers cannot get to their jobs and lose a paycheck, and the business community sees their livelihood threatened. As one local chamber of commerce executive said, lecturing a public works employee, "Business and industry are portions of the public domain most affected by impedances to the free flow of traffic when movement of employees and customers is ground to a halt . . . delay mean dollars, confusion spells cash." The business community has the most influence on government policy, and one APWA text put it bluntly: "Business tells the government how to do their job [since] business and industry are the portions of public domain most affected" by impediments to travel.[41]

Driving bans hurt individuals and businesses hardest in cities that have no interurban or subway transportation systems. In 1962 Edward Jurewicz, who worked for the Buffalo Streets Department, noted it "would be impossible to try for a total ban" on driving in Buffalo because the city had no primary metropolitan transit system to move people across town or in and out of suburbs. The best they could offer was "shutting down certain arteries" as long as they provided alternate routes for drivers.[42]

By the 1970s, the elements of a potential disaster were in place. Automobiles and buses had replaced earlier forms of transport and were more easily impeded by snow and ice. The use of road salt and more sophisticated plows allowed public works officials to overcome this impediment and universally adopt the bare pavement policy.

Cities in the northeastern United States spent a large portion of their annual budget on snow and ice control. The emphasis was mainly on keeping roads bare, with less concern about regulating driving or parking. Laws and regulations were in place to enforce parking and driving bans, but elected leaders were hesitant to deploy them because they delayed or halted commercial activity and led to public outrage.

Governmental preference had made car ownership and operation tantamount to an entitlement. A Department of Transportation (DOT) study of Buffalo in 1970 declared, "The car is so ubiquitous . . . the love for it so universal . . . that it is nearly incomprehensible to imagine that there are those in the U.S. that do not have one available whenever they want and for wherever they wish to go."[43] The study found that urban residents without cars were severely disadvantaged due to the rise of shopping centers, medical centers, and supermarkets in the suburbs accompanied by a steady decline of these services in the city of Buffalo. Like most urban areas, the carless population was higher in the city and lower in the suburbs. Those without cars tended to be unemployed, older female city residents who relied on bus lines to travel.

The DOT report was dismissive of the local bus lines. The cover of their report featured an illustration of a senior man waiting for a bus in the snow. The man waits with anticipation, but the cover suggests that the bus will never come. These examples, like the predictions by public works professional G. E. Taylor and urban historian Blake McKelvey, proved prescient for what happened in Buffalo during the Blizzard of 1977, when, for a time, everyone became carless and bus lines failed.[44]

3

The Blizzard of '77

Buffalo's Greatest Disaster

January 28, 1977, began as just another Friday morning for people across western New York. The temperature was expected to be twenty-six degrees Fahrenheit, and after a series of heavy snow flurries that beset the region on Thursday, Friday beckoned with the promise of the last day of the workweek. The morning was clear, and people went about their day's business—working, attending school, shopping, keeping appointments, running errands—only to be caught in a full-scale blizzard that erupted just after 11:00 a.m.

Drivers on the roads encountered walls of snow that obliterated their vision. Cars and buses stopped, then quickly became stranded as whiteout conditions or accidents made travel impossible. It took hours to get through a few city blocks, and many realized they would not be able to safely get out of the storm. They abandoned their vehicles but nearly froze in temperatures that had dropped to zero and wind chills that approached negative seventy degrees Fahrenheit.

Wind gusts knocked people off their feet, and icy snow clung to their coats as they sought shelter, safety, warmth, and food. Some hunkered down in office buildings, firehouses, taverns, and restaurants overnight; others, especially out in rural areas, were marooned for days. At least eighteen people died as a result of the blizzard, and many more were physically injured and emotionally scarred by the experience. Others were financially harmed by the storm due to property damage, lost wages, or lost income, all of which totaled hundreds of millions of dollars.

The Blizzard of '77 created the greatest disaster in the history of Buffalo, New York, and brought to life the frightening vision articulated a decade earlier of how a snowstorm could force an entire metropolitan region to grind to a halt. Along with Buffalo, cities including Batavia, Niagara Falls, and Watertown were paralyzed as transportation, utilities, and vital services all failed. Hundreds of thousands of people were stuck in their homes, some lacking heat, food, and medicine. Local governments faltered and failed in the ensuing crisis, and it fell to state and federal government agencies to assist the people of western and northern New York.[1]

The scale of the disaster that hit Buffalo in 1977 was in part due to public policies that had abandoned trains and interurban rail services in favor of automobiles that were more vulnerable to snowstorms. Another factor was a weather system that blew massive amounts of accumulated snow off Lake Erie that covered the metropolitan region. This phenomenon occurred during one of the coldest Januaries in Buffalo history and also amid one of the most frigid winters of the twentieth century. Below-average temperatures gripped the United States from December 1976 through February 1977. Blizzards and heavy snowfall battered the nation, and by January 1977, two-thirds of the country was covered in snow. Even the nation's capital suffered. Storms and cold threatened to cancel the outdoor inauguration of Jimmy Carter, who took his oath of office in temperatures hovering around the freezing mark. In Chicago, temperatures plunged to negative nineteen degrees Fahrenheit, and further south, Miami, Florida, saw the first recorded snow in its history.[2]

The extreme cold ignited a shortage of natural gas, a crisis that had been looming since 1970. Natural gas made up one-third of all energy demand in the United States and accounted for half of the energy used outside of transportation. Over forty million homes relied on natural gas for home heating and other domestic uses, and millions of commercial and business buildings did so as well. President Gerald Ford warned the nation in August 1975 that supplies of natural gas were lagging behind demand and that a severely cold winter would turn the shortage into a crisis. Fortunately for President

Ford, there were subsequently five mild winters in a row. That trend ended for President Jimmy Carter in the winter of 1976–77.

To deal with the crisis, President Carter convened a series of emergency meetings and appointed a federal energy coordinator, James Schlesinger, to oversee energy policy. Schlesinger was a seasoned administrator who had worked in both the Nixon and the Ford administrations. Carter eventually appointed him the first secretary of energy, where he worked with Congress to ration natural gas supplies and to facilitate the movement of natural gas across state lines. Since there was little the administration could do to increase the supply of natural gas, the Carter White House devised ideas for conservation and cutting back on usage, such as instituting a four-day workweek for industries.[3]

Natural gas shortages in the Mid-Atlantic states led governors in New Jersey, New York, and Pennsylvania to invoke emergency measures to deal with the situation. They imposed natural gas rationing for businesses, industrial plants, and schools to ensure that residential homes and apartments had sufficient heat for the winter. On January 27, 1977, the governor of New York, Hugh Carey, issued a fuel emergency that curtailed natural gas for everything but essential home heating.

The emergency order closed all gas-heated schools in the state for a week. Governor Carey issued a thirty-day suspension of laws mandating minimum temperature settings in public buildings. Meanwhile, the loss of natural gas supplies led to the layoff of a hundred thousand workers in the state. In western New York, the two principal utilities, Niagara Mohawk and National Fuel Gas, cut off natural gas supplies to hundreds of industries and curtailed supplies for an additional 29,000 commercial businesses. Buffalo-area malls remained open but kept their thermostats set at the low fifties, and some stores closed their suburban branches over the weekend.[4]

Amid the national and statewide natural gas crisis, Buffalo was experiencing one of its worst winters in recorded history. The average snowfall in Buffalo is forty-four inches of snow by late January, but in the winter of 1976–77 nearly 150 inches of snow had fallen before the end of January. By the end of the winter, Buffalo had received 199 inches of snow.

Winter began early that year with a foot of snow falling in October. From Thanksgiving through the first week of December 1976, forty inches of snow fell. Just after Christmas 1976, a storm dumped another two feet of snow on Buffalo, and it kept coming. Snow fell nearly every single day from December 20, 1976 until February 10, 1977. Compounding the misery, temperatures dropped below freezing just before Christmas and remained there until February. The average temperature from December to January was fourteen degrees Fahrenheit. Lake Erie froze and became buried under three feet of snow, which due to the subfreezing temperatures, remained on top of the frozen Lake.

Across the region, the cold kept the snow from melting, and it piled up along streets and in parking lots. Snow and parked cars clogged many of the city's side streets, which lay buried beneath the accumulated snow. Residents could not get to their buried cars, but even if they had managed to dig their cars out the streets remained snow-clogged and impassible.

The unrelenting weather blindsided streets commissioner James Lindner, whose crew could not keep up with snow removal.[5] Nonetheless, the city's Common Council blamed Lindner for failing to clear the streets. Lindner felt this accusation was unfair. Even during an average winter, removing snow from Buffalo's narrow side streets was a challenge, but the continual snowfall of 1976–77 made it an impossible task. In some spots, snow was piled as high as the tops of utility poles, and there was nowhere else to put the plowed snow. Cleared streets resembled mini-canyons as the snow piles along the streets grew higher and higher.

Lindner thought the best solution was to mount a massive ticketing and towing operation to enforce winter parking regulations. Buffalo, like many other cities, had adopted alternate street parking and snow emergency route protocols that required car owners to move their cars to facilitate the plows. However, in a perfect catch-22, people could not move their cars because of the snow-filled streets, which meant they remained illegally parked and blocked plows from clearing the streets. Lindner's solution was to ticket and tow these vehicles. Once the tow trucks removed the cars, the plows and other equipment and crews began clearing snow from along the streets and trucking it away.

Stanley Makowski, the mayor of Buffalo, was reluctant to launch this effort, fearing that it might upset residents. However, Lindner won the support of the Common Council, which empowered him to begin the massive ticketing and towing operation on Tuesday, January 25. For two days, the city towed and ticketed hundreds of cars, allowing public works personnel to clear Elmwood, Delaware, Main, Seneca, Swan, Genesee, and Niagara streets, which are the main arteries through Buffalo. Makowski's reluctance to support the ticketing and towing operation stemmed in part from the fact that he faced reelection in 1977. By the end of 1976, the mayor was unpopular with city residents who were angry about a series of decisions the mayor had made early in his administration.[6]

In 1975, the mayor had erected a wall around Buffalo's Lafayette Square, the city's central square, which earned the ire of residents who derisively called it "Fort Makowski." Under withering public criticism, the mayor removed the wall, but building and removing it cost taxpayers over $1.5 million, money that the city did not have. In 1976, the mayor urged the Common Council to pass a new occupancy tax on city residents to close the budget deficit in the Municipal Housing Authority. The new assessment proved so unpopular that the mayor, under pressure from the Common Council and the press, rescinded the measure in January 1977. The mayor had supported desegregation efforts in the city school system, which lost him the support of some of his blue-collar constituents.

Mayor Makowski was also hurting from a decision he made in December 1976 to impose a driving ban during one of the many snowstorms that beset the area that year. For retailers, the sales made in the weeks leading up to Christmas made the difference between profit and loss, solvency, or bankruptcy. Banning traffic in the city only diverted customers to the suburban malls located outside of the city. The commotion raised by the business community led the mayor to rescind the ban and discouraged him from issuing another one that winter. Thus, facing reelection, Makowski was hesitant about further alienating the people by ticketing and towing residents.[7]

By 1977, the citizens of Buffalo had taken the measure of Mayor Makowski's governing style. It was clear that Makowski preferred to be loved rather than feared, which meant he would quickly reverse unpopular decisions. "Stan the Man," as the public affectionately knew him, was a devoted father and devout Catholic who attended Mass daily. His rise to power in the blue-collar city of Buffalo reflected his working-class origins. Born in Buffalo in 1923, he was the son of Polish immigrants who raised him in "Polonia," the Polish neighborhood of the city. He worked in the grain mills around Buffalo, went to night school to study labor relations, and became active in the local union. He rose through the ranks of the association and then made the transition from union leader to an elected official.[8]

Makowski ran for office as a Democrat from the fourth ward, seeking a seat in the Erie County legislature. He served in that body until the late 1950s when he was appointed to an at-large seat on the Common Council, the legislative body of the city of Buffalo. Known for his compassion and ability to work with others, he was popular with voters and highly regarded by his peers, who elected him majority leader. Arthur O. Eve, a powerful Democrat in the State Assembly and perhaps the leading African American political figure in Buffalo, urged Makowski to run for mayor against incumbent Frank Sedita. It was not in Makowski's nature to be confrontational, so rather than run against Sedita, he joined forces with the administration as deputy mayor.

Sedita groomed Makowski to take his place, telling staffers in early 1972, "What Stanley directs, you accept." Health issues forced Sedita to resign from office in early 1973, and Makowski was acting mayor before winning the election outright in the fall. Ironically, one of his inaugural themes was to stress "good, capable, people in city government." A more realistic slogan might have been, "The city is broke."[9] Makowski was mayor of a city teetering on the brink of financial collapse. Buffalo was the epicenter of deindustrialization, and the city had been declining as a manufacturing and transportation center since the end of World War II. Many factors explained the decline, including the development of the Saint Lawrence Seaway, deindustrialization, and the concurrent rise of the Sunbelt.

The Buffalo metropolitan region lost 30,000 manufacturing jobs between 1954 and 1967. In one year alone, 1971, the area lost 9,000 jobs when Bethlehem Steel cut its workforce in half. By the mid-1970s, the city had an unemployment rate of 15 percent, which was the highest in New York State and one of the highest in the nation. Buffalo's plight gained the notice of the national press, and the *New York Times Magazine* featured the economic decline in a cover story in February 1975.

As the city bled jobs, residents were not far behind. The number of people living in the city peaked in 1950 with about 590,000 residents counted in the census, but by 1980 the city lost nearly 40 percent of residents and the population was down to just over 352,000. Some left the region to pursue jobs out of state, and others had moved from the city to the suburbs. The latter movement accelerated after the 1967 uprising by black residents. Wherever they went and for whatever reason, in the end, they took with them their property tax payments, which further depleted the city's ability to maintain essential government services, including snow removal.[10]

By December 1976, three times the average amount of snowfall had fallen, and the city had already spent its entire snow-removal budget. Because the city was insolvent, leaders had deferred maintenance or had failed to replace broken snow-removal equipment, leaving the city with less equipment for snow fighting. In a cost-cutting measure, the Common Council voted to freeze wages and imposed a hiring freeze at city hall, which eroded labor in the streets department and hindered the city's capacity to deal with the snow. A thousand workers were laid off or not replaced, reducing the municipal workforce. The austerity budget made it impossible for the city to buy new snow equipment. By January 1977, the city had at best seven functional snowplows available to clear 1,400 miles of streets.

Makowski lacked the budget to pay for removing the fallen snow. He had no money to buy more plows, no money to fix broken plows, and no money to hire additional public works employees or contract out some operations.

Near the end of January 1977, with the streets still snow-clogged and the snow-fighting ability debilitated, Makowski turned in desperation to the state of New York for assistance. Responding to the mayor's urgent request, Governor Hugh Carey announced that he would send snow-fighting equipment into Buffalo to aid the stricken city. Makowski predicted, "It looks like we are finally going to be able to beat the worst of it."[11]

One day later, the most severe blizzard in Buffalo's history struck the city. The morning of January 28, 1977, began with temperatures in the twenties and winds blowing at fifteen miles per hour. At 10:45 a.m., the Buffalo office of the National Weather Service issued a "blizzard warning for this afternoon and evening." Notably, this was the first time the local office had used the word "blizzard" in such a warning. The teletype had barely delivered the message when the skies around Buffalo darkened and the temperature dropped to zero. Winds over eighty-five miles per hour came blowing into the city, bringing a wind chill of negative sixty degrees. The storm itself contained only a foot of new snow, but the gale-force winds scoured the snow from atop frozen Lake Erie and drove it into the city. The effect was more like a dust storm than a typical snowstorm as a wall of snow enfolded the city, blocking out the sun and causing darkness at noon.[12]

Once the snow hit, stores, businesses, schools, and public agencies began to send workers home, creating chaos as thousands took to the roads at the same time. Public transportation ground to a halt; public buses stopped running; the airport closed, leaving planes stuck on runways with passengers in them; and trains became blocked by snow-clogged tracks. Those who tried driving found themselves stranded in the snow, facing zero-visibility whiteouts, which lasted for thirteen hours.

3. When the blizzard struck on January 28, 1977, people became stuck in their cars awaiting help. Fearing that some people were still trapped, the Red Cross sent out volunteers on snowmobiles who checked for survivors in abandoned cars such as this one, which was buried under a ten-foot snow drift. (Photo courtesy of the NOAA.)

With wind chills of sixty degrees below zero, drivers had a life-or-death decision to make. They could stay in their cars, where they were warm and protected from the elements, and hope that help would arrive before they ran out of gas and froze. Or they could abandon their vehicles, knowing that they would be searching for shelter with little or no visibility, all the time risking frostbite in the dangerously cold conditions. Nine people who chose to stay in their cars froze to death, awaiting help that did not arrive in time.

By late afternoon, thousands of cars, trucks, and buses were abandoned on streets and highways across the Buffalo Niagara region. Sixty thousand people were stranded in the city and across the Niagara Frontier. Whiteout conditions made it impossible for plow drivers to see the road and forced streets commissioner Lindner to stop all operations.[13] As the snow continued to envelop the region, Buffalo became isolated from the outside world with no means of transportation in or out by rail, car, or plane. Communication with the outside world failed when telephone circuits jammed from the thousands of people who tried to call loved ones at the same time. Power lines toppled from the sustained winds of sixty to seventy miles an hour. Seventeen thousand people were stranded in Buffalo alone, and these commuters sought refuge from the cold and snow in city locations such as the downtown department store, Adam Meldrum & Anderson; city hall; the *Buffalo News* office; and numerous hotels and taverns throughout the city. Thousands more spent the night at the Buffalo International Airport, located in the suburb of Cheektowaga, or at industrial plants across the metropolitan region from Niagara Falls to Hamburg. Ben Kolker of the National Weather Bureau, a Buffalo resident for thirty-eight years, claimed, "This is the worst storm I have ever seen."[14]

It was only the beginning. For the next week, another foot of snow fell on the region and winds continued to blow at over fifty miles per hour, sustaining the blizzard-like conditions and keeping temperatures near zero. Weather-related deaths reached twenty-nine, and the storm kept 450,000 people marooned in their homes for days on end. The postal service was curtailed, creating hardship for people waiting for their end-of-the-month social security and pension checks.

Weather conditions made the restoration of telephone and power services nearly impossible. It took crews hours to drive a few miles. Workers tried to work in the below-zero conditions and soon reported frostbite and exhaustion. When crews arrived on the scene, snowdrifts hampered them, and thousands of customers remained without power for several days after the storm. Economic activity nearly ceased in the region, travel became impossible, and many people feared for their safety and their lives.[15]

The snow hindered public safety efforts as the blowing and drifting snow stalled police, fire, and ambulance services. A crime spree erupted as criminals took advantage of the situation. Police made few arrests because they could not move about freely, nor could they stop the hit-and-run looters who were reported in every city and town in the region. Some broke into abandoned cars and took readily available property, but the boldest attempts were organized with sleds to steal the maximum amounts. One group broke into the local Salvation Army headquarters, ransacking eleven rooms, stripping a fleet of snowmobiles readied to assist the sick, and stealing a two-way radio used to reach out to the needy. On the East Side of Buffalo, looters in large gangs used sleds and wagons to methodically strip stores, homes, tractor-trailers, and cars. One police officer lamented, "They are hitting everywhere. We can't keep up."

Other vital services also faltered in the disaster. A dozen buildings became engulfed in flames on Buffalo's West Side, but fire-fighting equipment was stuck in snow or blocked by other vehicles. When crews got the fires under control in the below-zero temperatures, their hoses froze and created ice barriers that froze their trucks on the spot. Looters later stripped the trucks of all valuables. Ambulances were also ineffective in their attempt to reach people in an emergency. "We couldn't get out to the people," one doctor complained.

Zoos and farms struggled to operate in blizzard conditions. Although the animals were fed at local zoos, some died, and three reindeer made use of the foot-high piles of snow to escape. Dairy farmers trapped by the weather dumped 90 percent of the milk produced in Erie County.[16]

Emergency management in the modern sense was nonexistent in Erie County and virtually nonexistent throughout the state, which had no coordinated plan to deal with disasters. The civil defense program had been created to deal with the potential of nuclear warfare in the 1950s. By the 1960s public support for the organization had declined, and it languished in the 1970s. After civil defense failed during the March 1976 ice storm, county legislators defunded the organization and fired all but one employee. Officials were still debating whether to create a new organization to deal with local disasters when the blizzard struck, thereby leaving the county without an emergency services department.[17]

The county was under the steady leadership of Edward "Ned" Regan, the county executive. The forty-three-year-old Regan, who had been born and raised in the Buffalo area, swiftly rose in Erie County politics. He was elected to the Buffalo Common Council in 1965, ran unsuccessfully for state comptroller in 1970, and was elected Erie County executive in 1971 and again in 1975. He served as county executive until he was elected New York State Comptroller in 1978, a position he held until his retirement in 1993. Regan's county office was in downtown Buffalo, across from the mayor's office on Niagara Square.

After the blizzard struck, Regan stayed in his office for two days before strapping on cross-country skis and traveling around the area to get insights into conditions. Regan's office coordinated countywide activities and worked with volunteers who operated Citizens' Band radios to direct the tremendous force of volunteers who drove snowmobiles and four-wheel-drive cars to take homebound residents to hospitals or bring them medicine as needed. Volunteer fire crews and private contractors helped to deliver medicine, baby formula, and other necessities to those trapped by the storm. In hopes of rescuing people trapped in their cars, Red Cross volunteers used metal detectors to locate cars that were buried under thick layers of snow. Local governments from Cheektowaga to East Aurora were quick to impose a total driving ban.

Suburban residents relied on each other rather than on government assistance but had a higher opinion of their government than city residents. As Regan told the local press, people in the county did not need to be told "that there's an emergency and what to do about it. They don't hold a press conference . . . they just go out and get to work." County residents received less state and federal assistance, which Regan blamed on Governor Carey for underestimating "the magnitude of the crisis" and then procrastinating in getting equipment to anywhere but the city of Buffalo.[18]

Governor Carey may have been an object of scorn from the county executive, but most people in the region were delighted with his handling of the crisis. Carey was no stranger to crisis, having rescued New York City from bankruptcy and the state from economic disaster. Just before the blizzard roared into Buffalo, Governor Carey was in Washington, DC, to support President Carter's plan to send natural gas across state lines. When he heard about the storm, he declared a State of Emergency for Erie and surrounding counties and ordered 500 National Guardsmen to Buffalo to help with snow removal and restoration of services. Carey sent a telegram to the White House urging the president to declare a major disaster for Erie, Chautauqua, Cattaraugus, and Niagara counties. Carter agreed to call the situation in western New York an emergency but refused to declare it a disaster. Immediately, Carey began pressuring the president and insisted that these efforts were about saving lives and that the storm should be deemed a disaster.[19]

Taking advantage of a brief break in the storm, Governor Carey traveled to Buffalo aboard a C-130 cargo plane on January 30. After the requisite photo op, Carey met with Mayor Makowski, Erie County Executive Regan, and a representative of President Carter. Carey's decision to go to Buffalo was as much about politics as policy, and for his performance during the storm, Carey received an outpouring of letters from the community and politicians who acknowledged his leadership—precisely what Carey had hoped to gain from the crisis.

As a former member of Congress, Carey had learned that generous disaster relief could be parlayed into votes, but a weak response could be political suicide. His opponent in the 1974 gubernatorial election, Malcolm Wilson, had responded poorly to the gasoline shortages in 1973, thereby perpetuating an image of ineptitude. Aware of Wilson's bungling of the emergency, Carey's aides were unanimous in urging the governor to fly to snowbound Buffalo. The governor balked, fearing it would look like political grandstanding.

4. Buffalo was plagued by snow and blizzard conditions and needed assistance from the New York National Guard and US Air Force. Pictured here is a US Air Force cargo plane unloading equipment bound for Buffalo. (Archives & Special Collections Department, E. H. Butler Library, SUNY Buffalo State.)

His staff argued that the people of Buffalo would be comforted by his appearance and reminded him, "When you go there in bad weather, you've earned the right to go back in good weather." Carey ably demonstrated a concern for the plight of the people and showed that he was in charge.[20]

Carey called on President Jimmy Carter to declare a major disaster for Buffalo. He claimed that the people of western New York "have done so well, managing their lives and hanging in there to fight this disaster, that it's time for our government to respond on every level."[21] The governor not only seemed decisive and determined but also evinced compassion. Carey secured grants for the storm victims,

5. New York Governor Hugh Carey (right) arrived in Buffalo to assist Mayor Stanley Makowski (left). (Archives & Special Collections Department, E. H. Butler Library, SUNY Buffalo State.)

including over $2 million appropriated from state coffers. These grants allowed applicants to receive as much as $5,000 to replace or repair possessions lost or damaged by the storm.[22]

State operations in the region were overseen by a handpicked team that included Carey's special assistant, Ray Harding; William

Hennessey, a seasoned veteran of disasters from the Department of Transportation; and General Vito Castellano, who directed the agency responsible for handling natural disasters. This team remained in Buffalo until late February.[23]

In contrast to the governor, the mayor of Buffalo was stymied by the storm. Cars and trucks abandoned by their owners had to be moved before plowing could even begin on some streets, which meant towing thousands of cars to impoundment lots and private garages. Mayor Makowski was concerned that Buffalo could not pay for the towing. He also wondered where to put the snow. With streets so snow-packed, the snow would have to be hauled away, which meant additional costs for the city. The blizzard left the mayor physically and emotionally drained, and after the storm, he admitted to being gripped by fear: "We were going around the clock. Fear just gripped me. People and cars were stranded. That frightened me. There I was, the chief executive, and we'd never experienced this kind of blizzard before. There was nothing we could refer to to see what was done in the past. We had to start from scratch."[24]

Key to restoring services to Buffalo was to clear away illegally parked and abandoned cars to allow plows to get down side streets. Power could not be restored if lines were not accessible to utility crews. City streets commissioner James Lindner wanted the mayor to declare a total ban on driving so his crews could begin snow removal to reopen the roads. Lindner's crews worked from Friday through Sunday after the blizzard struck to keep main thoroughfares open, but to their dismay, this brought motorists out who then became stuck when conditions deteriorated, creating new obstacles to snow removal.

On Tuesday, February 1, under intense pressure from his political peers, the mayor declared a travel ban and authorized police to ticket anyone caught driving. Once imposed, the ban kept people off the streets and allowed effective snow removal operations. However, it led to more economic hardship for businesses and employees, and the mayor was besieged by complaints from industry, organized labor, banks, and retailers who asked the mayor to reopen the roads.

6. Buffalo police enforced the driving ban imposed by a reluctant Mayor Stanley Makowski. (Archives & Special Collections Department, E. H. Butler Library, SUNY Buffalo State.)

Bowing to pressure from business leaders, Makowski abruptly and unilaterally announced that, having weighed the inconvenience of snow removal efforts "against the potential losses to individuals and business people," he was lifting the driving ban starting at midnight on February 3.[25] The decision turned the next day's commute into a nightmare for those who tried to get downtown to work. Commuters found the streets still clogged with snow and abandoned cars, and their drive to and from work was made more treacherous by the four inches of snow that fell that day. The city became a giant parking lot as thousands of drivers were stalled in traffic jams that lasted for hours, and many feared that they would have to abandon their cars and seek shelter. Naturally, all the stalled and stranded vehicles made it impossible to clear away snow, open up streets, or haul in necessary supplies. Makowski then reimposed the ban for February 4, 1977. Once again, Makowski's indecisiveness made a bad situation worse.[26]

The mayor's unilateral decision hampered his ability to work with other governmental agencies. For example, when he lifted the driving ban, he informed neither Tom Casey from the Federal Disaster Assistance Administration nor Ray Harding from the governor's office. Harding told the press, "This was done without any prior consultation with us, and I understand without any consultation with the federal people." Nor did Makowski inform local agencies such as the Niagara Frontier Transit Authority (NFTA) before making his decision.

Makowski's failure to communicate is a classic example of the kind of fragmentation in intergovernmental relations that occurs during a catastrophe. "There is a total lack of coordination," one frustrated federal bureaucrat exploded. Meeting about the driving ban behind closed doors on February 1, Mayor Makowski and other government officials attempted to coordinate their efforts, but through either error or partisan politics they excluded the Erie County executive, Ned Regan, from the list of invitees to their meetings.[27]

Disasters have become political litmus tests for elected leaders. Natural disasters are widely covered by the media, which magnifies even the slightest mistake by an elected official. Governor Hugh Carey was a perceptive politician who used the disaster to showcase his leadership. The governor won the hearts and minds of the people of western New York that winter, while Mayor Makowski lost them. As disaster expert Richard Sylves noted, "In disasters, citizens need a voice of confidence." Mayor Makowski failed to impress the press and public and thus became an object of ridicule and scorn. He was not the first, nor would he be the last. Since the bare pavement policy was widely adopted in the 1960s, snowstorms have become the bane of elected officials, some of whom have lost political influence after they mishandled snow hazards.[28]

The poster child for snow failures was John V. Lindsay, a popular New York City mayor who was seen as a future presidential candidate. His reputation and career were severely wounded when he failed to respond adequately to an unexpected snowstorm in 1969. The forecast for New York City had called for rain, but instead fifteen inches of snow fell on the Big Apple, immobilizing the city for three days and leading to the deaths of forty-two people. Lindsay was unable to clear the streets in the boroughs for over a week. The mayor's popularity sank, and his competence was questioned. Lindsay's career stalled, and he was driven from the mayor's office. By the 1970s, this story had become political lore and was well-known to Stanley Makowski, who was desperate to fix the situation in Buffalo and to win reelection in the fall.[29]

The mayor received assistance from cities as far away as Toronto and New York City, which sent in snow removal equipment and personnel. According to some, the assistance was less than helpful. New York sent snowplows that were "vintage 1937," according to Deputy Streets Commissioner James Pierakos, and they "caused even more headaches." Toronto sent the most up-to-date snow melter they owned, but melted snow could not be dumped in the below-freezing temperatures. Even with assistance from local, state, and federal authorities who sent equipment into Buffalo, Makowski continued to fret. He was anxious over how the city was going to pay for the snow removal.[30]

The mayor made several calls to the White House seeking federal assistance speaking with Jack Watson, who was Carter's advisor on intergovernmental affairs. Makowski related to Watson the chaos that had descended upon the city—rampant looting, fire-fighting equipment broken down due to snow and cold, and few working snowplows. Public morale was low, and the city teetered on the brink of bankruptcy. Makowski pleaded with Watson: Buffalo was "fighting for its life, and now we're being flooded with bills." The city was in "a position where we can't help ourselves any longer."[31]

Watson assured the mayor that the president wanted to help but insisted that Makowski must first talk to Thomas Casey, who was an administrator with the Federal Disaster Assistance Administration (FDAA), the federal agency responsible for dealing with disasters.

Casey had arrived in Buffalo promising to protect "life and property," which were the parameters of the emergency declaration issued by President Carter. At a news conference following the phone call, the mayor publicly despaired over how to pay for the crisis and began openly to pray.[32]

Burdened with the financial woes of his city, Makowski showed both paralysis and despair in the face of the blizzard. Makowski was unable to meet the needs of his multiple and diverse constituencies. Assailed by press and public, Makowski's problems increased after fellow Democrats, smelling an opportunity to score politically, also piled on.

Erstwhile supporter Arthur Eve, a powerful member of the New York State Assembly, asserted that the mayor had "gotten more and more ridiculous" and "is not capable of running the city." At a press conference on February 4, 1977, Eve stated that should no other competent candidate appear by mid-March, he was going to run for office. He did not deny that he might support State Senator Jimmy Griffin if he ran. "The only person I'm saying now is not qualified or competent, is the present mayor," Eve told a gathering of reporters. He cited the occupancy tax debacle and the mayor's unilateral decision to lift the driving ban as evidence of incompetence. Eve also took a swipe at Erie County Democratic Party boss Joseph Crangle: "The office of mayor is controlled by a single individual, whose office is not even at City Hall."[33]

By late February 1977, as the crisis in Buffalo was easing, four Democrats emerged to challenge Makowski's reelection. All cited the mayor's poor decision-making before and during the blizzard as the basis of their decision to run. Makowski appeared before the press and complained that some people were trying to drive him out of office.[34] A survey of Erie County residents taken February 10–16, 1977, showed that 63 percent of the public gave Makowski low marks for his performance during the storm.

The career of "Stan the Man" ended in the piles of snow generated by the Blizzard of '77. In the aftermath of the blizzard debacle, Makowski was a liability to the Democratic Party. Erie County

Democratic leader Crangle and Governor Carey interceded with Makowski and told him it was time to walk away, promising him a state job if he would terminate his bid for reelection. In May of 1977, the once-popular mayor withdrew his candidacy, paving the way for a slugfest between fellow Democrats.[35] Eve saw an opportunity to become the city's first black mayor and ran with the support of the African American community and the liberal wing of the party. Senator Jimmy Griffin ran as a Conservative. Eve won the primary but lost the mayoral election to Griffin, who had been defeated in the Democratic primary and ran on a third-party line.

Makowski's last official act in the office on December 31, 1977, was to fire someone—something Makowski had never done before as mayor. In this case, it was James Lindner, the streets commissioner, who had endorsed Griffin for mayor. Makowski died four years after leaving office. His obituaries, while praising his character, inevitably noted his mishandling of the blizzard.

One reporter wrote, "In recalling the administration of former Mayor Stanley M. Makowski, there is an unfortunate tendency to equate it with the Blizzard of '77." Another reminded his readers that Makowski "was called on the carpet by the public" for his failures during the storm. Another reporter, who knew the mayor well, recalled, "The gentle mayor was done in by a cavalcade of political realities including his administration's handling of the blizzard of '77."[36]

4

Buffalo's Disaster Declaration and Presidential Politics

In early February 1977, Ohio Governor James Rhodes sent a telegram to President Jimmy Carter. The shortage of natural gas, below-freezing temperatures, and blizzard conditions prompted the governor to lead a fifteen-minute prayer session in the state capitol, asking God's deliverance from the extreme weather and then seeking help from secular powers. Rhodes telegraphed the White House imploring the need for federal assistance. He described the dire situation in his state, which was immobilized by the snow and cold. Rural areas were especially hard-hit. Rhodes told of a national guard unit that fought through the snow to rescue a family of eight who had run out of heating fuel and burned all their furniture in an attempt to stay alive. According to Rhodes, family members were throwing their shoes into the fire to keep warm when help finally arrived.[1]

Despite Rhodes's plea, Jimmy Carter rejected the request for a disaster declaration for Ohio, and he turned down a similar appeal from Milton Shapp, the governor of Pennsylvania. Carter approved Florida governor Reubin Askew's request for a disaster declaration based on the economic impact of the citrus crop failure, which threatened the livelihood of 50,000 migrant workers.[2] Ohio and Pennsylvania were rejected because Carter wished to avoid establishing a major disaster declaration for Buffalo as a precedent.[3]

A study of Carter's decision making reveals the general politics behind disaster declarations and the specific set of political factors that moved the president to take action in Buffalo but nowhere else.

From the outset of the crisis, President Carter was subject to intense political pressure to issue a disaster declaration for Buffalo. Carter calculated that bowing to pressure from party leaders in New York could gain him valuable support for his administration in the future.[4]

Carter had only been president for eight days when the blizzard struck, and he entered office lacking a clear mandate. His November 1976 victory had been slim, with Carter winning just 50.8 percent of the popular vote. Furthermore, he suffered from a reverse coattail effect—the forty million votes he received was one million less than votes cast for members of his party running for Congress, which diminished his standing with the party members.[5]

Despite the Watergate scandal, which led to a surge in Democrats elected to Congress in 1974 and 1976, Carter did not win a single state west of Missouri. A political outsider whose born-again Christianity resonated with evangelicals and those sickened by the corrupt antics of Richard Nixon, Carter was unpopular with labor groups and liberals within his party. He needed their support to achieve his policy goals. But to win them over, he would need to make concessions. A not-so-subtle reminder of this came during the 1977 blizzard when the president of the Buffalo Council of the AFL-CIO reminded elected officials that "we voted to put the guy in Washington and he'd better know it."[6]

Jimmy Carter had run and won the presidency as a political outsider, and official Washington did not see Carter as part of their world. Even though Democrats had a majority in Congress, the Democratic Party was not behind Carter.[7] Perhaps the lack of support for Carter was due to his notorious dislike of politics or politicians.[8] He imagined himself as a trustee for the national interest and not merely a partisan president, and he believed himself to be someone who would do what was right and not politically expedient.[9]

Many in Congress felt that the new administration was inept and not adept at prioritizing what and when things needed to be done. Carter himself once admitted to his aide, Stu Eizenstat, that domestic themes were not always "clear in my mind."[10] Carter was ill-served by his decision not to have a Chief of Staff, which Carter eschewed as too Nixonian. Instead, Carter acted as his own chief and allowed nine top aides equal access to him. When dealing with the crisis caused by the Buffalo blizzard, he relied mostly on Eizenstat, his domestic policy adviser, and Jack Watson, a savvy political operative who knew how to work Washington and served Carter as an intergovernmental affairs adviser and cabinet secretary. The two men did not get along and were often at odds. Eizenstat represented the young brash Georgians who ran Carter's campaign, and Watson represented the competent Washington insiders that ran Carter's transition team from election to the White House.[11]

The blizzard that struck Buffalo in January 1977 was part of a more extensive weather system that plunged wind-chill temperatures as low as one hundred degrees Fahrenheit below zero in Minnesota and generated blizzard conditions in Illinois, Indiana, Michigan, Ohio, New York, and Pennsylvania along with an ice storm in New Jersey. The storm created eleven-foot-high snowdrifts in Michigan; closed most of the thruways in northern Illinois; trapped 400 cars on a highway near Lafayette, Indiana; and forced Amtrak to stop service between Chicago and New York City. The entire nation suffered from an unprecedented blanket of arctic air that covered the continental United States. It was so cold that frost destroyed 95 percent of Florida's crops and put 50,000 migrant workers out of work. Governors in states battered by this weather clamored for their presidential disaster declaration.[12]

New York Governor Hugh Carey was in Washington, DC, to testify before Congress in favor of Carter's proposal to allow the interstate movement of natural gas. Governor Carey added his voice to the chorus of other state executives who sent telegrams to the White House asking President Carter for disaster declarations. These requests went to Thomas Dunne, the administrator of the Federal Disaster Assistance Administration (FDAA), which was located within the Department of Housing and Urban Development.

Dunne urged the White House to turn down disaster requests, fearing that such declarations would create a burdensome precedent for his agency. The Disaster Relief Act of 1974 gave President Carter an alternative to a disaster declaration; he could instead declare an emergency that empowered the federal government to intervene to save lives and property. This is the option Carter took on January 29, when he declared an emergency for Pennsylvania and four counties in New York, later adding and three other counties in New York to the list along with Indiana, Michigan, and Ohio.[13]

Carter, who relished delving into the details of whatever matter was before him, felt that he should and could know as much about an issue as any of his experts.[14] Thus, he asked William Wilcox from the FDAA to brief him on January 31. At the briefing, Wilcox detailed the function of the FDAA and described the philosophical and political problems associated with federal disaster assistance. He noted that the job of the FDAA was to respond to state requests for emergency or disaster declarations by assessing damage and resources to measure whether an event was beyond the capacity of state or local governments to respond.[15]

Wilcox reminded Carter that disaster assistance was *"always* supplemental to state, local and voluntary aid" with the intent to aid individuals and businesses and restore public facilities. Before this could happen, state and local officials had to show that they had committed resources to assist in disaster relief but remained overwhelmed and incapable of dealing with the situation without federal intervention. They also had to provide a detailed description of how federal money would be spent.[16]

In reality, Wilcox warned the president that despite the mandate that federal funds supplement state resources, states rarely committed to paying for a disaster because there was a "disincentive for a state to look internally for resources." Neither state legislators nor governors were willing to raise taxes to pay for disaster assistance, nor were they willing to take money from another program to assist citizens who had suffered in a disaster.[17] Besides, there was friction between state and federal agencies over jurisdiction and competing interests.

Wilcox instructed the president that emergency declarations were a new category in American disaster policy, which were added by Richard Nixon in the Disaster Relief Act of 1974. In the affected states, an emergency declaration allowed the federal government to assist in snow removal and restoration of transportation systems and utilities but permitted little else. On the other hand, if the president issued a disaster declaration, federal funds were available to rebuild infrastructures like roads and bridges. In the case of Buffalo this would have covered nearly the entire cost of snow removal, including overtime costs for personnel. A disaster declaration provided additional funds for businesses that suffered losses, unemployment benefits and food stamps to individuals who lost work during the crisis, and funds for people to pay their home heating bills.[18]

While Wilcox was detailing the reality of federal disaster policy, Tom Casey, the New York state regional director for the FDAA, was on the scene in Buffalo, assessing the damage and coordinating the emergency response.

Casey was a seminal figure in emergency management. For two decades, Casey found himself involved in every major disaster, including the Alaska earthquake of 1964, Hurricane Camille in 1969, Hurricane Agnes in 1972, and the Blizzard of 1977; later he oversaw federal operations at Love Canal in 1978 and the Mariel Boatlift in 1979. The president's rejection came as no surprise to Casey: "There never has been a major disaster declared for snow removal," he told newspaper reporters.[19]

Although Casey was not a political appointee, politics was intertwined with Casey's mission to deal with the crisis, beginning with the seemingly benign decision as to where to locate his headquarters. Initially, Casey established himself in the Management Information Center in Buffalo's City Hall, but this suggested to those in the towns that he was there only to help the city. Casey responded by moving to the Rath Building in downtown Buffalo, home of the county government. Still, since the county was under Republican control, Democratic leaders urged Casey to relocate to the Donovan building, which housed state government offices under control of the Democratic Party. Casey knew how to play politics and thus did as they requested.[20]

7. Tom Casey (center) was the Federal Disaster Assistance Administration coordinator sent to Buffalo to coordinate the federal response to the Blizzard of '77. (Archives & Special Collections Department, E. H. Butler Library, SUNY Buffalo State.)

Casey's search for a suitable headquarters illustrates the way politics permeated decision-making related to the blizzard. It also showcases the delicate nature of a government administrator, whose job was twofold—carrying out the administration of public policy but also diplomatically dealing with the politics of western New York.[21]

Even for a seasoned veteran of emergency management such as Casey, the situation in Buffalo was egregious and coordination proved to be difficult. "The Federal Disaster Assistance Administration (FDAA) is having difficulty getting reports from their personnel on the ground," one administrator wrote.[22] This was probably due to the many layers of government involved. Local officials knew which roads needed to be opened but could not talk directly to Casey.

They had to relay their data through New York state officials, who passed the information to the FDAA. The FDAA, in turn, worked through the United States Army Corps of Engineers (USACE) and Federal Highway Administration, who then hired private contractors to help remove snow. When this proved too slow, Tom Casey called up USACE personnel from Fort Bragg, North Carolina, to come to Buffalo and assist with snow removal, which was taking longer than expected.[23] Nature worked against government operations as well when weather conditions delayed arrival of the military units and heavy equipment from Fort Bragg until February 1, 1977. When they did arrive, the 300 troops, 50 pieces of heavy equipment, and 20 sanitation men were flown into Niagara Falls Airport, 29 miles north of Buffalo, because runways at the Buffalo Airport were too small for the C5 Galaxy, then the largest aircraft.[24] Once landed, the crews had to fight their way through the snow to Buffalo, which was 25 miles to the south. The Fort Bragg contingent added to the National Guard members in the Buffalo area, and the 353 USACE members already at work brought the total number of federal personnel to 900.[25]

Government operations were spread thin—outward from Buffalo south toward the Pennsylvania state line; north toward Ontario, Canada; and east to Jefferson and Lewis Counties in northern New York. The last two counties saw as much as a hundred inches of snowfall in twenty-four hours and broke all total snow records for the nation. Watertown was the largest city in the northern tier and had five feet of snowfall between January 28 and February 1. Adding to this was a wind chill that ranged from thirty-five degrees Fahrenheit below zero to forty-seven degrees Fahrenheit below zero.

The storm stranded thousands of motorists in Watertown, including hundreds of Canadians who were on their way to Florida. Storm victims were forced to seek shelter in hotels, office buildings, and farmsteads. Residents were trapped in their workplaces and forced to hunker down in office buildings and retail outlets. The second floor of the state office building in Watertown became a giant dormitory for about a hundred workers. With no transportation in or out of the region, grocery stores became depleted, and food was scarce. Officials considered imposing rationing and appealed to nearby Fort Drum for C rations.[26]

To alleviate the food shortage, Watertown officials temporarily lifted the travel ban on February 2 and allowed the 2,000 stranded travelers to leave the city. Personnel and equipment from Fort Drum assisted in rescue operations, and armored personnel carriers loaded with food, medicine, and baby formula were sent out across Jefferson and Lewis counties.[27]

Unaware of the logistical difficulties in communicating and coordinating such far-flung efforts, local officials were often critical of the assistance provided. James Pierakos, who served in the Buffalo Streets Department, had little good to say about the federal response. Pierakos disparaged the FDAA and claimed they had hired tornado experts from Puerto Rico to run the operation. He was unhappy with the myriad governmental forms and rules needed to get federal assistance. When the USACE arrived to help, Pierakos claimed they brought in "useless machinery that would have been more appropriate for plowing sand in Florida." Army personnel helping with snow removal were less careful than plow operators, and they caused two million dollars in damage to city streets, streets signs, trash bins, and trees.[28]

State and local officials argued that the emergency declaration failed to meet the needs of the Buffalo metropolitan region, and they urged Casey to recommend that western and northern New York be declared significant disaster areas. Casey demurred, telling officials that before considering such action, federal authorities needed a detailed survey of actual storm damage.[29]

Elected officials in western New York knew that responding to the disaster was crucial for their political future. Congressional representatives, sensitive to the political ramifications of a disaster, showed their concern for constituents by traveling to the devastated region and conducting helicopter tours of the area, during which they landed in a stricken city or town to meet local officials. Representatives promised to contact President Carter and add their voice to Governor Carey's request for a disaster declaration.

Jack Kemp (R-Hamburg) exemplified the work of congressional representatives. He served the southern portion of Erie County from 1971 to 1989. Kemp was a well-known figure in western New York, having been the quarterback of the Buffalo Bills football team in the 1960s. Kemp flew to Buffalo from Washington on February 3, 1977. He met with Erie County executive Ned Regan to plan his tour of Erie County, including the towns of Hamburg, Orchard Park, and East Aurora. An aide told Kemp that the weather conditions were turning bad and he should abandon the helicopter tour. Ned Regan told Kemp to go. "You had better get out there and see your people," Regan said astutely, "I have five friends waiting to run for your seat."[30] Perhaps Regan said this tongue-in-cheek, but the advice was sound as constituents demanded that representatives show concern for their plight.

Senator Daniel Patrick Moynihan also traveled to Buffalo during the crisis. Moynihan was new to the Senate, having been sworn in on January 1, 1977. He owed his election, in large part, to Erie County Democratic chairman Joseph F. Crangle. Crangle had been one of the first to support Moynihan in his Senate bid in 1976 and played a crucial role in Moynihan's victory over Representative Bella Abzug in the Democratic primary that year. Crangle's influence on Moynihan extended to twenty-six-year-old Tim Russert, who was in charge of Moynihan's Buffalo office. The Buffalo-born-and-bred Russert was Crangle's protégé.[31] Russert, perhaps speaking for Crangle, urged Moynihan to come to Buffalo as soon as possible to show his compassion for the plight of the storm victims.

While awaiting the arrival of the senator, Russert handled the press and worked with local political figures on the senator's behalf. Moynihan was so delighted with Russert's public relations effort that he took Russert back to Washington with him. On the plane to Washington, DC, the senator's wife, Elizabeth Moynihan, suggested that the young man stay in DC and "help us out with the press," which led directly to Russert's future career as a journalist.[32]

Joseph Crangle had political clout in Erie County, across New York State, and among national Democrats. From 1965 until 1988,

Crangle served as Erie County's Democratic Party chair. Erie County had the largest pool of reliable Democratic voters outside of New York City, which made Crangle a player in statewide elections. Crangle chaired the New York State Democratic Party from 1972 to 1974, and in 1977, he served as Chief of Staff and Special Counsel to the Speaker of the New York State Assembly.[33] As a member of the Democratic National Committee (DNC) from 1967 through 1989, Crangle influenced Democratic politics on the national stage as well. Just a few years after the blizzard, Crangle came within a few votes of being elected chair of the Democratic National Committee.

The Erie County chair aided Carter's victory in New York State in 1976. Carter won the state by less than 200,000 votes, which is surprising considering how much animus Gerald Ford created when he rejected New York City's request for a federal bailout. Indeed, the *New York Daily News* famously posted a headline that read "Ford to City: Drop Dead."[34] With Crangle's support, Erie County was one of three counties outside of New York City that voted for Carter in 1976.[35] Although his power waned in the late 1980s, in 1977 Crangle was at the height of his influence. Like a powerful political magnet, he drew Moynihan to Buffalo and worked behind the scenes to induce the reluctant president to declare a disaster for western New York.[36]

While Crangle worked on President Carter behind the scenes, other elected officials used local and national television to pressure federal officials. Unable to exert influence on Tom Casey, elected officials circumvented official channels and went directly to President Carter.[37] Jack Watson, one of Carter's close aides,[38] warned the president that "the congressional delegation and Governors of states that were declared eligible for emergency assistance have begun what seems to be a major lobbying effort." The delegation claimed that federal help was essential for the "economic survival" of these States: "Because of this political pressure, you may be forced to make a decision soon."[39]

Pressure on the White House came from Buffalo's mayor as well. Makowski made several calls to the White House appealing for a disaster declaration in Buffalo. The mayor told Carter aide Jack Watson that the city was "fighting for its life."[40] Watson reassured the mayor that the president wanted to help but under the law had to wait for Tom Casey's assessment. Casey did not see a need for disaster status for snow. "There is no way anybody can rip me off," he warned.[41] Despite the political pressure exerted on the president, Carter's advisers cautioned him against declaring a disaster, warning him that "it will set a precedent for all snow removal problems." They reminded Carter that there had only been a handful of similar declarations, and only for ice storms, in the history of federal disasters.[42]

As a former governor, Jimmy Carter knew that a precedent-setting declaration would encourage governors to seek federal disaster assistance whenever there was a heavy snowfall. This went against his "New Democrat" agenda of achieving liberal social ends without excessive spending. Carter wanted to create a more efficient, fiscally restrained government and was himself a fiscal conservative.[43] A disaster declaration would be expensive and would make the work of federal emergency managers that much harder and less efficient. William Wilcox reminded the president at his briefing that 70 percent of disaster assistance requests were "marginal" and therefore did not meet FDAA criteria for disaster assistance, but nonetheless only one in three of these were ever turned down by presidents.[44]

When determining whether a situation is a disaster, presidents often rely more on politics than on policy.[45] Presidents since Lyndon Johnson have found that disaster declarations reap political rewards. Johnson was the first disaster-in-chief president, and he created the expectation that the sitting president will visit the site of a disaster, give a rhetorical nod to the victims, and provide generous funding for disaster relief and recovery.

Failure to follow Johnson's script could lead to political blowback, something that Chief of Staff Jody Powell was already worried about on January 28 when he noted that the "delay and confusion" regarding the situation in Buffalo was incurring negative press. Members of Carter's administration were sensitive about bad press and cited the case of Richard Nixon. "One of the Worst PR efforts by the Nixon administration was its initial handling of the Agnes flood. Nixon's tour of the state by helicopter was viewed by many as too little, too late," Powell wrote to Carter.[46]

As policymakers and politicians were dealing with the snow, citizens in western New York waited for Jimmy Carter to fulfill his presidential duty to tour the disaster area. The public knew that Lyndon Johnson toured New Orleans after Hurricane Betsy in 1965, and Richard Nixon toured areas devastated by Hurricane Camille in 1969 and Hurricane Agnes in 1972. Residents of Erie County, New York, therefore, expected a similar recognition of their situation by President Carter.[47] They were dismayed when Carter, unable to make the trip to Buffalo due to the extreme weather, flew by helicopter to Pittsburgh to see how people in that sizable industrial city were faring.[48] Their surprise turned to anger when Carter made clear that he was not going to visit but instead chose to send his son James Earl "Chip" Carter to Buffalo in his stead. "What's Chip Carter going to do here," one veteran Democratic politician groused, "shovel snow?"[49] Chip did not salve the wound when he told the press, "I'm the second-best thing that could come." The people of western New York did not want second best.[50]

On February 4, 1977, the weather cleared and allowed Chip Carter to travel into Buffalo accompanied by Margaret "Midge" Costanza. Costanza was the former deputy mayor of Rochester, a city just seventy-five miles northeast of Buffalo, and she was familiar with the area and local political figures. As one of the directors for Carter's New York presidential campaign, she was a key player in orchestrating the trip to western New York. and was well aware of the situation. "It goes beyond what you see with the naked eye— the city that hasn't the budget to cope with the added expense and people with no jobs trying to cope with impossible heating bills," Costanza said.[51]

Costanza headed the Public Liaison Office for Carter, and her office was near the Oval Office, a sign of the power and influence she wielded with Carter. She and the president had met when she made an unsuccessful bid for the House in 1974. Two years later,

8. President Carter did not visit Buffalo during the crisis and instead sent his son Chip and White House aide Midge Costanza. (Archives & Special Collections Department, E. H. Butler Library, SUNY Buffalo State.)

she cochaired Carter's campaign in New York. In 1977 she could influence President Carter, but within a year she was ousted from her position and left politics altogether. Some blamed her fall from grace on her tendency to be reactive rather than proactive in dealing with constituent groups; others said it was because she lost the support of Carter's Georgian contingent after calling on Bert Lance to resign over a banking scandal.[52]

In 1977 she spoke for the president, and she and Chip Carter spent four hours in the Buffalo metropolitan area with New York senators Jacob Javits and Daniel Moynihan and congressional representatives John LaFalce and Henry Nowak, all of whom lobbied for a disaster declaration. Residents were pleased to see Chip, but officials fretted that the bright sunshine and newly opened roads might not convey the true nature of the conditions Buffalo had faced. Some feared that because Carter was a southerner, he might suppose that Buffalonians were used to harsh winters.[53] Chip, only twenty-six years old, expressed his shock at the amount of snow he saw: "I've never seen so much snow in my life," he exclaimed. The brief tour led to a press conference in which Senator Javits opined, "I don't see how the president can fail to declare this a disaster area."[54]

During the tour, Chip met with local business, labor, and political leaders who testified on the plight of western New York. Moynihan created a transcript and had aides prepare a written report that was sent to the president by special messenger, timing it to arrive before their return to Washington, DC.[55] The report stressed the unique context of the area that made a disaster declaration appropriate, stating, "More snow has fallen than at any time in this century, indeed at any time since the National Weather Service began keeping records almost a century ago." To this was added the unprecedented cold and wind, which were "worse than at any time since records began." Towns still had snowdrifts six to fifteen feet and higher clogging their sidewalks, parking lots, and buildings. The main roads were still closed. The region was already mired in 12 to 13 percent chronic unemployment, and combined with the natural gas shortage constricting business it now faced tremendous economic losses due to the snowstorm, which had the potential of generating a mass exodus of more businesses from the region.

In words reminiscent of the Old Testament book of Jeremiah, the report prophesied dire consequences: "Unless the Federal Government moves with dispatch and determination to undo the damage and regain the initiative, there is, quite frankly, the prospect of quantum decline. Jobs could hemorrhage, industries could disappear." Because of the storm, unemployment reached 50 percent in the city, with as many as 15,000 buildings damaged by the storm and a death toll that had climbed to twenty.[56] The report was signed by a veritable Who's Who of New York State political and economic elite, adding more pressure on the White House.[57]

Some have suggested that Carter sent Chip to Buffalo, rather than await the recommendation from Casey of the FDAA, because he had already resigned himself to declare a disaster for Buffalo. This interpretation is supported by a memo that domestic policy staffer Lynn Daft sent to Eizenstat on February 4, which stated: "Chip Carter understands the situation."[58] However, evidence also points to the fact that Jimmy Carter had not made his mind up as of February 3, 1977. On that date, Daft noted in a memo to Eizenstat, "To date, the Federal Government has played a limited role in dealing with the recent weather-related problems in North Carolina and the North Eastern States," to which Carter added in pen, "Let's continue to be conservative."[59]

Upon returning to Washington, Senator Moynihan placed a call to the White House but missed speaking with the president who was unavailable. The president's staff assistant, Nellie Yates, took the call and informed Carter that Moynihan planned to call back. She wanted to know if she should send the call to the private residence. She may have hesitated to do so without Carter's okay since the president had made clear in a memo that family and private time were necessary to function well in Washington. He had already told staff he needed more alone time in the morning and moved national security briefings to 8:30 a.m. to allow for this. Carter had sent a memo to all staff telling them to spend time with their families.

The political influence of the New York delegation proved stronger than Carter's resolve, and he told his aide to send the call to the residence. Carter took the call, which lasted about two minutes, during which time Carter told Moynihan that he would declare Buffalo and several counties major disasters, thereby making them eligible for a raft of federal benefits.[60] For example, local governments were assured that most of the cost of cleanups would be reimbursed and that businesses could apply for low-interest loans to get back into operation. Special unemployment compensation was provided for individuals who were out of work from storms beginning on January 16, 1977, and food stamps were given out to anyone who signed a sworn statement indicating that they had missed at least one day of work from the snowstorms.

It is possible that Carter had not yet made up his mind on February 4. Carter detested politics and often agonized about making decisions. A procrastinator, he was comfortable passing the final decision-making to another. In this case, he had to be the one to decide.[61] In the end, politics outweighed policy. Carter's staff made it clear to the president that by February 4 the crisis in Buffalo was over. Daft, a member of the domestic policy staff, wrote, "Snow removal in Buffalo is well in hand. Many roads are now snow-free. Public services are being restored. Some areas in the country are still isolated, but roads are being cleared there too." However, he continued, due to the "very strong political pressure from State, city and county governments to declare a major disaster, politically, there is probably no alternative but to declare a major disaster for at least a portion of the area." The memo made it clear that this was "a political decision at this point. If a major disaster is declared, it will be important to specify it in such a way that it establishes a precedent we are willing to live with in the future."[62]

David Rubenstein, Carter's deputy assistant for domestic policy, told the president that the FDAA would be willing to recommend a disaster for Buffalo, but it was only because of the snow and not the energy crisis. Rubenstein also suggested that Pennsylvania's request for a disaster declaration be turned down.[63] Daft warned the president that the cost of including Pennsylvania was too high: "Pennsylvania was not so hard hit by snow," he said, but the fuel shortage and unemployment costs could run $90 million. Daft warned Carter, "Should Pennsylvania be declared a major disaster, many other states would be sure to follow."[64]

On February 5, President Carter declared nine counties in western and northern New York disaster areas but crafted his remarks to tie the decision to the economic plight of Buffalo and western New York.[65] The declaration stated, "On February 3, Governor Carey requested that the nine counties were to be declared major disaster areas to provide financial assistance in addition to the direct federal assistance being provided under the emergency declaration. A major disaster was declared on February 5. With this declaration, the FDAA was directed to develop a cost-sharing program to alleviate the burden on government budgets caused by snow removal costs. Under the announced formula, when communities exceed their budgets, the Federal government will pay 75% of the additional cost until expenditure reaches twice the normal budget. Beyond this, the government will bear the entire cost."[66] After signing the declaration, President Carter called Makowski and informed him of the declaration so the mayor would have the benefit of announcing it to the local press.[67]

Many people in western New York were ecstatic at the president's decision. The declaration was psychologically beneficial for the people of the region, who now felt Washington understood what they were going through. Naturally, Makowski was delighted and declared that he could now stop worrying about "how we are going to pay" for snow-fighting operations. Makowski thought Costanza was a key player behind the decision and wrote to her on February 9: "It is obvious that you played an important role in encouraging President Jimmy Carter to declare the Buffalo area as a Major Disaster Area . . . May God Almighty Bless you for helping Buffalo during its battle for survival: Best personal wishes, Stan."[68] Henry Nowak also singled out Costanza for her assistance.[69]

Other grateful leaders thought Chip had been the key to the disaster declaration. The Pendleton town supervisor wrote to Carter, "I personally met your son, Chip, at the Harrison Radiator plant meeting, and I left immensely impressed with his dignity and poise under the pressure of the press and local officials. Please pass our THANKS on to him for his personal attention to Niagara County's problems during our disaster. God bless both of you and thanks again."[70] Perhaps the most significant "thank you" to the Carter White House came from the powerful Democratic Party leader Joe Crangle who held power at the county, state, and national levels. He warmly thanked Costanza and then went on to acknowledge

Carter's speed and thoroughness of action.[71] This was an indication to Carter that his disaster declaration would bring political rewards.

It Is a Snow Problem

Carter's decision was politically expedient but caused a number of problems in the immediate and long term. Not everyone was happy with Carter's decision. Carter may have won points in Buffalo and with the New York congressional delegation, but he earned the wrath of governors and citizens in states who were turned down for disaster assistance.[72] Nor were people within his administration pleased with his decision. Casey, the disaster expert who had served four presidents, was reported by one eyewitness as having been vexed because the president rejected his argument for denying the call for a disaster declaration.[73] Carter's political decision created a new category of disaster, which required new regulations, inspired another reorganization of federal disaster agencies, and provided future presidents with opportunities to declare a disaster for even marginal snowfalls that might enhance their electability.

The paperwork needed to get the disaster relief baffled local officials, according to James Pierakos, who worked for the city of Buffalo. In this he was in agreement with the village board of Sinclairville, New York, which sent a letter to Senators Javits and Moynihan and congressional representative Stanley Lundine, indicating they were "totally disenchanted" with Carter. The president promised to send money but three months had passed, and the federal government still had not refunded the village for snow removal.[74] Les Foschio, who led the Buffalo Corporation Council, later testified to Congress that small businesspersons felt stymied by the paperwork, and it took officials at all levels of government to explain exactly what benefits individuals could claim. Both the mayor's office and the chamber of commerce had to publish a fact sheet to help area business communities. Federal regulations barred consultants from meeting with the owners of small businesses.[75]

The food stamp distribution in Buffalo and other areas led to widespread fraud and brought negative press on the White House, forcing Costanza to return to Buffalo to assess the political damage and put things back into order.[76] Food stamps covering the entire month were given out to anyone who had lost even a day's wages, with no consideration of financial means. This excluded many senior citizens from receiving this benefit even though they suffered financially from the blizzard.

The cost share of the federal assistance remained under dispute through spring. Casey of the FDAA rejected a $43 million proposal to clear the parks of the snow that had been dumped there rather than in the Niagara River. Casey suggested he had no authority to provide the money and proposed that the county allow the snow to melt on its own. On the other hand, the Common Council of Buffalo was under enormous pressure from residents of the city who wanted the snow removed so the parks could reopen, and these demands spilled out into the pages of the local newspapers and on the airwaves of local television and radio stations. The political debacle required an intervention from Senator Moynihan with Casey, who finally agreed to remove the snow from the parks. The entire operation did not end until April 22, 1978.[77]

Jimmy Carter had given in to those clamoring for a disaster declaration for Buffalo, but in so doing, he set a precedent for American disaster policy, which he hoped could be limited to the unique situation of Buffalo and western New York. In exchange for this, Carter believed that he could gain political traction with the more liberal groups within the Democratic Party and Congress. It seems that neither of these hoped-for outcomes was realized, and Carter was swept from office in 1980 after serving only one term.

5

A Blizzard of Change

Jimmy Carter Remakes Emergency Management

In the immediate aftermath of the Blizzard of 1977, President Jimmy Carter declared a disaster in Buffalo, New York. Perhaps, due to his penchant for micromanagement, he might have liked to have managed the event himself. From the outset of his presidency, Carter sought to control disaster policy. Just five days into his term, Carter castigated the Federal Disaster Assistance Administration (FDAA) for merely providing a rough estimate of the cost of declaring a disaster for Maryland and Virginia. Carter wrote on the memo that he wanted more exact figures "in the future, [and] be sure to state estimates are part of the application." Carter demanded that the FDAA prepare a monthly summary of the ongoing cost of emergency and disaster declarations. Reviewing the month of February 1977, which included the Buffalo disaster, he noted the costs to the government and said they were "excessive. Tighten up all of them."[1]

President Carter not only was troubled by the preparation of paperwork and financial issues but also was not satisfied with the intergovernmental conflict and bad publicity that ensued during the Blizzard of 1977. The president was struck by how deeply political this disaster became in its impact and outcome.[2] At one point during the crisis in Buffalo, disaster specialist Tom Casey tried to reason with the press and politicians, saying, "I'm neither for nor against the major disaster declaration. . . . I'm an apolitical professional who has worked under seven presidents." However, Casey worked for the Federal Disaster Assistance Administration, an agency that lacked autonomy, and he spoke from a position of political weakness as his agency's fortunes remained tied to those of the president.[3]

Carter, who liked to micromanage, reasoned that the White House needed greater oversight of emergency and disaster declarations and more direct control over the disaster experts who dealt with state and local government officials.[4] To increase White House control, Carter overhauled the entire emergency management system then in place. In 1977 he laid out his course of action by creating an executive office working group. After they completed their work, Carter issued Reorganization Plan No. 3 in 1978 and provided the outline for a new emergency management agency. After significant input from local and state governments, Congress, and members of executive departments, the president created the Federal Emergency Management Agency (FEMA) on April 1, 1979. FEMA consolidated the agencies involved in emergency management into one entity, run by a director who reported directly to the president.[5]

Carter and FEMA

The seeds of FEMA began in 1977 when President Carter called on all agency directors to assess US disaster preparedness. He ordered the Office of Management and Budget (OMB) "to carry out a comprehensive study of the Federal Government's role in preparing for and responding to natural, accidental, and wartime civil disasters." Carter's memo noted that three different departments had primary responsibility for disaster and civil defense preparedness. Many other federal organizations were involved in planning, relief, or recovery responsibilities.[6]

James T. McIntyre, deputy director of OMB, responded to the president with a sobering memo criticizing the convoluted nature of American disaster policy. McIntyre was particularly harsh in addressing the governmental reorganization plan of former President Richard Nixon. McIntyre suggested that Nixon had created serious problems by eliminating the Office of Emergency Preparedness (OEP) in the White House and distributing its functions across the federal bureaucracy. The OEP's functions had been given out piecemeal to the General Services Administration, the Department of Housing and Urban Development, the Department of the Treasury, and the Department of Commerce, which produced the "greatest degree of fragmentation of these authorities" ever.[7] McIntyre blamed Congress for complicating disaster assistance. Each time a large-scale emergency occurred, Congress responded by adding new programs and more generous funds for disaster assistance.[8]

Greg Schneider, Assistant to the President for Communications, agreed with McIntyre's assessment. He described US disaster policy as "confused, overlapping, duplicative, wasteful, and, most importantly, dangerously ineffective." Schneider noted that the brokenness of the overlapping agency jurisdiction encouraged fragmentation. "Many of the agencies charged with responsibility in this area do not carry it out because they received no guidance or too much from too many different people."[9]

The National Governors Association (NGA) also criticized federal disaster policy, blaming not their own state organizations but the lack of centrality within the federal government. The NGA created a select committee to look into US disaster policy and asked Mike O'Callaghan, a former regional director in the OEP, to chair it. They found that most state emergency operations were fragmented and lacked coordination with federal offices. Following a natural disaster, governors invariably had to turn to their congressional delegations to secure federal aid or to obtain a presidential declaration of disaster. The governors were also unhappy with the multitude of federal agencies involved in assisting after a disaster.[10] The report acknowledged that politics played a role in how state leaders responded to emergencies: "In a large majority of civil emergencies of limited impact, governors take no action other than keeping informed, unless an unusual event occurs or it happens during an election season."[11] In their final report the NGA urged the president to consolidate the functions of disaster management into one agency located in the executive office of the president.[12]

Carter's decision to revamp federal disaster policy was, much like his decision regarding Buffalo in 1977, a mixture of his innate desire for efficiency and politics. Schneider wrote to Jack Watson in February 1978 that "politically, this is a plan whose time has come—to coin a phrase. The Hill is anxiously awaiting it and will, by-and-large, commend the president for sending it to them. Outside of the bureaucracy itself, there is little or no opposition to the plan." Schneider believed it was an "opportunity for the president to provide strong leadership in an area that has a great popular appeal with little downside risk."[13] Carter's plan had the approval of the NGA.[14] The only opposition came from civil servants within the FDAA,[15] who were concerned that overpoliticizing the agency could dilute its effectiveness.[16]

Carter, who disliked politicians and politicking, was not overly fond of the Washington bureaucracy either. During his 1976 campaign for the White House, Carter had railed against the bureaucracy as undemocratic. Once in office, Carter renamed the Civil Service Commission as the Office of Personnel Management and reformed it to give himself, and future presidents, greater control over the career civil servants who worked within the executive branch.[17]

Creating FEMA was potentially a political liability for presidents because it might function outside their control: "Consideration must be given to the downside risk to the president, creating yet another independent agency."[18] Presidents since Franklin Delano Roosevelt (FDR) have learned the hard lesson that independent agencies may bedevil a president. When he became president, Roosevelt sought to fire the director of the Federal Trade Commission, an appointee of President Herbert Hoover, who refused to carry out FDR's policies. The director refused to resign, and the case went to the Supreme Court, which in 1935 ruled against the president in *Humphrey's Executor v. United States*, asserting that the president's removal power was not absolute and limiting the removal powers of the chief executive. Ever since then, presidents have sought ways to control independent agencies through the process of politicization or adding political appointees to direct agencies.[19]

9. In the aftermath of the Blizzard of '77, President Jimmy Carter issued the first major disaster declaration for snow in US history. He then refashioned disaster policy and created the Federal Emergency Management Agency. Pictured here, left to right, are President Carter, Stu Eizenstat, Jack Watson, unknown, James McIntyre, unknown. (Photo courtesy of the National Archives.)

Because of Carter's sensitivity to this politics of the situation, and his mistrust of bureaucracy, FEMA became one of the most politicized agencies within the federal government. In his initial reorganization plan, Carter had eight political appointees for the agency. Still, by the time he left office, thirty-one political appointees were managing an agency with 3,400 employees, which is three times the average political staff for an agency of that size.[20]

It was not only the number of appointees but the quality of those running FEMA that Carter had to consider. The president understood that even if the new agency included political appointees, he could not always count on their loyalty. Political appointees were as likely to be overly influenced by bureaucrats within the agency they directed as they were by directives of the White House, and these could lead to friction and negative publicity for a president.[21] On the other hand, if the political appointee did not command the respect of the career civil servants working in the agency, this created problems in implementing official policy.

Thus President Carter needed an agency head that would remain loyal, win the respect of the agency's staff, and also be politically savvy. The director had to "have high personal stature to command the attention of departments which control most emergency-relevant resources, [and] an ability to handle political pressure. Political skill was also needed if the President, like his predecessors, wants FEMA to concentrate on political interactions and to gain credit for the Administration."[22]

The list of potential directors included Dick Clark, a first-term senator from Iowa;[23] George Elsey, who had served in the administrations of Franklin Roosevelt and Harry Truman and headed the American Red Cross from 1970 to 1983;[24] Mike O'Callaghan, governor of Nevada and author of the NGA report on reforming US disaster policy;[25] and Wesley Posvar, a former Air Force brigadier general.[26] The debate over the candidates divided Georgian loyalists Carter brought to the White House and Washington insiders he hired after he was elected president. On the one side were those who favored skill above politics. The National Security Council and the Communications Office wanted Posvar. Washington insiders such as Tim Kraft, Anne Wexler, and Jack Watson stressed the political sensitivity of emergency planning and disaster response. They believed political skills were the principal requisite for handling the job. The insiders wanted Governor O'Callaghan.[27]

Robert Lipshutz, White House counsel and one of the Georgians brought to Washington, warned that "eighty percent of the FEMA budget involves domestic disaster relief. The director should have political skills to deal with Governors and Mayors. The Federal Government's response to a domestic disaster can be the source of political praise or severe criticism."[28] Nye Stevens, who had worked on Carter's campaign, wrote that the Office of Management and

Budget was "unimpressed with O'Callaghan and Elsey may be past his prime."[29]

Perhaps because of the infighting, none of the individuals on the shortlist were hired. Instead, Carter brought in on an interim basis Gordon Vickery, who created the paramedic program that became a model for the United States and the world. Following Vickery's departure, Tom Casey, who had been in emergency management since the days of Lyndon Johnson, briefly served until the appointment of permanent director John Macy in July 1979.[30] Macy was a Washington insider who had shown great loyalty to the party and held many positions across the federal spectrum, none of which were directly connected with disaster management. Macy was savvy enough to bring in an expert—his associate director in charge of natural disasters was William Wilcox, who had done similar work within the FDAA.[31]

Carter established FEMA to replace what he saw as the ineffectual FDAA, located in the Department of Housing and Urban Development. The new agency was no panacea for emergency management. First, the overly politicized nature of the new agency reflected Carter's philosophy and concerns at that time. However, since the president staffed so many of the positions, the effectiveness of FEMA depended on the quality of these political appointees, which was not always high. In fact, according to some experts, FEMA became a dumping ground for lower-echelon partisan loyalists with virtually no emergency management experience, which undercut its mission during crises such as Hurricane Hugo (1989), the Loma Prieta earthquake (1989), Hurricane Andrew (1992), and Hurricane Katrina (2005).[32]

Secondly, the new agency pulled together the FDAA, the Civil Defense Preparedness Agency, the Federal Insurance Administration, the National Fire and Control Administration, and dozens of other agencies in the executive branch. To appease the interest groups and congressional committees involved in the many facets of disaster relief and recovery, Carter's reorganizational plan transferred every single existing political appointee to FEMA. Although this gave the president a platform for political patronage and leverage with members of congress, it also created stove-piped offices that had more connection with specific congressional committees than departments within FEMA. It took some time before these agencies worked smoothly together.[33]

Third, Carter rejected President Nixon's Disaster Relief Act of 1974 that intentionally separated the civil defense and disaster response functions of the government. The former was primarily a military concern related to nuclear war and invasion, and the latter was a civilian agency focused on strengthening mitigation and preparation by local and state agencies for disaster.[34] This created internal friction within the agency, which one political scientist characterized as an "internecine" struggle, as the civil defense components within FEMA refused to cooperate or share resources with those working on disaster response and recovery.[35] As one agency staffer remarked, FEMA worked about as well as "trying to make a cake by mixing the milk, still in the bottle, with the flour, still in the sack, and the eggs still in the carton."[36]

Despite the problems that were inherent in the FDAA and later in FEMA, President Carter utilized his emergency management agencies for crisis management, including the toxic dumpsite known as Love Canal in Niagara Falls, New York 1978–79; the near-meltdown of the nuclear power plant at Three Mile Island near Harrisburg, Pennsylvania, in March 1979; and the 1980 Mariel Boatlift.[37]

Carter's expansive use of FEMA to tackle all hazards was not popular with Congress, which passed the Robert T. Stafford Disaster Relief and Emergency Assistance Act in 1988, which amended the Disaster Relief Act of 1974. The Stafford Act, as it is routinely called, narrowed the definition of disaster intending to limit the president's ability to declare anything a disaster. This provided insurance that future presidents would not use FEMA for disaster management in the same vein as Jimmy Carter.[38] The Stafford Act deepened Carter's idea of making the agency more malleable to the president while curtailing the bureaucracy. It provided the president with more latitude in determining whether an incident was an emergency or not, granted the chief executive the right to suspend environmental laws, and provided the president with the power to direct any agency of the government to assist during a disaster. It further eroded the power of career civil servants in FEMA by requiring that all requests for resources had first to be approved by the Office of Management and Budget.[39]

No Dough for Snow

The Blizzard of 1977 and the chaos that it provoked in the Buffalo region, led Jimmy Carter to issue the first major disaster declaration for snow in American history. Carter's decision had been political, aiming to strengthen his legislative agenda and to save Buffalo from bankruptcy. Still, in consequence, a domino effect began as governors across the United States sought to exploit this new disaster category.[40] It is no surprise, given Carter's attempts to control the budget and to manage disaster/emergency declarations, that the president refused all subsequent major disaster requests for excessive snowfall. Jimmy Carter tied with Ronald Reagan as having the most turndowns, or rejections of applications for federal disaster aid, of any president from Harry S. Truman to Donald Trump.[41] Employing stringent standards, President Carter issued no major disaster declarations, but he did grant fourteen emergency declarations for snow-related disasters after the Blizzard of 1977.[42]

The winter of 1978 was as severe as the winter of 1977. A series of disastrous storms struck the United States, beginning in January when three low-pressure systems collided over the Midwest. One moved north from the Gulf Coast, another surged south from Canada, and one more headed east from the Southwest, creating one of the worst snowstorms the Midwest had ever seen. Winds as high as one hundred miles an hour dumped and blew one to three feet of snow on Ohio, Indiana, and Michigan. The storm paralyzed the region and stranded thousands of motorists, and seventy people died. One week later, the Great New England Blizzard of 1978 occurred, bringing over two feet of snow to the Northeast. Winds between 80 and 110 miles per hour whipped the snow and reduced visibility to zero. Coastal waves fifteen feet higher than usual crashed over coastal towns and villages. This storm damaged or destroyed thousands of homes and businesses and killed a hundred people.[43] A month later, the Great Easter Weekend Ice Storm of March 1978 swept across the Midwest, toppling power lines and leaving a million people without electricity, some for weeks on end.[44]

Governors clamored for major disaster declarations and made their requests through the FDAA, which followed Carter's instructions to be conservative with declarations and denied dozens of applications. Carter himself reminded governors that "snow removal is the responsibility of the State and local government. Federal aid is supplementary and should be limited to that which is necessary to provide emergency access to vital transportation arteries, the reopening of blocked supply routes to agricultural, educational, governmental, commercial and industrial establishments."[45]

To ensure that major declarations were rare, the FDAA created a three-part test to determine eligibility for emergency or disaster declarations. First, did the storm pose a threat to public health and safety of catastrophic proportions? Second, did the state or local government commit resources to fight the disaster? Third, could it be demonstrated that federal assistance was necessary for effective relief from the disaster?[46] The FDAA limited any financial assistance to the time period beginning from 12:01 a.m. on the day an emergency was declared until 11:59 p.m. on the day the main thoroughfares were once again open. Thus, no expenses incurred before a presidential declaration were eligible for reimbursement. Irrespective of how extreme or extraordinary the winter storm was, the FDAA would not assist a region if they had already opened at least one lane of their major roads and highways.[47]

William Wilcox, who replaced Thomas Dunne as administrator of the FDAA in 1978, had experience in both local and state politics. He spent twenty years as the executive director for the Greater Philadelphia Movement, a business organization dedicated to ending corruption and promoting social justice in Philadelphia. Pennsylvania governor Milton Shapp appointed Wilcox director for community affairs, and it was in this role that Wilcox developed expertise in disaster policy. After Hurricane Agnes devastated Pennsylvania in 1972, Wilcox oversaw state recovery operations. Wilcox's experience led to appointments as a disaster director within HUD, then as administrator of the FDAA, and eventually as an associate director in FEMA.[48]

The FDAA and later FEMA served two masters—the president in the White House and 535 representatives in the Capitol, most of whom were ambivalent about emergency management. Congressional representatives need an agency that works, but they are quick to condemn it when it fails to assist their constituents in what they see as a timely fashion.[49] Members are quick to forget that Congress writes the legislation under which the FDAA and later FEMA operated. Before the Stafford Act in 1988, this meant following the Disaster Relief Act of 1974, which stated the federal government could act only if a snow event went beyond the capacity of state and local governments to open roads for emergency services. Even so, turndowns were unpopular with congressional delegations from the affected states, and they hounded the FDAA and White House staff. As one aide noted in a memo, "Congressmen are still leaning on the president."[50]

The FDAA, however, lacked the bureaucratic autonomy that would have shielded it from congressional interference. As we have seen, the president, the executive staff, members of congress, and state political leaders lacked confidence in the FDAA, and they were all pleased with Carter's decision to scrap it and create FEMA. Indeed, the FDAA had a reputation for inefficiency, problems in delivering services, and lack of expertise in emergency management. Therefore the FDAA administrator Wilcox took the brunt of congressional anger at the president's "no dough for snow" policy.[51]

Congressional hearings placed Wilcox in a bind. He had to carry out the policy directives of President Carter, who wanted to keep a lid on paying for snow removal and was wary of declaring another snow disaster. Wilcox also had to maintain favorable relations with Congress, which controlled his department's budget. Additionally, Wilcox had to mollify state and local officials who might complain about FDAA policy directly to the president or Congress, which could lead to more hearings and bad publicity for the White House.[52] Personally, Wilcox was concerned about the domino effect in disaster declarations. Anytime the president granted emergency status to one state for snow or ice, surrounding states clamored for their own declarations, even for limited amounts of snow.[53]

State officials told Congress that the FDAA policy was ungenerous, inequitable, and unclear. They wanted a different standard to trigger federal aid and believed that eligibility for snow assistance should be based on measurable criteria such as the total accumulation of snow, not whether the state or locality had the necessary resources available. The latter criteria, they argued, penalized states for being too prepared for winter and rewarded states that remained unprepared.[54] Wilcox weakly reminded them that disaster relief money was not intended to provide budgetary relief when snowfall led to budget overruns in state or local governments.[55]

Other officials wanted the FDAA to take into account that the blizzard conditions hindered travel and communications, which made it impossible for some regions to gather the data needed to request federal assistance in a timely fashion. Government leaders knew that any delay in applying for federal aid cost them money, which was available only after the president issued an emergency or disaster declaration and did not cover expenses incurred before the disaster declaration.[56]

Dr. Robert M. Ward, an Eastern Michigan University geographer, testified to Congress that this was the case for the city of Ypsilanti, Michigan. On January 26, 1978, between eighteen and twenty-six inches of snow fell on Michigan, and strong winds created drifts of twenty-five to thirty feet in rural areas. Statewide the blizzard caused 700 injuries and 40 deaths and an estimated $18.7 million in property damage. About 290,000 people had to seek public shelter, and up to 100,000 vehicles became stranded on highways. Based on the weather forecast, officials in Ypsilanti began snow-fighting measures before the storm hit.

On January 26, Governor William Milliken declared the state a disaster, and the next day President Carter issued an emergency declaration for Michigan. The FDAA marked the period of eligible expense from one minute after midnight the day the president made the declaration, or from 00:01 a.m. on January 28 to midnight on February 1, 1978. Whatever the expense, the city had committed to snow-fighting operations when the storm hit, but before the emergency declaration those costs could not be recovered. Dr. Ward noted, "Ypsilanti lost money from the Federal Government because it acted too quickly."[57]

As Wilcox feared, frustrated state and local officials took their case to congressional representatives who insisted on a series of hearings on federal snow removal policy. On March 7, 1978, Wilcox testified to a subcommittee of the US Senate Committee on Environment and Public Works to explain the federal response to the Great New England Blizzard of 1978.[58]

Wilcox testified that he was only following the law which they had written. Wilcox stated that federal assistance was merely supplemental to that of the state and local funding. Wilcox mentioned that during the Blizzard of 1978, the FDAA waived requirements for Rhode Island and activated the Army Corps of Engineers to prepare for snow removal operation before President Carter issued an emergency declaration. Within fifteen minutes of President Carter's declaration, the Army Corps issued its first contract to start snow removal. Wilcox noted that on his recommendation, President Carter approved a disaster declaration for Rhode Island, not for snow removal but for the storm surge and coastal wave destruction that wreaked havoc with homes and businesses.[59]

The House likewise held hearings into snow disaster policy. When asked why he rejected Ohio's request for disaster assistance in January 1978, Wilcox noted that the FDAA provided $10 million in snow removal assistance to open major roads and alleviate human suffering. And he could not declare a disaster simply because a state was financially stressed. He recalled that on April 21, 1977, the House of Representatives had voted down $20 million in snow removal costs for six states that had applied for assistance based on fiscal overruns.[60]

Perhaps in hope that he might avoid future hearings, Wilcox sent state government officials the specifics of the federal snow removal policy.[61] He presented a session on natural disaster policy to members of the International Public Works Congress, and he reminded those in attendance that proper documentation was the key to gaining federal assistance after a disaster. Since the attendees were on the frontlines of snow control, he suggested they could be of great help to their local governments and the FDAA: "There is a place for working alliance between the department of public works and the FDAA." Wilcox went on a series of local talk shows; he also created educational pamphlets and instructional materials and mailed them to all forty states that had annual measurable snowfall.[62]

It was not just Congress or local governments that had a problem with the FDAA's snow removal policy. The Comptroller General of the United States, who oversaw the General Accounting Office (GAO), claimed that the FDAA policy was overly generous. The GAO is an independent agency, created to keep Congress informed about government finances, to guard the US Treasury from fraud, and to put a check on presidential spending. In 1978, the Comptroller General was Elmer B. Staats, who held that position from 1966 until 1981.

Staats was a significant figure in American political history. He had a long and distinguished career in government service beginning in 1939 when he started at the Bureau of Budget, known today as the Office of Management and Budget. Once he became the Comptroller General, he used his office to conduct audits and issue reports focused on making the government more efficient and effective.[63] The White House treated GAO reports with a mix of respect, concern, and sometimes fear.[64]

The GAO report *Federal Snow Removal Reimbursement Policy: Improvement Needed* (1979) concluded that many local and state governments that had received federal funding between 1977 and 1979 could have, and therefore should have, paid for snow removal out of their own budgets. The report suggested an even more stringent application of the snow removal reimbursement policy to safeguard the federal purse.[65] The report recommended that the FDAA discourage states from submitting "inappropriate requests" for assistance.[66] It also recommended that Congress pass legislation making federal assistance for snow removal a loan rather than a grant, with a provision that in cases of genuine hardship the FDAA would have the ability to forgive loans.[67]

The FDAA, elected state officials, and members of Congress found little use for the report. The FDAA argued that their policies and procedures were clear and consistent and that they had no power to stop states from requesting assistance. Nor could they define what an "inappropriate request" was. State officials objected to the idea that they were seeking a handout and were aghast at the suggestion that the FDAA standards were too lax, as they believed the FDAA guidelines were too restrictive. Nor were state leaders happy with the idea that government assistance might come in the form of a loan rather than an outright grant. Members of Congress also dismissed the idea of turning grants into loans.[68] The GAO report was more welcome in the White House, which incorporated it into their "no dough for snow" policy.

Emergency Management in New York

Carter's reorganization of emergency management and tight control of snow-related expenditures led New York State, among others, to revamp their emergency management agency and to better prepare for snow-related disasters. Reviewing the lack of equipment in Buffalo after the Blizzard of 1977, Raymond Schuler, chairman of the New York State Department of Transportation (NYSDOT), recommended to Governor Carey that New York State acquire more heavy snow removal equipment to lend to local governments in future emergencies.[69] However, the state was slow to adopt these recommendations, and two downstate blizzards in 1978 and one in 1979 caught the governor unprepared.[70]

The media and many state legislatures were angry at the inadequate state response to the blizzards from 1977 until 1979. Stung by the criticism, NYSDOT inaugurated a "Heavy Snow Fighting School" in 1979 to train public work employees in state's transportation department on how to deal with heavy snow. Newly appointed NYSDOT commissioner, William C. Hennessey, who had spent a month in Buffalo helping fight the blizzard and restore order, emphasized that the school was about being prepared for winter. "The purpose of the snow-fighting classes is to give snowplow operations from the normally milder climate of our state, such as Long Island, Westchester, Hudson Valley, an opportunity to have the experience to learn about the method of dealing with heavy snow accumulations," he told reporters.[71]

The Blizzard of 1977 prompted a refocusing of the state disaster agency, which many legislators saw as overly attuned to military threats and not sufficiently capable of dealing with a natural disaster. The New York State Senate had been battling with governors since 1972 over the lack of preparation and response to natural disasters. After an anemic response to Hurricane Agnes in 1972, a select Senate committee had looked into deficiencies in the state response to the disaster and forced Nelson Rockefeller, who governed the state from 1959 to 1974, to create the Office of Disaster Preparedness (ODP). Rockefeller placed this within the Division of Military and Naval Affairs, again signaling the emphasis on military attack rather than natural disaster.[72]

The ODP maintained that the initial response to any disaster had to be local. The state emphasized the need for more training for the seventy-one local civil defense organizations scattered throughout the state. Training before 1977 was focused almost wholly on preparation for a nuclear attack and not natural disasters.[73] At the time the blizzard struck Buffalo in 1977, there were only six district offices scattered across the state.[74]

State Senate Majority Leader Warren Anderson (R-Binghamton) noted that the "Senate had a long history of attempting to prevent the type of unplanned and uncoordinated disaster response by the state and had attempted on several occasions in recent years to get such a plan accepted into law, only to have such legislation vetoed."[75] Unhappy with the state response to the Buffalo blizzard and a series of snowstorms that struck downstate, the Senate created a special commission under the auspices of Bernard Smith (R-Long Island) to investigate disaster preparedness.

The Senate report, issued in 1979, concluded that a need for better preparedness and coordination at local, city, county and state government levels, and it criticized Governor Hugh Carey for an overreliance on the National Guard during an emergency.[76]

The Senate report condemned the state's "inertia" on disaster policy and suggested a revision and greater state responsibility.[77] Unimpressed with the senatorial indignation, Carey, who governed the state from 1975 until 1982, vetoed the bill. In his veto message, Carey indicated that the legislation did little to provide incentives to local governments to prepare for a disaster, nor did it resolve to the governor's satisfaction the need for centralization of disaster coordination at the state level.[78]

What Carey did not say explicitly was that many governors saw a catch-22 in federal disaster policy. The more resources a state put toward coping with disaster, the less federal aid they received after a disaster. This issue kept cropping up in debates about FDAA and FEMA snow policy in the late 1970s and beyond. The catch-22 was that FDAA/FEMA seemed to penalize states for being too prepared for winter when it came time to declare an emergency or disaster declaration for snow and ice.

Governor Carey launched a study of disaster policy and appointed secretary of state Mario Cuomo and chief of staff Vito Castellano to lead it. Their study prompted new legislation that formed the core of Executive Law 2-B in 1978. Under this act, Governor Carey created the Disaster Planning Commission to work in tandem with the

ST. JOHN THE BAPTIST PARISH LIBRARY
2920 NEW HIGHWAY 51
LAPLACE, LOUISIANA 70068

FDAA and later with FEMA. The Disaster Planning Commission emphasized comprehensive emergency management for all hazards. The new agency, the State Emergency Management Office (SEMO), reflected the changing ethos of professional response to disasters and placed greater emphasis on training first responders and local emergency managers.[79]

At the local level, these efforts led both the Erie County government and the City of Buffalo to restore and refashion their emergency management agencies. The Erie County legislature enacted legislation creating an emergency management department in 1978, and by 1980 Buffalo recreated an emergency services agency.[80]

6

"Grab a Six-Pack"

Snow Control Policy in Buffalo after 1977

In the aftermath of the Blizzard of 1977, Buffalo's mayors and New York's governors became even more focused on keeping roads open and people and goods moving during extreme snow events, fearful that they might make the same missteps as Stanley Makowski. Speaking at the 1987 North American Snow Conference, one commissioner noted that "elections are won and lost on ice and snow, and many of you have seen it." Anecdotal evidence is rife with stories of municipal leaders who slipped in the polls when they failed to clear streets in a timely fashion and, as a result, faced political disaster when they were cast out of office.[1]

Snow politics defies the accepted logic of disaster experts, who find that most disasters have such low political salience and come and go so quickly that "officials and public are quick to forget" about the problems and, therefore, are less likely to ascribe blame for problems encountered during a disaster.[2] This has not been the case for Snowbelt regions where snowstorms and blizzard conditions are expected and where subsequent economic and social dislocations have grave economic and social effects.[3] Thus voters in the Snowbelt are less forgiving when public officials appear incompetent in the face of snow.[4]

The Blizzard of 1977 put public servants on notice that snow clearance had to be a priority lest elected officials go the way of Makowski, who was for a time the poster child for snow failure. He was not the only one; within a half-dozen years following the Buffalo blizzard, at least two other big-city mayors were credited with losing reelection due to their inept handling of blizzards.[5]

A combination of savvy politics and the adoption of the latest technology has significantly enhanced snow control in Buffalo and other Snowbelt cities. These techniques include more precise weather forecasting, global positioning systems (GPS) or geographic information systems (GIS) to indicate where to plow, road sensors to show the correct amount of salt to spread, and the development of anti-icing techniques.[6]

City officials in Buffalo have avoided the political pitfalls of a bungled snowstorm by emphasizing better cooperation, communication, and preparation. After 1977 the city organized a special snow removal task force made up of representatives from the city council and the police, fire, and sanitation departments.[7] To this day, according to one streets commissioner, public works employees hold regular "meetings for winter prep, and when we have an emergency, everyone understands what they need to do."[8]

Mayors grasped the importance of cultivating the media before and during winter storms. Citing Makowski's bad press, one speaker at an APWA Snow Conference warned his audience to develop good public relations with the media: "In Buffalo, NY the mayor did very poorly, and other town administrators did very poor PR during a major 1977 snowstorm, the mayor was trying to run the department, and as a result, everything got confused and bungled. Moreover, the upshot was he lost the election big time."[9]

The Buffalo Blizzard of 1977 laid bare the importance of keeping the public informed even before a crisis begins, which led to an emphasis on communication and public relations at the APWA-sponsored Snow Conference. One attendee recalled how they were "impressed by the growing interest shown in the so-called public relations aspect of the snow fighter." Constance Wilder, the director of public information for the city of Rochester, New York, appeared at the 1986 Snow Conference and told her audience that Rochester cultivated good media relations by scheduling tours of the facilities;

they also allowed reporters to ride along with plow drivers to gain a better understanding of, and more sympathy for, the work they did.[10]

Thomas Low, who oversaw street clearing operations in Greece, New York, a suburb of Rochester, warned fellow public works employees against getting sandbagged by reporters. "Picture this," he told his audience at the 1986 Snow Conference. "You are on the six o'clock news explaining the amount of equipment, number of personnel and hours you are spending trying to clear the roads after a major snowstorm. The reporter, relaxed, rested and showered, thanks you, and then runs a story showing traffic snarled on a downtown bridge and interviews 'taxpayers who swear they haven't seen a plow all winter.'" By the 1980s, Low said, "Good equipment, long hours, and good planning are not enough"; one also has to have good media relations.[11] Buffalo's mayors took this advice to heart. Every single mayor since the Makowski era has held an annual press conference to showcase their preparation for winter.[12]

Public officials have also been served by the rise of improved weather forecasting, which grew dramatically since the Blizzard of 1977. By the late 1960s the National Weather Bureau had computers and an orbiting satellite station to track weather, but forecasting remained limited. Meanwhile, the federal government ambitiously sought a means to control snow by controlling the weather. Weather control began with seeding clouds to make rain, an idea discovered by accident at the General Electric labs in Schenectady, New York, when Vincent Schaefer discovered that dry ice dropped into a conventional freezer created clouds of ice crystals.

In the late 1960s, the federal government sponsored a program called "Project Lake Effect." The National Oceanic and Atmospheric Administration (NOAA) seeded clouds around the Erie and Ontario lakes, hypothesizing that they could alter the weather and induce snow to fall inland away from industrialized cities and concentrated populations near the lakes. Initially the project saw positive results, but public concern brought legislative hearings and a call for regulation by New York State officials, which dampened enthusiasm for the project. The government abandoned Project Lake Effect in 1977, the same year the United States signed onto a United Nations pledge to ban military control of the weather.[13]

So limited was forecasting in 1977, only one television station in the Buffalo area predicted the storm. WKBW foretold the snowstorm two days in advance because they paid a private weather service called AccuWeather for weather models. To keep up with private forecasters, the National Weather Service (NWS) adopted new technology, including satellite coverage of the earth provided by the Geostationary Operational Environmental Satellite (GOES), Doppler radar, and a global network of weather-gathering stations that use advanced computers to generate data for better precision in forecasting storms.[14]

Today, forecasters can issue warnings anywhere from three to five days ahead of a significant storm, and thanks to the careful lake effect research of meteorologists such as Robert J. Sykes, they can predict not just what, or how much, but also where the snow may fall. The result has been that both citizens and governments are better prepared for blizzards and snowstorms now than they were in 1977. For example, in 1978, forecasters missed the New England Blizzard of 1978 that killed ninety-nine people, stranded thousands of cars and trucks, and shut down transportation for a week or more. In contrast, a similar blizzard that struck New England in 2013 was forecast days ahead, and the government instituted a driving ban ahead of the storm that cut down on fatalities and injuries.[15]

Television and radio coverage of the weather increased in the 1970s, just as suburbanization and urban sprawl made daily commutes longer and more treacherous in winter. The anxiety of commuters about their daily travels have led to an increase in the amount of weather coverage on local news stations and generated entire channels devoted to covering weather events. In Buffalo, this focus has also changed everyday habits. At one point, the business community urged NWS personnel to tone down their weather warnings because it was "scaring people, and they were staying home," rather than going to work or shopping.[16]

Most local news programs begin with a weather teaser and then return to talk about the weather in the middle of a broadcast and again at the end. Radio stations often provide weather and traffic reports at regular intervals during morning and afternoon commutes. With the advent of digital channels, some stations now carry a local weather report twenty-four hours a day. Information for these broadcasts comes from both the NWS and one of the hundreds of private firms that sell weather consulting services. The best known of these firms is AccuWeather, which began operating in State College, Pennsylvania, in 1962 and sold forecasts to local television and radio stations. Two decades later the Weather Channel launched and provided around-the-clock weather information.[17]

Weather news, especially severe weather, increases viewership and listenership.[18] The effect of this has been mixed, with media critics suggesting that meteorologists hype forecasts.[19] Others have countered that the protection of lives and property demands such warnings, even if they prove to be faulty. Storm warnings lead people to become fearful of being stuck indoors, so they descend on local grocery stores and purchase days' worth of bread, milk, and other staples.[20]

To sort the hype from reality, some municipalities have turned to a tool called the "Maintenance Decision Support System" to provide accurate information on weather conditions and the kind of snow that is going fall. As road managers know, there is no such thing as generic snow. Snow contains various degrees of water, and this affects the way street departments approach road conditions.[21]

In addition to improved weather forecasting, twenty-first-century cities, counties, and states have adopted smart snowplows that use sophisticated technology to measure pavement temperature and the amount of residual salt still on the road. Twenty-first-century plows display the many technological modifications adopted for plows since the 1960s. Hydraulics turn the blades to match road conditions. Plows often work in tandem, a procedure in which two plow teams work the same street to clear it more rapidly. Many public works trucks include winged plows, which eliminate the need for tandem plowing.[22]

Global positioning systems and geographic information systems direct plows to the most efficient pathways and note every landmark, from guardrails to county lines, that plows are likely to encounter and must avoid. Computer software tracks weather conditions, allowing plows to make real-time adjustments to meet changing road conditions. This technology provides the driver with essential information on how much salt is needed to reduce or prevent icing. Preventive anti-icing has replaced simple deicing because it reduces the amount of salt required and the effort it takes to clear roadways. Creating a brine of salt and water will reduce the bouncing effect of dry salt, and laying brine down two hours before a snowfall will prevent icing from occurring in the first place. Adding beet or pickle juice makes the brine mix stickier, which aids in disrupting ice formation.[23]

Snow Control in Buffalo after 1977

New emergency management agencies in the city and county, increased use of technology, better weather forecasts, and a knowledge that both state and federal governments would provide resources in case of emergencies have given city officials in Buffalo the ability to avoid a repetition of Buffalo's Blizzard of 1977, even when they faced winter storms that were even more severe.

Jimmy Griffin succeeded Stanley Makowski as mayor of Buffalo. Born and raised in the First Ward, where the bulk of Buffalo's Irish had come to settle, Griffin was a balding, belligerent politician who had gone from high school dropout to a seat on the Common Council and then into the New York State Senate. A political maverick, he bucked the party system by running for mayor. Democratic Party Chair Joseph Crangle endorsed Arthur Eve, who won the Democratic primary. Griffin ran and won the 1977 election on the Conservative Party line, and the rift between Crangle and Griffin never healed.[24]

Griffin, whose politics emphasized Buffalo's past accomplishments, and he appealed to the working class by keeping taxes and expenditures low. He focused his efforts as mayor into redeveloping Buffalo's downtown and waterfront. Griffin easily won reelection in 1981 with the endorsements and ballot lines of the Democrat, Republican, Conservative, and Independent parties.[25]

Griffin may have won over the Democratic Party in his second term in office, but Mother Nature was less forgiving. He faced his first significant snowstorm in 1982. The snow began late Sunday night on January 10, 1982, and continued into the Monday commute. The airport shut down, the New York State Thruway closed from Rochester to the Pennsylvania state line, and motorists became stranded on the Thruway. At least five people died.[26] Griffin did not declare an emergency, nor did he issue a travel ban, mainly because the snow struck on a weekend and schools and businesses voluntarily closed on Monday. By Tuesday morning, January 12, 1982, roads were open and the streets cleared.[27]

A mild winter allowed moisture from unfrozen Lake Erie to build and led to the two-day Leap Year Storm of February 27–29, 1984. The storm dropped more than two feet of snow on the Buffalo metropolitan region, killed nine people, closed schools and businesses, and trapped citizens in their cars overnight. Griffin, alerted to the storm while on vacation in Florida, quickly returned to assume command of the snow-fighting efforts. Aware of the need to cultivate the media, he held a press conference to reassure people that he had things under control.

He also had to fend off being undermined by his political rivals. The mayor learned that, in his absence, the Common Council, headed by political rival George K. Arthur (who was an ally of Joe Crangle), had assumed control of snow-fighting efforts and voted an additional sum of $250,000 to fight the snow. Returning to the city, Griffin instituted the "Buffalo plan" and brought equipment from the surrounding towns into the city, which alleviated the crisis. He conducted a massive towing operation and removed 900 cars from Buffalo's streets but did not impose any fines.[28]

The worst blizzard of the Griffin era occurred in 1985 when a subarctic air mass, known as an Alberta Clipper, came sweeping down into the region and plunged temperatures thirty degrees below zero. Lake Erie had not frozen that year, and the moisture from the lake turned into thirty-five inches of snow accompanied by subzero temperatures and winds over fifty miles an hour. The storm paralyzed the city from January 19 until 21. Zero visibility rendered the fleet of eighty plows useless and, in a replay of 1977, cars and trucks stalled on roads and highways, which forced people to wait in their vehicles for rescue or to abandon their vehicles in dangerously cold conditions and desperately search for shelter.

Griffin showed no fear or indecision. Drawing on lessons learned during the Blizzard of 1977, the city leader told the people of Buffalo to "stay inside, grab a six-pack, and watch a good football game."[29] Griffin imposed a total driving ban that lasted the entire week, and he enforced it with police roadblocks and minimum fines of twenty-five dollars.[30]

Griffin's actions displeased some. Buffalo merchants worried about lost revenue due to the driving ban, and on a national scale General Motors was concerned that closing the Buffalo plant would delay shipments to their operations across the country. Common Council members complained that the mayor lacked a clear snow removal plan and that most side streets remained clogged with snow: "I could build an igloo on my street," one council member declared.[31]

The storm was a potential threat to Griffin's political career. The mayor's pugnacious attitude had already irked members of the Common Council whom he called "goofs" and "liars." His reputation with the media was rocky, as everyone recalled how he once threw a local news crew out of his house. Crangle gleefully noted that Griffin had "alienated a number of community members."[32] African American leaders were especially critical of Griffin. City Council President George Arthur claimed Griffin ignored the needs of the black community. Despite the impressive development in Buffalo, which included a new convention center, a light rail rapid transit system, a new ball field for the local AAA baseball team, hotels, and condominiums on the waterfront, the federal dollars were not flowing into all neighborhoods. James Pitts, who represented a majority-minority district on Buffalo's East Side, estimated 40 percent of African Americans were unemployed in spite of the construction work.

Arthur, who planned to run against the two-term incumbent mayor in the fall, used the snowstorm as a chance to attack Griffin. Citing the bungled storm response as an example of Griffin's incompetence, Arthur claimed that Griffin lacked a comprehensive plan for snowstorms other than closing schools and public agencies. The mayor, he charged, failed to think about the people who needed to get to work but could not because of the lack of public transportation.[33]

Griffin's popularity with independents, Republicans, and some Democrats led him to easily win a third term in November 1985. Overall, Mayor Griffin's ability to deal with the threat to mobility by snow was of significant advantage. Despite criticism that he did not attend to the needs of the black community, Griffin won an unprecedented fourth term in office in 1989 with 79 percent of the vote.[34]

It was not only the mayor's office that showed improved skill in dealing with winter. All across Erie County, towns and villages showed better preparation for extreme snowfall. James Pierakos, the deputy street commissioner in Buffalo, urged the towns and villages around Buffalo to adopt and enforce new powers to declare emergencies and snow holidays.[35] Erie County Sheriff Kenneth Braun purchased twenty-four new four-wheel-drive cars and trucks to prepare for a future snow emergency.[36] The county and the city of Buffalo created the Buffalo Plan of mutual aid between regional and city governments for all political subdivisions to share their equipment during a storm.[37]

In 1978, after suffering two major disasters, the ice storm of 1976 and the Blizzard of 1977, Erie County retooled its disaster response agency, the Office of Disaster Preparedness, which was placed in the division of environmental planning.[38] This agency became the center for disaster response from twenty-five towns and villages, whereas the three cities in Erie County—Buffalo, Lackawanna, and Tonawanda—have their own separate disaster preparedness offices.[39]

Erie County Executive Ed Rutkowski, who succeeded Ned Regan, was attending Ronald Reagan's second inauguration when the 1985 blizzard struck. He issued a countywide emergency declaration and initiated the Buffalo Plan of mutual assistance. The all-wheel drives purchased after 1977 gave sheriff deputies greater mobility to deal with the crisis. New York State, under the authority of Governor Mario Cuomo, responded with alacrity and initiated the Emergency Operations Center in Albany, which provided better coordination among state, federal, county, and local officials than was seen in 1977.[40]

The action by all levels of government, the fact that the storm came on a weekend when fewer people needed to travel, and the shorter duration of the event left citizens satisfied and also gained the respect of the national press.[41] FEMA turned down a request by Governor Cuomo for a disaster declaration. The FEMA representatives found that the emergency was not beyond the means of state and local officials to handle. Although Governor Cuomo objected, in the era of "no dough for snow," the decision was upheld, and Buffalo received no federal assistance.

President Clinton was more generous with federal snow declarations, in part because the Stafford Act of 1988 gave the president more power to control what constituted an emergency or disaster, and also because Clinton gave higher priority to natural disasters compared to his predecessors. Clinton appointed James Lee Witt to helm FEMA. Witt was the first professional emergency manager to run FEMA, and he replaced a third of the inexperienced political appointees with experienced professionals drawn from the civil service. As he remembered it, "The White House didn't like that, but the president didn't mind."[42]

Clinton may also have been more generous because he calculated, as Carter had in the Buffalo blizzard, that there would be a political benefit for his generosity. Much like Carter, Clinton needed all the political support he could muster due to his close election and reverse coattail effect. Bill Clinton was elected president with just 43 percent of the popular vote, and except for Arkansas and the District of Columbia, he failed to get 50 percent of the vote in any of the states. Worse for Clinton, in the midterm election of 1994 his party lost fifty-four seats in the House of Representatives and ceded control to the Republican Party.[43]

As president, Clinton granted twenty-four major disaster declarations for snow and ice; he also declared twenty-eight emergencies, some for the most marginal of storms.[44] Buffalo had few snowstorms during Clinton's time in office. The winter storms that battered Buffalo fell on the weekends or were of such short duration that there was little disruption to the social and economic life of the city or region. It also helped that the man who ran Buffalo in the Clinton era was Anthony "Tony" Masiello. Masiello was born and raised on Buffalo's West Side. As the son of a former public works employee, he understood his father's mantra, which was "stay ahead of the storm." Anytime storms threatened the region, Masiello quickly imposed a driving ban and positioned plows ahead of the winter weather. During his tenure in office, Masiello installed the latest GIS equipment on plows to better plot snow-fighting efforts. He kept city offices in communication with the NWS, which had perfected a forecasting model, aptly named "BUFKIT," which predicted lake-effect snow patterns.[45]

When cars blocked the narrow city streets and prevented plowing, the mayor had them towed to city lots, but knowing the furor that occurred when Makowski ticketed and towed back in 1977, Masiello wisely granted owners a seventy-two-hour grace period to pick them up for free. Masiello's policies kept weather dislocations to a minimum, even in the winter of 1999, when the region lay beneath five feet of snow and President Bill Clinton declared an emergency for the period January 1 through January 15, 1999. The mayor's response to the storms earned Buffalo a national reputation as a city that knew how to deal with snow.[46]

This was true even when the unexpected happened. During Thanksgiving week in 2000, Buffalo received more snow in twenty-four hours than had ever been recorded. The storm began on Monday, November 20, 2000, and fell at a rate of four inches an hour, and by the time the snow from the "Gridlock Monday Storm" ended, it had dropped thirty-five inches of snow on Buffalo. The timing of the snow could not have been worse. It began during the afternoon commute home and created chaos and desperation as people abandoned their cars and sought shelter across western New York. As many as two hundred school buses full of children became stuck in the snow, forcing the children to take refuge across the city in retail outlets, fire halls, city halls, and restaurants. Many other motorists followed suit, finding shelter where they could. Some people chose to stay in their car but had a long wait. Meredith McDowall from East Aurora had been on her way to Buffalo when the storm hit. She remained in her car for twenty hours, awaiting rescue.

The mayor and city streets operators remained upbeat since they had a plan for digging out. The Buffalo Parks Department and the Streets and Public Works Commission had merged into one large department that year, which doubled the size of the winter crew. The city and county had the most up-to-date equipment available and, during the height of the crisis, borrowed material from as far away as Toronto. The mayor banned all nonemergency travel and set up police roadblocks on the outskirts of the city to keep people from trying to drive in. Governor George Pataki sent in the National Guard with snow-fighting equipment and dump trucks to haul the snow away. By Wednesday, public officials restored order, and people resumed making plans for Thanksgiving.[47]

A blizzard that began on Christmas Eve 2001 and lasted five days dropped 82.3 inches of snow and covered the region in 7 feet of snow. The storm closed the New York State Thruway and the Buffalo Niagara Airport and brought crews south from Toronto and west from Rochester. Governor Pataki dispatched the National Guard to help, and he, along with area congressional representatives, called on President George W. Bush to declare the area a disaster. However, the response by state and local officials was adequate, there was little disruption to travel, and the event never reached crisis proportions.[48]

Tony Masiello managed snow and politics well during his three terms in office. Like his predecessor Jimmy Griffin, Masiello was a popular mayor endorsed by the Republican and Democratic parties alike when he ran for reelection in 1997 and 2001. This kind of political capital gave Masiello independence from any one political party, and he felt secure in endorsing Pataki, the Republican governor of New York, in 1998 and 2002.

What Masiello could not manage was the decreased population and economic decline of Buffalo and western New York. He tried economic development to revitalize the city, but his efforts failed to bring Buffalo back to economic vitality. The city continued to borrow and its deficit ballooned. By 2003 the city was nearly bankrupt, and the state, with the endorsement of Masiello's ally Governor Pataki, imposed a state financial control board on the city that stripped powers from elected officials to spend and tax. This did not endear the mayor to the public, and Masiello wisely chose to retire from office in 2005 rather than lose reelection.[49]

In 2005, the public elected Byron K. Brown, the first African American mayor of Buffalo. Brown was not a native to Buffalo; he was born in Queens, New York, and then moved to the Buffalo region to attend Buffalo State College. After graduation, Brown found mentors in African American leaders such as George K. Arthur and Arthur Eve, who encouraged Brown to run for office in 1995. Brown was on the Common Council for five years before he pursued and won a seat in the New York State Senate. Brown was the first African American elected to the New York State Senate outside of New York City and the first to win in a white-majority district.[50]

Brown found himself facing an economy that might have been familiar to Stanley Makowski. Buffalo's deficit soared, and the mayor had no control over city finances. Worse yet, Erie County's debt approached $100 million, and it was placed under a fiscal control board imposed by the State of New York in 2005.[51]

Rather than focus exclusively on downtown development, which was the view of his predecessors in office, Brown set out to make the city more livable as a means to attract investment. He received a tremendous boost when Andrew Cuomo was elected governor in 2010. Cuomo provided a billion dollars in state redevelopment funding for the Buffalo metropolitan area, which resulted in, among other things, Canalside, a mixed recreational and entertainment district that opened up the river and harbor to area residents for the first time in nearly a hundred years. Brown did not neglect the various communities, and he spread funds throughout the city.[52] Brown easily won reelection in 2009, 2013, and 2017.[53]

Brown initially appeared to be less adept at handling winter storms than former mayors and native Buffalonians Jimmy Griffin and Tony Masiello. Brown faced a significant winter storm in 2006, which began in the late afternoon on Thursday, October 12, and lasted through early Friday, October 13. The weather service had called for rain, but instead as much as two feet of heavy wet snow fell at a rate of three inches an hour. The event left commuters and public officials caught off guard. Cars, trucks, and buses slid about in the heavy wet snow, creating a ten-mile-long traffic jam on the New York State Thruway. Some motorists remained trapped for over twenty-four hours awaiting rescue.

Trees across western New York, laden with leaves, were brought down by the heavy snow blocking roads and bringing down power lines that left more than 400,000 people in the dark and cold. There was also a danger of being without water as the county water authority nearly ran dry without power. The power remained off for days and even weeks for some, and spoiled food from stores and homes had to be tossed, leaving the poorest residents in desperate need of food. Food was slow to get into the region because the downed tree limbs and trees made travel impossible. Public works officials across the area had not converted their leaf collection trucks to snowplows, an operation that can take two hours per vehicle. Thus they had less equipment available when the storm struck, and city and town residents remained trapped in their unheated homes for days. Thirteen people died from this storm.[54]

Erie County Executive Joel Giambra and Mayor Brown, who rarely agreed on anything before the storm, worked in tandem during the crisis. Governor Pataki declared an emergency and sent in National Guard troops and equipment to help clean up the trees and limbs.[55] At the federal level, President Bush declared an emergency for western New York and sent in FEMA to assess the damage and assist in cleanup operations. During his presidency, Bush issued fewer snow-related declarations than his predecessor Bill Clinton—just five major disasters and twenty-nine emergency declarations for winter storms.[56]

The local congressional delegation, which included Louise Slaughter (D-Fairport), Brian Higgins (D-Buffalo), Tom Reynolds (R-Clarence), and Senators Hillary Clinton and Charles Schumer, pressured President Bush for a major disaster declaration. President Bush was quick to comply. The storm came with the midterm election just weeks away, and many felt a disaster declaration would enhance the standing of Republican Tom Reynolds.[57]

Bush declared the region a major disaster on October 25, 2006, and sent $45 million in aid, but much of this assistance went to the suburbs. Within Buffalo, the bulk of the money went to the poorest residents in the majority-minority East Side of the city rather than to the upper- and middle-class citizens of North Buffalo, who saw more damage. Federal aid also led to a prolonged dispute between FEMA and city officials over how the city spent money for cleanup damage.[58]

Some criticized Brown for failing to ask for help from Pataki, who deployed National Guard troops to the suburbs but not the city. Critics also wanted to know why the city was unprepared for winter and had no plows ready in mid-October. Brown sent out a press release reassuring the public on how "the equipment and crews [were] doing an excellent job; we're still working on leaf and refuse removal across the city. Since then, the snow-fighting equipment has been reassessed and thoroughly prepared for the coming winter season." Pressured by public disapproval, over the next ten years, the mayor spent an additional $10 million on new snow-fighting equipment for the public works department, all of which had the latest technology for tracking the vehicles and measuring the pavement for temperature and salt. Included in this are ATVs and snowmobiles so that services could continue even during the worst of storms.[59] He also reviewed past procedures and instituted new snow removal protocols, including deploying AmeriCorps volunteers to shovel the walks of the aged and infirm.[60]

Buffalo mayors learned from the Blizzard of 1977, but it came with a price. The budgets used for snow fighting continue to grow, as does the city's dependency on the use of road salt to combat snow and ice during the winter months. During his tenure in office, Mayor Brown's budget for snow removal rose from $6.7 million, of which $750,000 was earmarked for salt and sand, to $8.9 million in the 2018 budget, of which $1.1 million was allotted for salt and sand. On average, the city uses 7,000 tons of salt annually.[61]

Road salt accounts for nearly half of all salt sales in the United States, and the cost of salt has been an issue for local governments since at least the 1970s. But fearful of a repeat of the Blizzard of 1977, few dare to face the winter without salt. In justifying the expense, most cite a Salt Institute–sponsored study from Marquette University that offers data proving road salt pays for itself by reducing accidents, injuries, and costly delays. The American Highway Users Alliance, another trade advocacy group in Washington, DC, has calculated that just one day of closed roads will cost a city $300 to $700 million in lost wages and economic activity.[62]

Salt is necessary but not always available. Shortages have caused panic for those responsible "to ease the flow of traffic in winter by removing snow and ice and by salting the streets."[63] In the 1970s, a series of harsh winters reduced the regular stockpile of salt at the same time there were production problems in the salt mines and winter storm disruptions in transportation systems. Some public works officials made plans to switch back to abrasives, such as sand and cinders, or use alternatives on roadways such as beet juice. These factors sufficiently concerned William Dickinson of the Salt Institute that he asked to speak to public works personnel at the APWA North American Salt Conference. Dickinson assured the attendees that the shortage was temporary and suggested that in the future officials should preorder and stockpile salt.[64]

In 1994 another shortage loomed after the collapse of the world's largest salt mine. The Restof mine, located near Rochester, New York, once contributed a third or more of all salt used in the Northeast and was the leading supplier to the states of Vermont, New

Hampshire, Maine, Massachusetts, New York, New Jersey, Rhode Island, Connecticut, and Pennsylvania. After the mine collapsed, panicky public works personnel had to secure sufficient supplies for the winter of 1994–95 from other sources. Severe winters led to salt shortages again in 2008 and 2014.[65]

Shortages not only cause stress for highway superintendents but also can deplete a local government's budget by increasing the cost of snow removal. A salt shortage in 2008 led to the per-ton price jumping from 45 dollars to 70 dollars a ton. This put stress on state and local budgets, which were already experiencing economic upheaval due to the near-collapse of the financial industry that year.[66]

The industry standard is for salt contracts to be issued in the fall, long before the snow falls, thereby requiring public officials to estimate how much salt they think they will need for the upcoming winter. Salt contracts are subject to an 80 percent acceptance rate, meaning that highway department officials have to buy 80 percent of the salt they ordered, even if they do not need it. It is a risky situation because if they do not order enough salt before winter, the salt they buy during winter can cost twice as much per ton as they paid in their fall contract.[67]

There is another cost to salt. Salt corrodes metal on cars, bridges, and the steel reinforcements beneath modern roadways and parking garages. It is estimated that in addition to the $2.3 billion spent on salt every year, the damage inflicted by salt corrosion may cost the United States between $16 and $19 billion a year.[68] This cost will rise as more salt is added to our nation's roadways.

7

No Thruway

Automobility in Decline

By the year 2014, nearly forty years after the Blizzard of 1977, the city of Buffalo had earned a reputation (that some felt was undeserved) of being a city of snow and ice. It had also earned a reputation (that many felt was well-deserved) of being a city capable of handling snowstorms that would have paralyzed nearly any other city. A major snowstorm in November 2014 solidified Buffalo's image as a winter "ice bowl" and challenged its reputation for competence.

Beginning late Monday on November 17 and then continuing early Tuesday morning on November 18, 2014, snow began falling in the Buffalo region at a rate of three to five inches an hour. Within twenty-four hours, seven feet of snow had fallen on Buffalo and in towns south of the city. The lake-effect snow fell in a pattern not usually seen, creating a sheer line separating streets that saw snow mounded on one side of a street and virtually no snow on the other. While towns south of Buffalo were buried beneath the snow, cities to the north remained snow-free and road crews picked up fallen leaves. Dubbed "the high wall of snow" or "the Knife" by locals, the storm killed a dozen people, collapsed over thirty roofs, trapped motorists in their cars for up to two days, and isolated people in their homes for almost a week.

Although there was a warning of an impending snowstorm, the forecast did not indicate the magnitude of snow that befell the city. On November 17, 2014, the National Weather Service (NWS) and local meteorologists had warned of a lake-effect snowstorm that was expected to bring about two feet of snow.[1] The storm swept in with gale-force winds, picking up snow from Lake Erie and creating snowdrifts as high as houses. Some compared it to the Blizzard of 1977. Jack Fasanella, a sixty-year-old lifelong resident of Buffalo, was trapped in his home for days and said that the 2014 storm was "worse than the Blizzard of '77." The blizzard of 1977, he recalled, made driving impossible but not walking. "You can't walk through this stuff," Fasanella said of the seven feet of snow that fell in 2014. Unlike in 1977, when most people had a week's worth of food on hand at any one time, generational changes made people more vulnerable in 2014. Panic gripped people who were trapped in their houses with food for only a few days, and in some cases they lacked heat because the snow covered their heating vents and people lacked the tools to get on their roofs to clear the snow.[2]

Despite an emergency ban on travel issued countywide, many people tried to drive. They became stuck in the snow, which compounded the difficulty for plow drivers, who could not get down roads to remove snow due to abandoned automobiles.[3] Buffalo's mayor, Byron Brown, told the public that clearing the snow would be a slow process; he said "there is a long way to go" before the situation would be under control. Erie County officials warned people to stay off the roads. Abandoned cars made plowing impossible after the storm hit. Deputy County Executive Richard Tobe told the public to expect the travel ban to last at least seventy-two hours while officials cleared streets of abandoned cars and removed the snow.[4]

The combined efforts of local public works officials removed well over five thousand tons of snow from roads.[5] Unable to dump the snow in the sewers or truck it to the Niagara River as they might have done after the Blizzard of 1977, city workers piled the snow in designated lots such as the lot near Buffalo's Central Terminal, where it remained throughout the cold winter of 2014–15. The snow pile did not melt until after July 2015. The filthy snow pile accumulated more snow throughout the winter, and the dirt reflected the sun's rays making it even more difficult to melt.[6]

The endurance of the snow, which did finally melt, was no match for the improved response of Buffalo to storms since 1977. Greater coordination and cooperation, updates to equipment, and larger budgets for winter have made a significant difference for the region, which has earned a reputation as a city that knows how to handle snow. One local author even showcased Buffalo's snow-fighting ability in a children's book titled *Max Meets the Mayor*.[7]

Buffalo and other Snowbelt cities reduced their vulnerability to winter through technological solutions and by mitigation methods such as imposing driving bans; however, extreme weather events such as those in 2006 and 2014 continued to endanger lives and property. Still, the highest risk is no longer in the city but on the roads between towns and their suburbs and exurbs, where mobility continues to be subjected to threats from winter on the multiple roads leading into and out of the city. In fact, many of the worst snow disasters have befallen people trapped on the New York State Thruway or one of its offshoots.

In the second decade of the twenty-first century, anyone driving on New York State's section of I-90, or spurs such as 190, 290, 390, 490, or 590, have seen signs erected by New York State meant to provide vital information to motorists such as amber alerts, lane closures, and warnings about the potential for winter driving hazards. Some people may have noticed gates installed by the state to keep people from entering the Thruway when winter hazards are realized. These devices are twenty-first-century responses to winter's continual threat to mobility.

Death on the Highway

Transportation paralysis and death on the highways stirred the first imaginings that snow was a disaster. After back-to-back winters during 1978–79, which featured storms that trapped motorists in their cars for two or three days at a time, Michigan State Department of Transportation Director John P. Woodford took action to combat the human suffering and economic loss. "It is not only a danger to people to be stranded on the enclosed freeway, but the vehicles, often abandoned, make snow clearing an impossibility," Woodford said. In 1975, Michigan piloted the idea of closing freeways during snowstorms. Due to its success, after the blizzards of 1977–78, the plan was implemented statewide and then across the Snowbelt.[8]

The power to close freeways and the political will to close highways are two very different things. Until the twenty-first century, officials only closed the New York State Thruway after a snow event, never before one occurred.

This policy changed after the press and public expressed outrage at Governor Andrew Cuomo for failing to close the Thruway when a three-day snowstorm brought three feet of snow to Buffalo beginning on December 1, 2010. Rain turned to snow without warning, and trucks on the New York State Thruway slipped and jackknifed, effectively blocking the road and causing a massive backup. Oblivious to the danger, drivers continued to enter the Thruway but were unable to get off, and they remained stuck in their cars as the road became covered in several feet of snow, leaving them stranded for over seventeen hours.[9]

Public anger led to a call for better closing procedures for the Thruway. Initially, the state placed New York State Troopers at key entrance ramps in case of snow, but this entailed massive communication and labor resources, leading the state to install remote-controlled gates to close access to the Thruway.[10] The first test of the system happened in 2011 when forecasters predicted a massive storm would strike western New York. Thruway authorities closed the roadway to tandem trucks, stationed heavy wreckers in case trucks jackknifed, and closed the gates to prevent cars from entering the road. The precautions proved unnecessary because the forecast proved erroneous, and many people criticized the governor for acting too quickly.[11]

When the November 2014 storm dropped seven feet of snow on the area in less than two days, plowing became ineffective. One emergency responder who looked at the abandoned and stuck cars suggested it was "like Beirut here."[12] The heavy snow closed the Thruway from the Pennsylvania state line to Rochester, and those unfortunate enough to be on it when the storm hit were there for over a day and some longer.

The storm trapped the entire women's basketball team from Niagara University on the Thruway for nearly two days.[13] Nor was being stuck in a car a mere inconvenience; one man trapped in his car tried to use his cell phone to get assistance, first to the AAA Automobile Club and then to police, but no help came, and he was found dead in his car the next day.[14]

The local response was heroic. One police captain, Jeff Hartman, led fifty stranded motorists from route 170 on a one-mile walk to a warm gas station. The Lackawanna Toll Plaza became a haven for over two dozen motorists stuck there overnight. Residents in the Buffalo area responded by volunteering their time and snowmobiles to rescue trapped strangers and bring food and medicine to neighbors. Much like the Blizzard of 1977, people opened their homes to help strangers stranded by the storm.[15]

Governor Andrew Cuomo flew to the scene on Friday, November 21, to inspect the damage and to urge President Barack Obama to issue a major disaster declaration. The local congressional delegation accompanied Cuomo and expressed the belief that the damage would reach the necessary threshold of $27 million statewide to qualify for disaster relief money from the federal government.

Yet Cuomo's failure to close the Thruway quickly enough in November 2014 led to widespread criticism. Although the governor declared an emergency and sent in National Guard troops, he failed to close the Thruway before the storm, and many cars and trucks became stuck there. The installation of barriers and other mechanisms would have been a practical and straightforward means of protecting lives.[16]

Over 150 cars were stuck, leaving hundreds of people trapped in their vehicles for thirty to forty-eight hours at a time. This inspired a state senate investigation of the governor and the Thruway Authority and led to the resignation of key leaders of the Thruway Authority, including the chairman, executive director, and chief financial officer.[17]

At a press conference during the height of the storm, a reporter asked Cuomo why he had not closed the Thruway immediately. The governor defended his lack of action by reminding the press that in 2011 he had closed the Thruway when conditions were not that severe. Cuomo said he was damned if he did and damned if he did not. Rather than accept the blame, the governor tried to deflect it to others, such as blaming motorists themselves for becoming stuck on the road by suggesting they had somehow bypassed the gates and illegally entered the Thruway after it closed.[18]

When he received negative press for blaming the victims of the Thruway debacle, Governor Cuomo suggested the event was an act of God and an extraordinary circumstance beyond his control. "Mother Nature is showing us who's boss once again," he told reporters. He also blamed the NWS for failing to warn the government and citizens of the impending storm. Cuomo said that "no one had an idea" that Buffalo was in danger, claiming that the NWS "was off" on its forecasts.[19]

The snowstorm of 2014 refocused state and local authority on the problem of snow fighting. After the seventy inches of snow in November, Cuomo called for the state to spend an additional $50 million to buy equipment in advance of winter. The program, called "N.Y. Response," included online tools and technology to bring rural and urban areas affected by heavy snow into contact with the latest information. In a press release, New York State Department of Transportation Commissioner Matthew Driscoll announced that sixty-two state-of-the-art plows would be added to the state's fleet and included tow plows attached to plow trucks that would allow them to clear two thruway lanes at once.[20]

Concerned about the political cost of another transportation debacle, the state showed an immediate response in 2015 when up to three feet of snow was forecast to fall over a three-hour period. Responding to the forecast, the state's Emergency Operations Center closed the Thruway at 9:00 p.m. in advance of the projected three feet of snow. They assembled an armada of equipment to combat the storm, including 793 snowplows and 48,000 tons of salt.

Not only did state authorities close the New York State Thruway, but they also closed Route 219, Route 400, and several other significant roads long before the snow fell. By the next day, plows had cleared the streets down to the bare pavement, but the Thruway remained closed for several hours after the snow blitz, suggesting a "new normal" of caution in responding to lake-effect snowstorms. Lieutenant Governor Kathleen Hochul, referring to the 2014 incident, said: "There were a lot of lessons learned from the last experience." The state was not going to "run the risk of another situation with children and families stranded."[21]

Since 2014 the governor has preemptively closed the New York State Thruway several times in advance of winter storms. In some cases, the government has banned all vehicles and, in others, just tandem trucks and trailers.[22] This policy is in stark contrast to the prevailing concerns of the 1960s and 1970s that driving bans would infuriate commuters, anger the business community, and cause economic hardship due to lost wages and productivity. It reflects a turning away not only of old policy but also of the hegemonic control that cars have had in defining mobility for Americans. The rise of the internet led to a revolution in mobility that has dethroned the car and remade the American economy. By 2017 a Gallup Poll showed that, of employed Americans, 43 percent said they worked at least part of the time remotely. E-commerce is rapidly replacing brick and mortar stores, thus making the automobile no longer as economically vital as it once was.[23] Mobility has made the necessity of the car less important and raised new awareness about the environmental hazards from road salt.

Salt and the Environment

Although environmentalists and public health officials began raising questions about the potential for health and environmental risks from the use of road salt in the 1960s, it was not until the twenty-first century that these concerns were taken seriously. This was mainly because the Salt Institute dismissed such matters, and public works employees became more concerned about the short-term goal of keeping traffic flowing in the winter rather than the long-term effects on the environment.

One early opponent of salt was Carolyn Whittle of Massachusetts, who advocated for a total ban on road salt. Whittle found no statistical evidence that salt cut down on motor accidents during winter, but she did notice that it contributed to the corrosion of cars. She was concerned about the potential for health and environmental problems. Despite her lobbying effort, Massachusetts did not ban the use of road salt but bowed to public pressure and cut down on its use.[24]

Environmental concerns led the National Academy of Sciences (NAS) to study salt's effects. The NAS found that road salt did hurt roadside vegetation as well as pine, hemlock, sugar maple, red maple, and other ornamental trees. They found evidence that salt interfered with photosynthesis in plants. A study funded by the Environmental Protection Agency (EPA) discovered road salt in groundwater, which made its way into streams and harmed freshwater organisms. The same survey echoed the NAS findings by showing that brine runoff from salt on pavement scorched and killed roadside vegetation. The EPA report estimated that the total cost from salt damage was $2.8 billion, but added a disclaimer that the figure would be much higher if they calculated the effects on health.[25]

To disarm opponents, the Salt Institute produced a twenty-five-minute color film, which they premiered at the annual snow conference in 1973. The film depicted the parents of a girl who died in an accident on an unsalted road. The mother in the movie acknowledged that there might have been some environmental damage from road salt but stated, "You can replace a tree, but we'll never be able to replace our daughter." The institute reinforced this dramatic depiction of the life-saving properties of salt with data collected from one of their funded research programs showing that salt saved 500 lives a year and $18.4 billion in economic and property losses.[26]

A 1980 story in the *New York Times* claimed road salt endangered the lives of pets and children who consumed salted snow at the roadside. Salt Institute president William Dickinson scoffed at the idea. "Why a child or pet would want to eat salted snow is unknown. However, the salt used in roadways is chemically the same as the salt used on potatoes," Dickinson told the *New York Times*. For the less than one percent of the population who might be harmed by salt-contaminated water, Dickinson suggested they should drink bottled water instead.[27]

By the 1980s, it was evident that snow control policies had created a new hazard. A study of urban snow piles found that these contained chemicals and a great deal of sodium and calcium from road salt. In response, many states passed laws prohibiting the dumping of snow into creeks, streams, and rivers, which was common practice until the 1970s. Instead of disposing of snow in waterways, municipalities created dumping sites and snow farms in places where snow was unlikely to affect groundwater.[28]

Concerned about the danger of road salt led Burlington, Massachusetts, to issue a ban on road salt. Concord, Woburn, and Winchester, Massachusetts, followed. Two Rivers, Wisconsin and Tulsa, Oklahoma, later issued their bans. Boulder, Colorado, and Anchorage, Alaska (the fifth- and sixth-snowiest cities in the United States) switched from sodium chloride to the more expensive magnesium chloride to limit environmental degradation, and some towns experimented with beet brine as a safer alternative to salt. The Salt Institute dismissed these concerns, claiming that salt was a natural element found in rainwater and would eventually make its way back to the ocean. The Institute blamed Burlington and other municipalities for not storing their salt correctly and offered new guidelines on how to store salt safely and how to use it more sparingly. Thus was born the Salt Institute's "sensible salting program," which was meant to use salt more efficiently, and thereby save money, while also overcoming objections by environmental groups.[29]

The Salt Institute published *The Salt Storage Handbook* to instruct highway personnel on how to properly store salt to eliminate environmental hazards and methods to cut down on oversalting roadways. The Salt Institute proudly points to two studies; one by the University of Waterloo and Environment Canada showed chloride levels were cut in half when these best practices of salt storage and spreading were employed.[30]

In addition to publications, the Salt Institute developed seminars for trade shows and regional public works conferences. Backed by data showing that salt saved lives, Dickinson labeled antisalt diatribes as the result of "an emotionally charged atmosphere created by . . . environmentalists," a feeling shared by many road managers. At the annual snow conference in 1991, Paul Stirzek told attendees that the salt ban in Tulsa, Oklahoma, was a disaster. After Tulsa abandoned salt, it began to use abrasive sand, but sand lost its abrasive qualities and caused numerous accidents while also clogging the sewers. The media, he told his audience, had a field day with editorial cartoons lambasting the city. The public was outraged, and many letters to the editor pressured local officials into rescinding the ban. Fran Carr from the Massachusetts Department of Transportation scoffed at replacing road salt and asked, "What do you want, highways or skating rinks?"[31]

Objections to road salt have grown since the 1990s. A study by the Cary Institute of Ecosystem Studies found that 60 to 90 percent of salt in local groundwater came from salt used on the roads. The report pointed to the health risks associated with higher concentrations of salt in drinking water and the effects on freshwater organisms when salt levels rose in the Mohawk River. A similar study by the Rensselaer Polytechnic Institute found salt-infused groundwater harmed zooplankton by upsetting their circadian rhythms. In 2004 the Canadian government classified road salt as a toxin, and a 2005 study from Duke University showed that salt intrusion into groundwater was increasing and presented severe problems for sensitive plants.[32]

A US Geological Survey reported increasing levels of chloride in streams and groundwater was harming aquatic life and found that, in some urban areas, chlorine levels were becoming toxic. The Carey Institute teamed with the National Academy of Sciences for a report issued in April 2017 that detailed the growing chlorination of freshwater streams and rivers, which threatened wildlife—leading some legal scholars to lay out an agenda for regulating the use of road salt.[33] That agenda culminated in a test case in 2020, when a lawsuit in New York State courts charged that oversalting the Thruway killed an entire herd of dairy cows. An Ontario County farmer claimed that oversalting on the nearby New York State Thruway contaminated the groundwater on his farm and polluted his wells. He sought $250,000 in damages from New York State.[34] In the face of such opposition, the Salt Institute closed its doors abruptly and without explanation in March 2019. The dissolution of this trade group is another sign of the declining power of the automobility regime.[35]

The inclination of political leaders to close expressways and ban travel, along with rising concern about the use of road salt, reinforces the idea held by some scholars that the American love affair with the private automobile is over.[36] Signs that Americans are not as obsessed with cars seem to be everywhere. Travel by private automobile peaked and has declined throughout the United States. The climax of hours of private car ownership was in 2000 when forty-eight of the fifty states reached their peak. Since 2004, vehicle miles traveled per person have fallen or remained flat despite the growing American population. Miles driven since 2000 have fallen 10 percent.[37]

Obtaining a driver's license, the rite of passage to adulthood for Americans born in the twentieth century, does not have the same cachet for millennials and Generation Z. Obtaining one's first cell phone is now considered to be a sign of growing adulthood. The decline in the number of people with driver's licenses manifests this generational shift. Only 69 percent of nineteen-year-olds have a driver's license, compared with the 1980s when 90 percent of nineteen-year-olds had a license.[38]

Thirty- and forty-year-olds are less likely to have driver's licenses than those in earlier eras. People born after 1980 show a preference for sustainable forms of public transportation and have embraced the shared economy of Uber and Lyft. "There's been a shift publicly for people to move to things like public transportation that just wasn't there back in the '80s and '90s, partly because there's sometimes better public transportation in certain areas than there were a few decades ago, and a little more concern about the environment," said Brandon Schoettle, a University of Michigan researcher. Uber and Lyft are also attempting to create driverless cars.

Driverless cars also offer the chance of less traffic congestion and fewer automobile accidents. They may also be useful in terms of dealing with snow and ice by driving more slowly or utilizing advanced technology and sophisticated GPS to avoid entering certain highways. The advent of driverless cars betokens the revolution against automobility.[39]

Cities, which were once under the rule of the automobile regime, are now taking steps to reduce traffic flow. They show less desire to accommodate cars and more preference for pedestrians and bikers. Current practice in city planning is to promote pedestrians and biking. Most moderate to large cities already have bike lanes. Cities have shortened crosswalks by adding pedestrian islands, which take the road away from the car and allocate it to walkers. Most cities have reduced speed limits and become more aggressive in enforcing existing laws to protect pedestrians. Restricting vehicles is a "huge departure from how culturally [we have] thought about this over the years," said Dr. Kari Watkins, a civil and environmental engineer. In addition to accommodating people, some cities have begun to punish drivers with congestion pricing to discourage using private automobiles.[40]

Reversing the trend of building new roads, some cities and suburbs are reclaiming space once reserved for cars.[41] Rochester, New York, closed its inner-loop roadway system, which had opened to great fanfare in 1965. City leaders filled in the below-ground-level roadway to create space for new housing, parks, hotels, and retail outlets to bring people back to the downtown and to make the city more livable. Rochester's decision reflects an international trend. Evanston, Illinois, which once embraced the automobile, remade the town to become independent from the car. Evanston has half the amount of car traffic as its surrounding cities and has increased the use of public transportation. Cities in New York that also plan to demolish highways include Buffalo, Niagara Falls, Syracuse, and the Bronx.[42]

In Buffalo, the emblematic and closure-prone Skyway will be torn down, and its access ramps restored to city lots, adding twelve acres of downtown real estate for development. Although 42,300 people use the Skyway every day, city and state officials are unconcerned with diverting them to existing streets, and they claim this adds a maximum of five minutes to the daily commute. The 198, which divided the city economically and racially, is also being considered for a redesign.[43] Buffalo is also in the midst of a debate on a rising crisis in available downtown parking. In the post-automobility era, loud voices are advocating for less parking downtown because cheap parking encourages private cars at the expense of public transportation.[44]

In Toronto, Alphabet, Google's parent company, whose internet mobility may be responsible for toppling the regime of automobility, has agreed to create a mini-version of the city of the future. Self-driving cars will replace automobiles, walking, cycling, and public transportation. The company is exploring an idea first promoted in the 1960s—heated walkways to melt the snow in winter.[45]

If public policy continues to shift in the direction of increasing population density in cities and the development of public transportation that runs on track systems, then the risks of winter hazards may be reduced. Imagine interurban tracks that are heated to eliminate snow and ice. Fewer miles driven means fewer tons of road salt needed in the winter, potentially removing this environmental hazard. Increasing the number of goods delivered by train in the Northeast could reduce products and services that are now dependent on rubber-tired vehicles.[46]

Despite this rosy vision in which winter becomes potentially less disastrous, the rising threat of global climate change portends an increase in winter disasters in cities outside of the traditional Snowbelt. One example is the bomb cyclone that brought winter to the South in 2018.[47] Large-scale snow events and blizzards continue to be an existential threat to mobility. The snow that falls at the rate of several inches an hour overwhelms current technology and the ability to keep snow off the roads. Blowing snow creates whiteout conditions that force plows to wait until the roads are clear. Both types of conditions make it likely that cars, trucks, and buses will become stuck in the snow and create an impasse that hinders plowing. Anthropocene climate change has created new snow events south of the Snowbelt, which makes it all the more likely that immobility and paralysis of commerce and society will continue to be an issue for years to come. To better prepare for such events, it would behoove policymakers to look with care on the experience of Snowbelt cities in the twentieth century and begin implementing the lessons learned from the Blizzard of 1977.

Epilogue

Fixed in Memory

Near the end of my research I was contacted by my friend, J. P. Dyson, vice president for exhibits and director of the International Center for the History of Electronic Games at the Strong National Museum of Play. He invited me to review a new game from their collection that had not yet been played—the Blizzard of '77 Travel Game. Looking over the game, I was amazed at how perfectly it reflected the key elements of my work on the Blizzard of 1977.

Created just after the blizzard by C. P. Marino, the game comes in a rectangular cardboard box decorated with photographs of cars buried in snow, a stalled bus, and pedestrians walking in whiteout conditions. The images suggest to would-be players that the game will be a battle between snow and mobility. Upon opening up the box, one finds the contents include a two-sided game board that features a sunny side and a blizzard side. The game also includes thirty destination cards, twenty-two blizzard cards, twenty-two weather cards, six wooden tokens shaped like vehicles, and two standard six-sided dice.

The game consists of a board with spaces that the players must circumnavigate to get from start to finish. Game tokens are shaped like cars, buses, or trucks, thereby underscoring the importance of automobility in the movement from space to space. The goal of the game is to be the first player to make it back home after completing a series of tasks such as driving to the bank, the grocery store, the hardware store, and the pharmacy or making it into work.

10. The Blizzard of '77 Travel Game is one artifact of the blizzard. (Photo courtesy of the author.)

The game board has two sides. Players begin on side one, which features a sunny day in Buffalo. Players roll the dice and move a set number of spaces as they wind their way to each task before returning home. At five different intervals on the game, board players encounter a weather space and must draw a card, which has various instructions players must follow. Everything remains normal until a player draws the blizzard card. Once this happens, the entire game board must be flipped from its sunny side to the blizzard side, resetting the game and causing players to fight for survival in blizzard conditions.

Players now draw blizzard cards, and everywhere they turn, they encounter new obstacles that set them back, cause them to lose a turn, or wind up in jail for violating a ban on driving. Barriers include whiteouts, stalled cars, zero visibility, the driving ban, and snowdrifts—the very things that immobilized the people of Buffalo in 1977. The first player who circumnavigates these obstacles to complete all their tasks and reach "home" wins the game.[1]

The game captures the widespread view that the Blizzard of 1977 was a struggle between people and nature that threatened to disrupt their ordinary lives. What the players seek is to return to the normalcy of home. The game also provides a metaphor for public policy. Games are played by rules constructed by game designers, much like the public policy that is created by politicians and bureaucrats who shape outcomes for political and social interactions. Like people who subscribe to the rules of games, people rarely question how policies develop our dependence on cars or how this might threaten us and our natural environment.

The game is an artifact of the Blizzard of 1977; it is part of the image and memory created by that event but also reflects the struggle for identity that the people of Buffalo have experienced since the 1977 debacle. On the one hand, the city has tried to redefine itself as the "Miami of the North," while at the same time boasting of its ability to take on winter.[2] This struggle is an excellent example for how the environment and this particular storm shaped regional identity and memory.

The Blizzard of 1977 has become a fixture in the collective memory of Buffalo. For those who lived through it, the blizzard is a trauma seared in their minds. Yet individual consciousness is not the same as public memory of the disaster, which, as Don Glynn aptly put it, is "Frozen in Memory."[3] Since 1977 the blizzard has been routinely memorialized and recollected in the media, and the event remains the standard by which all other snowstorms are measured.[4] The persistence of this memory reflects how the storm of 1977 threatened the normal by redefining the city and not in a positive way.

Jimmy Carter declared the blizzard a disaster, not because of the snow totals, although they were extreme, but because of Buffalo's economic catastrophe that the blizzard exacerbated. The blizzard occurred amid deindustrialization and economic decline in the region; it jarred people within the community who were already grappling with an identity crisis. At one time, Buffalo was the largest inland port in the United States. Nicknamed the "Queen City of the Lakes," or simply the "Queen City," this identity was upended after the Saint Lawrence Seaway opened in 1957.[5]

Deindustrialization in the form of a decline in manufacturing and the loss of unionized jobs hit the region hard. The domestic steel and American auto industries were two of the largest industries hurt by global competition and the availability of cheaper labor in the Global South and Asia. As these industries declined, they eroded the economic base of the region. Bethlehem Steel, which was responsible for creating the city of Lackawanna just south of Buffalo, closed forever in 1983.[6] The loss of the steel industry created a host of secondary job losses as well. "It would be hard to overstate the sense of despair that enveloped western New York in the late 1970s and early 1980s," said former Erie County executive Dennis Gorski.[7]

The Blizzard of 1977, combined with the decline of manufacturing, left Buffalo with abandoned plants and brownfields, just as a new identity for Buffalo was fashioned in the aftermath of the blizzard. Buffalo became known as the "snow capital of the United States," the equivalent of an American Siberia. Don Sabo, a sociology professor at D'Youville College in Buffalo, noted that "Western New York has always had a chip on its shoulder," but it grew after the Blizzard of 1977. Whereas the 1930s musical *42nd Street* happily suggested that people "shuffle off to Buffalo," by the 1970s the musical *A Chorus Line* told audiences that "to commit suicide in Buffalo would be redundant."[8]

Some blamed their new image on late-night comedians, such as Johnny Carson, who hosted the *Tonight Show*. Carson's writers made the first jokes about snow and ice in Buffalo on February 10, 1977, and crafted the image of Buffalo as a city perpetually buried in snow and ice. Gorski, who served as Erie County executive from 1988 until 1999, was one of those who blamed Carson. For a long time, he said, Buffalonians were embarrassed by the "snow jokes on the Johnny Carson show."[9] And Buffalo mayor Jimmy Griffin claimed, "Johnny Carson caused many of our problems. If people want an easy joke, they mention our snow."[10] Indeed, Johnny Carson was influential. He hosted the *Tonight Show* for thirty years, and his monologues and shtick were, in the days before the internet, the topic of conversation around office watercoolers and coffee klatches across the country.[11] The image was so widespread that snow became synonymous with Buffalo. Television shows such as *Jesse*, a short-lived comedy set in Buffalo in the late 1990s, and movies such as *Best Friends* also equated Buffalo with snow jokes.[12]

For decades after the blizzard, citizens fought the negative stereotype of their city. Buffalo residents complained that no matter where they traveled, people poked fun at Buffalo for the snow.[13] The city unsuccessfully tried to change the arc through a public service campaign in the 1980s called "Talking Proud."[14] "For 37 years we've had to dig out from the frigid reputation left by the Blizzard of '77," complained local newspaper columnist, Denise Jewell Gee. Gee wanted to know why there was not more emphasis on the positive elements of the storm, such as neighborhood shovel brigades, volunteers using snowmobiles to deliver medicine, and the overwhelming sense of community.[15]

Unlike some disasters, such as floods or fires, the Blizzard of 1977 does not have a commemorative marker or monument. The memory of the blizzard is instead perpetuated through news articles and broadcast media. At regular intervals, anniversary stories appear that suggest a history of the blizzard as a terrifying but surmountable event. Every decade newspaper and television stories follow a well-scripted format of recollecting the emergency by detailing the extreme weather and the resilient and caring people who overcame it. Typical of such stories is the headline for the twenty-fifth anniversary of the blizzard: "Blizzard of '77 Brought Out the Best in Us."[16]

The desire to remember a disaster in a positive way is common after a disaster. Remembering disasters as "acts of God" beyond human culpability is particularly useful to elected officials.[17] Conceived in this way, the memory of a disaster may serve local leaders who want to avoid responsibility for actions or policies that contributed to a disaster. Policy failures included the decision by Erie County to eliminate civil defense in 1976, the city of Buffalo's deferred maintenance and hiring freeze on personnel for snow removal operations, and the bare pavement policy that made commuters more vulnerable to winter storms.[18]

Although rarely rewarded for spending tax dollars for preparation for a disaster, elected leaders are punished at the ballot box for real or perceived failures in dealing with a natural disaster. Thus, elected officials and community leaders focused on the positive memory of Buffalonians coming together and making a collective sacrifice for others during the disaster. For the people of Buffalo, the blizzard became part of their self-image as a resilient people capable of dealing with a destructive force of nature, and perhaps capable of surmounting the economic forces conspiring against the area.[19]

The public memory of the blizzard was expertly crafted to counter the narrative of economic decline and regional self-doubt that plagued Buffalo throughout the 1980s. As Judge Penny Wolfgang told a *New York Times* reporter, "We're saying: 'We made it. We'll make it again. And we'll always make it, no matter what they throw at us.'"[20]

Politicians asserted a celebratory view of the 1977 blizzard immediately after the event. President Carter took the lead when he sent a message to the people of Buffalo on February 8, 1977: "When Midge Costanza and my son Chip came back to tell what they'd seen in your city, they told me about police and firemen who were frostbitten rescuing motorists from the stalled cars . . . and about a community helping one another."[21] Another opinion leader, former television anchor Rich Kellman, echoed this by claiming that the storm "brought out the best in us" and "defined us as a community you can count on."[22]

The process may have begun with politicians but was solidified by Erno Rossi, a Canadian social studies teacher who wrote and self-published the first book on the storm in 1978. His book, *White Death: The Blizzard of '77*, is a collection of interviews with political leaders, first responders, and ordinary citizens in Canada and the United States. The respondents all have three things in common: an emphasis on the extreme and unexpected nature of the life-threatening storm, the resilience of the people in response to the blizzard, and the sense of community and camaraderie that emerged as people assisted one another.[23]

The book, like the Blizzard of '77 Travel Game, is another artifact of the blizzard. Rossi's book became an overnight success, selling 5,000 hardcover copies and 10,000 paperbacks in the first year alone, and altogether it has sold over 100,000 copies. Since writing the book, Rossi has taken up the role of memory keeper of the blizzard. The memory he created is one of the stories that highlight the "the human spirit" rising to "crush adversity" and "to restore faith in human nature."[24] He became the expert for US and Canadian regional news media outlets marking anniversaries of the event.[25] Rossi administers a Facebook page dedicated to the Blizzard of '77 that is run out of Welland, Ontario, and has over six thousand subscribers.[26]

Rossi's book was the first but not the only book on the blizzard. Tellingly, other histories of the blizzard have been far more critical of the situation in Buffalo, and perhaps because of this have been less successful with the public than Rossi's. Robert Bahr's *The Blizzard* was published in 1980 and provided a critical view of those involved in the storm. The book alludes to adulterous relations that developed as people found themselves thrown together overnight during the storm and exposes the incompetence of political leadership during the crisis. The media did not embrace his take on human foibles. Bahr is absent from most news stories, was never interviewed, and his book is out of print. His version of the storm is all but forgotten.

Bahr was the pseudonym for Harold Litten, who wrote and was an editor for Rodale Press. Bahr had greater success with a children's book on the blizzard called *Blizzard at the Zoo*, published in 1982. This book turns animals into heroes as they struggle but successfully overcome the blizzard.[27]

The storm also had a central role in Dr. Ruth M. Stratton's academic study, *Disaster Relief: The Politics of Intergovernmental Relations*, published in 1989. Tragically, Dr. Stratton died in the 1990s and was not available to continue her work and offer a counternarrative to the popular memory of the blizzard. Her book delves deeply into the politics and policies that contextualized the disaster and is well-respected in academic circles, but it is virtually unknown by the public.[28]

The triumph of the public memory of the disaster occurred because, according to Pierre Nora, memory "remains in permanent evolution, open to the dialectic of remembering and forgetting" and is vulnerable to "manipulation and appropriation."[29] Thus, individuals' memories of an event may be in sharp contrast to one another. Individual memory is susceptible to revision, but public memory is the product of elites within a community who mold memory into local history and then work to maintain its form into the next generation when it becomes the official memory of the event.[30]

The story of the Blizzard of '77 told here serves as a challenge to the public memory of the event and a reminder that disasters are the combination of natural hazards and public policies that place people into the path of these hazards. The Blizzard of '77 resulted from a combination of factors, such as the rise of automobility and the decline of other forms of public transportation; the development of suburbanization and snow control policies that encouraged people to travel as freely in winter as in summer; the impact of deindustrialization and decision making by elected officials of that time; and the unique weather conditions that prevailed in the winter of 1976–77.

Furthermore, the consequences of the blizzard lasted through the present. Carter's decision to declare a disaster for snow led to a chess-like series of policy moves among local officials, Congress, and the president over what constituted a snow disaster. Like other elements in federal policymaking, Congress liberalized the threshold so that now any snowfall might be eligible for an emergency or disaster declaration. Meanwhile, the fate of Stanley Makowski loomed over political leaders in Buffalo who made great strides in preparing for winter—suggesting that studying the underpinnings of a disaster may be the best means of preventing a repeat in the future.

Glossary

Notes

Bibliography

Index

Glossary

blizzard. A snowstorm in which the following conditions prevail for a period of three hours or longer: sustained winds or frequent gusts up to thirty-five miles an hour or greater, and considerable falling and/or blowing snow that reduces visibility to less than a quarter mile.

horizontal fragmentation. Describes a breakdown in communications between government officials and offices on the same governmental level (local, state, or federal).

lake-effect snow. Snow showers that are created when cold, dry air passes over a large, warmer lake, such as one of the Great Lakes, and picks up moisture and heat.

moral hazard. Refers to instances in which a government policy encourages greater risk on the part of citizens.

road salt. A type of salt used for winter road maintenance. It consists of chloride salts of sodium, calcium, magnesium, and potassium.

snowbelts. Regions near the Great Lakes where heavy snowfall in the form of lake-effect snow is particularly common. Snowbelts are typically found downwind of the lakes, principally off the eastern and southern shores.

snow flurries. Intermittent light snowfall of short duration (generally light snow showers) with no measurable accumulation.

snow squalls. Intense periods of moderate to heavy snowfall, usually of limited duration and accompanied by strong, gusty surface winds and possibly lightning. The snow showers are generally moderate to heavy. Snow accumulation may be significant.

vertical fragmentation. Describes the breakdown of communication between officials at different levels of government, such as local and federal miscommunications.

Notes

Introduction

1. *A Charlie Brown Christmas*, dir. Bill Melendez, Warner Brothers, 1965. More information on this animated television short can be found at the Internet Movie Database: https://www.imdb.com/title/tt0059026/.

2. G. E. Taylor Address, Box 23, Folder 71, American Public Works Association Records (K0651), State Historical Society of Missouri Research Center–Kansas City (hereafter SHSMO-KC).

3. Brouillette and Ross, *Organizational Response to the Great Chicago Snowstorm of 1967*.

4. McKelvey, "Snowstorms and Snow Fighting," 21–22. Rooney, "Urban Snow Hazard in the United States," 538–59.

5. "Automobility" was a term first used by John C. Burnham in 1961. See Burnham, "Gasoline Tax and the Automobile Revolution," 435–39; Flink, "Three Stages of Automobile Consciousness," 457–59. Automobility studies exploded in the 1990s as new forms of mobility such as the internet and a relative decline in the automobility regime arose. See Sheller and Urry, "City and the Car," 737–57. The regime concept first appears in Bohm, Jones, Land, and Paterson, *Against Automobility*; Conley and McLaren, *Car Troubles*; Geels, Kemp, Dudley, and Lyons, *Automobility in Transition*.

6. Association for Safe International Road Travel, "Road Safety Facts," https://www.asirt.org/safe-travel/road-safety-facts/.

7. "Federal Funds Available for Improved Highways," *Buffalo Live Wire* 10, no. 2 (1919): 48. Highway funds came from an excise tax on gasoline sales; see Burnham, "Gasoline Tax and the Automobile Revolution," 435–59.

8. Shane, *Down the Asphalt Path*.

9. David Williams, Public Works Director, Latrobe Pennsylvania, "Upper Limits," April 8, 1987, Folder 2, Box 295, Snow Conference 1987, American Public Works Association, SHSMO-KC.

10. New York Port Authority, "History of the Holland Tunnel," http://www.panynj.gov/bridges-tunnels/holland-tunnel-history.html.

11. Sara Rimer, "Upheaval and Calm as Big Dig Transforms Boston," *New York Times*, April 28, 1996, https://www.nytimes.com/1996/04/28/us/upheaval -and-calm-as-big-dig-transforms-boston.html; Barthes, "New Citroen," 88.

12. Caro, *Power Broker*, 5–9, 850–920.

13. Wickstrom, "History and Consequences of the Interstate," 3; Seely, "Interstate System," 2; Schulz, "Benefits of the Interstates Undeniable," 4; Melosi, "Automobile Shapes the City."

14. For a history of American energy politics, see Yergin, *The Prize*; Patterson, *Restless Giant*, 232–33.

15. "Alfred P. Sloan Jr. Dead at 90; G.M. Leader and Philanthropist," *New York Times*, February 18, 1966, https://www.nytimes.com/1966/02/18/archives /alfred-p-sloan-jr-dead-at-90-gm-leader-and-philanthropist-alfred-p.html; Sheller and Urry, "Car and the City," 738.

16. Automotive idealization is discussed in Urry, "Inhabiting the Car"; Eyerman and Löfgren, "Romancing the Road," 53–79; Smoak, "Framing the Automobile in Twentieth-Century American Literature." Besides, one need only turn to the History Channel to find shows such as *Ice Road Truckers*. Also see Marc Fisher, "Cruising toward Oblivion, America's Once Magical—Now Mundane—Love Affair with Cars," *Washington Post*, September 2, 2015, http://www.washington post.com/sf/style/2015/09/02/americas-fading-car-culture/. For a history of NASCAR that tackles the myths and reality, see Beekman, *NASCAR Nation*.

17. McDonogh, "Coming of Age," 174–75. This is changing, according to public interest group researcher Andrea Bernstein; see "Young People Are Driving WAY Less," *NPR*, April 5, 2012, http://www.wnyc.org/story/286823-report-young -people-are-driving-way-less; Melosi, "Automobile Shapes the City"; Jain, "Violent Submission," 186–214.

18. Cochran, *American Business System*, 44. Suburbs arose in the early nineteenth century and inexorably spread away from the city with the development of the streetcar. The classic study of Boston is Warner, *Streetcar Suburbs*; see also Melosi, "Automobile Shapes the City," 10.

19. David Call combines geography and meteorology in his study of winter on society. Call's publications include Call et al., "Meteorological and Social Comparison of the New England Blizzards of 1978 and 2013," 1–10; Call, "Rethinking Snowstorms as 'Snow Events,'" 1783–93. Geographers John F. Rooney and Stanley Changnon have contributed insights as well. See Rooney, "Urban Snow Hazard in the United States," 538–59; Changnon and Changnon, "Lessons from the Unusual Impacts of an Abnormal Winter in the USA," 187–91. Environmentalists have been less active in this discussion, although an intriguing theoretical framework with implications for this study is an idea proposed by James Feldman and Lynne Heasley of creating a specific transnational environmental history field centered on the

Great Lakes; see Feldman and Heasley, "Recentering North American Environmental History," 951–58.

20. As environmental historian Donald Worster put it, environmental history is about "how humans are affected by their natural environment and how they have affected that environment and with what results." Worster, "Appendix: Doing Environmental History," 290–91.

21. People from Buffalo boast about their ability to deal with the many feet of snow they annually receive but also struggle to redefine their city as more than just a place of snow and cold. For environmental identity see Worster, "Doing Environmental History," 293.

22. Chris Dolce, "These Southern U.S. Cities Have Had More Snowfall through Early December Than Anchorage, Alaska," The Weather Channel, accessed December 21, 2018, https://weather.com/storms/winter/news/2018-12-10-southern -cities-more-snow-than-anchorage. The intersection of environmental sustainability and policy is explored in Dovers and Hussey, *Environment and Sustainability: A Policy Handbook.*

1. Buffalo and Snow Control

1. Common Council, *Manual of the Common Council City of Buffalo for 1896*, 1–9, 15; Leary and Sholes, *Buffalo's Waterfront.*

2. Mergen, *Snow in America*, xiv.

3. Monmonier, *Lake Effect*, 2. Of course, larger weather systems such as Nor'easters and Alberta Clippers occur throughout the winter.

4. Michelle Karas, "From Planting Advice to Weather Predictions, Old Farmers Almanac a Gardener's Favorite for 227 Years," *TCA Regional News*, September 15, 2018, https://search-proquest-com.ezproxy.naz.edu/docview/2104136888 ?accountid=28167; "NOAA's National Weather Service Celebrates 135th Anniversary," http://www.nws.noaa.gov/pa/history/135anniversary.php; Shea, *History of the NOAA*; Steinberg, *Acts of God*, 192–93.

5. Of course dramatic storms such as the Great Blizzard of 1888, which killed 400 people, are notable exceptions; see Cable, *Blizzard of '88.*

6. One researcher has found a strong correlation between snowfall and compactness of American cities. See Guterbock, "Effect of Snow on Urban Density Patterns in the United States," 358–86.

7. McKelvey, *Snow in the Cities*, xv; Warner, *Streetcar Suburbs*; National Snow and Ice Data Center, "Snow Removal," accessed December 17, 2014, https:// nsidc.org/cryosphere/snow/removal.html.

8. Moore, *Buffalo Blizzard Book*, 26. As the title suggests, this is a collection of primary source material from an array of newspapers.

9. Moore, *Buffalo Blizzard Book*, 31.

10. They are quoted in Morrison, "Conquering Winter," 219.

11. Mergen, *Snow in America*, 45–50; Monmonier, *Lake Effect*, 98.

12. International Railway Company, *Comprehensive Transit Plan for Buffalo*, 6.

13. Blake McKelvey details the history of Rochester in McKelvey, "Snowstorms and Snow Fighting." At one point, the city saw nearly four feet of snowfall within hours, but the trolley service was interrupted for only one day.

14. National Snow and Ice Data Center, "Snow Removal," accessed December 17, 2014, https://nsidc.org/cryosphere/snow/removal.html; Sara Morrison, "Of Snowtron and Snowzilla: How Boston Removed Snow from Its Streets Throughout History," Boston.com, January 24, 2015, http://www.boston.com/news/local/massachusetts/2015/01/24/snowtron-and-snowzilla-how-boston-removed-snow-from-its-streets-throughout-history/v8455vpxuBjJ8KmRFDPguK/story.html.

15. "Here Is the Story of a Storm That Broke All Records for Viciousness," *Buffalo Morning Express*, February 9, 1895; "City and State Experience Phenomenal Fall of Snow," *Buffalo Courier*, January 23, 1902; "Fierce Storm Sweeps across State; Cry for Coal," *Buffalo Courier*, December 14, 1902; "Buffalo and All Northern New York in Storm King's Grip," *Buffalo Courier*, January 12, 1903.

16. Kostof, *America by Design*, 176; Moore, *Buffalo Blizzard Book*, 96.

17. "Lives and Property Destroyed," *The Buffalo Enquirer*, October 11, 1906, 1. Of course, the city was still compact enough that walking was possible.

18. Ibid.

19. Moore, *Buffalo Blizzard Book*, 60.

20. Ibid., 75–77.

21. Ibid.

22. Ibid., 78–80. Such incidents were not isolated to Buffalo; Rochester had a similar struggle in the 1880s between their street commissioner and their interurban railway. See Mergen, *Snow in America*, 57–58.

23. Moore, *Buffalo Blizzard Book*, 31.

24. Street cleaning quote in Fetherston, "Discussion of Street Cleaning," 187–91. Janet Ward, "'Snow Problem' Buffalo Knows How to Deal with Winter," *American City and County*, April 1, 1999, https://www.americancityandcounty.com/1999/04/01/snow-problem-buffalo-knows-how-to-deal-with-winter/.

25. Kostof, *America by Design*, 176.

26. McShane, "Transforming the Use of Urban Space," 298.

27. Ibid., 295.

28. *Manual of the Common Council City of Buffalo 1896*, 129.

29. Ibid., 194–95.

30. McShane, "Transforming the Use of Urban Space," 281–83.

31. Parker, "Good Roads Movement," 51–57; Melosi, "The Automobile Shapes the City," 5–9; Timothy O'Leary, Boston Streets Commissioner, article, "Snow Removal and Ice Control," Folder 23, Box 71, American Public Works Association Papers, State Historical Society of Missouri–Kansas City (SHSMO-KC). The development of road technology is described in McShane, *Down the Asphalt Path*.

32. McShane notes a correlation in asphalt paving and the rise of car culture. The three cities with the most asphalt roads were Detroit, Cleveland, and Buffalo, all early innovators in manufacturing automobiles; see McShane, "Transforming the Use of Urban Space," 282.

33. "WNY Has Helped Fuel Auto Industry Growth," *Buffalo Business First*, November 29, 1999, https://www.bizjournals.com/buffalo/stories/1999/11/29/focus4.html.

34. Buffalo and Erie County Historical Society, "Pierce-Arrow Motor Company," 57–84; Ralston, *Pierce-Arrow*; Bob English, "Pierce-Arrow, King of the Limos," *Globe and Mail*, July 3, 2008, G6; Bob Tomaine, "Birdcages to Iceboxes to Cars," *Autoweek*, June 5, 2006, 37.

35. Sass, *Stewart Motor Corporation of Buffalo*.

36. Szafranski, "Atterbury Motor Car Company," 6; Goldman, *City on the Edge*, 292–93.

37. Criticism of the railways can be found in *Buffalo Live Wire* 10, no. 1 (January 1919): 1; *Buffalo Live Wire* 10, no. 9 (September 1919): 1; *Buffalo Live Wire* 12, no. 1 (January 1921): 1.

38. Dispenza, *From Elite Social Club to Motoring Service Organization*.

39. Norton, "Street Rivals," 337–45; *Buffalo Live Wire* 10, no. 12 (December 1919): 1; "Finished Thruway Forecast for 1954," *New York Times*, May 6, 1950, http://www.nytimes.com/1950/05/06/archives/finished-thruway-forecast-by-1954-state-official-tells-engineers.html.

40. The replacement of mass transit by automobiles and trucks occurred piecemeal as incremental policy changes subsidized autos at the expense of mass transit. See Slater "General Motors and the Demise of Streetcars," 45–66.

41. *Manual of the Common Council*, 16; International Railway Company, *Comprehensive Transit Plan*, 10; Ahlstrom, *Last Decade of Buffalo Trolleys*, 3.

42. International Railway Company, *Comprehensive Transit Plan*, 16.

43. "No Cars Will Run Today," *Commercial Advertiser*, July 3, 1922, 1; Rizzo, *Through the Mayor's Eye*, 238.

44. Bentham, *International Railway Strike of 1922*, 49 and 61. Bentham takes a sympathetic view of the union and the mayor and relies heavily on the *Buffalo Times*, a pro-labor newspaper, for much of his information. In contrast, the *Commercial Advertiser* supported the IRC and called the mayor's attempted actions during the strike "Schwabbery"; *Commercial Advertiser*, August 1, 1922, 12.

45. "I.R.C. Is after Jitneys," *Commercial Advertiser*, July 31, 1922, 1; "Jitneys Orders Off, Schwab Request for Stay Denied," *Commercial Advertiser*, August 7, 1922, 1 (unable to resist a dig, the newspaper labeled the mayor "Schwab, the Law Breaker"). "Grants I.R.C. Second-Order Against Jits," *Commercial Advertiser*, September 12, 1922, 3.

46. "Schwab to Fight for City Buses," *Commercial Advertiser*, August 1, 1922, 1.

47. "Questions Go to People," *Commercial Advertiser*, October 24, 1922, 3.

48. Rizzo, *Through the Mayor's Eyes*, 238–45.

49. "Mayor Wants I.R.C. to Co-operate to Set 5c Fare," *Commercial Advertiser*, September 25, 1922, 3.

50. Rizzo, *Through the Mayor's Eyes*, 238–45.

51. Goldman, *City on the Edge*, 89–91, 121; Charles Burchfield, *Civic Improvement*, watercolor on paper, available at the Burchfield Penney Art Gallery at SUNY Buffalo State, https://www.burchfieldpenney.org/collection/object:v2013 -0420-001-civic-improvement/; Price, "Urban Renewal," 129–30.

52. Post, "Myth Behind the Street Car Revival," 95–100; Schrag, "'The Bus Is Young and Honest,'" 51–79.

53. Bentham, *International Railway Strike of 1922*. As for snow removal, automobile drivers did not have to pay for this service on Buffalo roadways, while transit lines still had to plow and hire gangs of men to shovel snow off the tracks. For example, the *Evening News*, February 3, 1908, reports that after a winter storm the IRC had to hire scores of men to clean their tracks, while all other roads were cleared by Buffalo's Department of Streets; Moore, *Buffalo Blizzard Book*, 138.

54. Cichon, "Buffalo You Should Know"; Goldman, *City on the Edge*, 150; Ahlstrom, *Last Decade of Buffalo Trolleys*, 3, 6.

55. Quoted in Moore, *Buffalo Blizzard Book*, 119. Dorr did not live to see the error of his thinking as he died suddenly in May 1901. See "Recent Deaths," *Boston Medical and Surgical Journal* 144, no. 19 (May 1901): 462.

56. *Evening News*, November 17, 1920, reported that cars followed cleared trolley lines and "added to the difficulties of the streetcar, for as soon as the plow passed, the damp snow was packed into space between the rails by the autos." Quoted in Moore, *Buffalo Blizzard Book*, 146.

57. Moore, *Buffalo Blizzard Book*, 156.

58. *Evening News* quoted in Moore, *Buffalo Blizzard Book*, 146; for additional examples of private cars hindering mass transit see ibid., 139–40, 156.

59. *Report on the Problem of Snow Removal in the City of Rochester*.

60. Edholm, "New York's Army of Snow Fighters," 547. The term "snow-fighting" is indicative of the fondness for military metaphors among those employed

in public works. It may be due to the masculinized culture of these departments or merely tied into the mechanical, organic dialectic explored by scholars such as Merchant, *Death of Nature*; Fetherston, "Street Cleaning," 668.

61. Longville, "New York's Snow-Fighting Tractor Plows," 85. Experts in Rochester complained not only about the lack of available men but also of their quality; see *Report on the Problem of Snow Removal in the City of Rochester.*

62. Dispenza, "From Elite Social Club to Motoring Service Organization," 236–47.

63. Moore, *Buffalo Blizzard Book*, 155.

64. For the 1927 storm see Moore, *Buffalo Blizzard Book*, 158; "Blizzard Up-State Maroons 2,500 Cars," *New York Times*, October 19, 1930, 1; "Snow Covers Area Near Buffalo—Four Feet Fall Blankets Highways," *Washington Post*, October 20, 1930, 1; see also Moore, *Buffalo Blizzard Book*, 162–65.

65. Moore, *Buffalo Blizzard Book*, 173; Call, "Rethinking Snowstorms as Snow Events."

66. The 1936 storm is discussed in McKelvey, *Snow in the Cities*, 107; Moore, *Buffalo Blizzard Book*, 173–80.

67. A snowstorm that struck the city on December 15–17, 1945, caused transportation havoc for a day or so. The city and state responded with alacrity and, during the war years, when automobile use was discouraged by the government, city officials were more tolerant of the IRC and railroads were still in operation. Moore, *Buffalo Blizzard Book*, 186–89; Ahlstrom, *Last Decade of Buffalo Trolleys*, 3.

2. Buffalo and Snow Control in the Age of the Automobile

1. Doris R. Kimbrough, "Salting Roads: The Solution for Winter Driving," *ChemMatters* (February 2006), https://www.acs.org/content/dam/acsorg/education /resources/highschool/chemmatters/articlesbytopic/solutions/chemmatters-feb2006 -salting-roads.pdf.

2. Fetherston, "Discussion of Street Cleaning," 187–91.

3. Schwartz and Schmidlin, "Climatology of Blizzards in the Conterminous United States, 1959–2000," 1765. The authors suggest that the term "blizzard" was coined after the advent of the railroad and became common in the 1880s. Leon M. Despres, "Why Doesn't the City Clear My Block?" January 1964, Folder 22, Box 71, American Public Works Association Records, State Historical Society of Missouri–Kansas City (hereafter APWA-SHSMO-KC).

4. Robert Lockwood, *Snow Removal and Ice Control in Urban Areas*, Research Project Number 114, Progress Report 4 (Chicago: American Public Works Association, 1965), no folder, Box 720, APWA-SHSMO-KC. Geographer John F. Rooney Jr. reached a similar conclusion; see Rooney, "Urban Snow Hazard in

the United States"; Schrag, "Motorization of Manhattan Surface Transit," 59; *Report on the Problem of Snow Removal in the City of Rochester* (Rochester 1917), 30–31; Making drivers responsible for their own automobility was a behavioral solution to the problem of congestion. Some localities required snow tires and snow chains. If a driver became stuck in snow they might be fined for failing to comply with road regulations; see American Public Works Association, *Special Report Number 25, Proceedings of the Northeast Conference on Urban Snow Removal* (Washington, DC: American Public Works Association, 1962), Folder 9, Box 720, APWA-SHSMO-KC.

5. Post, "Myth Behind the Street Car Revival," 95–100; Schrag, "'The Bus Is Young and Honest': Transportation Politics, Technical Choice, and the Motorization of Manhattan Surface Transit, 1919–1936," 51–79.

6. Robert Moses was critical in brokering the deal between the city and the state that produced the Thruway deal in 1950. See Caro, *The Power Broker*, 817; Thruway Authority Act, accessed November 13, 2016, http://www.thruway .ny.gov/about/compliance/thruwaystatutes.pdf; Charles Bennett, "Thruway Feeders: Lag in Finishing Terminals Could Create Serious Traffic Problems," *New York Times*, June 20, 1954, 9.

7. Price, "Urban Renewal," 132; Buffalo Olmstead Parks Conservancy, *BOPC Position Statement on Route 198 Scajaquada Expressway*, last updated July 2015, https://www.bfloparks.org/positions/198-scajaquada/; Steve Cichon, "The Buffalo You Should Know: The Slow Death of Humboldt Parkway in Building the 33 & 198," *Buffalo News*, May 18; October 18, 2016, http://buffalonews.com/2016/05/08 /buffalo-know-slow-death-humboldt-parkway-building-33-198-2/.

8. "Buffalo Skyway," *Western New York Heritage*, https://www.wnyheritage press.org/content/buffalo_skyway_1950s/index.html; Kowsky, "Municipal Parks and City Planning," 49–64; Moore, *Buffalo Blizzard Book*, 198.

9. The concept of the Kensingston as a canyon can be found in Deidre Williams, "Covering the Kensington Canyon; Groups Seek to Restore Olmsted Green Space," *Buffalo News*, March 9, 2012, https://buffalonews.com/news/covering-the -kensington-caynon-groups-seek-to-restore-olmsted-green-space/article_03a6d993 -7ce2-5a51-8580-4dd949e7fa64.html; Kowsky, "Municipal Parks and City Planning," 49–64; Dan Reitz, "Humboldt Parkway and the Kensington Expressway: A History," July 16, 2010, http://danreitz.com/gridplan/?p=36; Kraus, *Race, Neighborhoods, and Community Power*, 124–26.

10. Henderson, "Secessionist Automobility," 293–307; Boustan, "Was Postwar Suburbanization 'White Flight'? Evidence from the Black Migration," 417–43; Goldman, *City in the Edge*, 160. Also see Kraus, *Race, Neighborhoods, and Community Power*, 126; Domonique Griffin, "'They Were Never Silent, You Just Weren't

Listening': Buffalo's Black Activists in the Age of Urban Renewal" (Senior Thesis, Trinity College, 2017), 14–19. http://digitalrepository.trincoll.edu/theses/641.

11. Goldman, *City in the Edge*, 169–72.

12. Western New York Heritage, "Thruway Plaza: Western New York's Pioneer Suburban Shopping Plaza," https://www.wnyheritagepress.org/content/thru way_plaza_western_new_yorks_pioneer_suburban_shopping_plaza/index.html.

13. An informative site about the life and death of malls is available at Dead Malls.com. For Western New York, see http://www.deadmalls.com/stories.html #NY.

14. Moore, *Buffalo Blizzard Book*, 205–7; 214–18.

15. Ibid., 220–22.

16. "Snow Removal," Folder 48, Box 36, APWA-SHSMO-KC; "Torts," Folder 30, Box 71, APWA-SHSMO-KC.

17. Shan Wang, "Road Salt: Where Does It Come From, Where Does It Go?" Boston.com, http://www.boston.com/news/local/massachusetts/2015/01/16/road -salt-where-does-come-from-where-does/ i3aGKBEppiysZVkXt8cIMJ/story.html.

18. Fleming, "Snow-Fighting's New Techniques," 83–85, 110, 112; Lawrence O'Kane, "Snow Removers Plotting Tactics," *New York Times*, November 14, 1961, 41; Wang, "Road Salt: Where Does It Come From, Where Does It Go?"

19. *Snow Removal and Ice Control in Urban Areas*, no folder, Box 720, APWA-SHSMO-KC; Louis Drasler, Department of Public Services, Cleveland, "Highway and Bridge Design for Snow and Ice Control for 1985 Traffic," April 7, 1965, Folder 2, Box 72, APWA-SHSMO-KC. The American Public Works Association supported these efforts; see Folder "Snow Melters," Box 72, APWA-SHSMO-KC; see also "Snow and Ice Removal from Road Surfaces by Electronic Heating," *Highway Research Record* 94 (1965): 45–60; "Snow Removal Procedures," Folder 11, Box 191, APWA-SHSMO-KC; Henry Liebman, "Turn on the Heat Lamps—IT'S SNOWING," *Public Works* (August 1965): 103–6; Vince Lattanzio, "Why Can't We Just Melt the Snow?" March, 10, 2014, http://www.nbcphiladelphia.com/weather/stories /Why-Cant-We-Just-Melt-the-Snow-246222371.html.

20. Hunt, "Winning the Battle with Snow," 19; Miller, "Ice Control in Rochester," 21 and 24. For more on Rochester, New York, which adopted salt early on, see McKelvey, *Snow in the Cities*, 115.

21. Calcium chloride may also be used on roads but is more expensive and less common. Unlike table salt, calcium chloride is not safe for humans to ingest.

22. Transportation Research Board, *Road Salt Use in the United States*, 19.

23. Joseph Stromberg, "What Happens to All the Salt We Dump On the Roads?" *Smithsonian*, (January 2014), http://www.smithsonianmag.com/science -nature/what-happens-to-all-the-salt-we-dump-on-the-roads-180948079.

24. The move to Washington, DC, represents the shifting nature of public advocacy groups in the 1960s and 1970s. See Scholzman and Tierney, "More of the Same," 351. Kurlansky, *Salt: A World History*; Long, Jacuqes, and Kepos, "Morton Salt, Inc."

25. McKelvey, "Snowstorms and Snowfighting," 7.

26. Sanitation Committee American Public Works Association, *Street Cleaning Practice* (Chicago: APWA, 1938).

27. Transportation Research Board, *Road Salt Use in the United States;* Miller, "Ice Control in Rochester," 21; Mergen, *Snow in America*, 66.

28. The Salt Institute, *The Sensible Salting Program* (1971), Box 721, APWA-SHSMO-KC. The Salt Institute has its roots in the late nineteenth century. Salt is a valuable commodity and has been the subject of monopolization and deregulation. See Jenks, "Michigan Salt Association," 78–98.

29. Booth, *Standardization Activities in the United States*, 74; *Directory of U.S. Standardization Activities*, 145.

30. The influence of the Salt Institute can be seen in the invitation by the British Medical Journal to allow William Hanneman, president of the Salt Institute, to refute the scientific findings that salt intake is linked to with hypertension. Open Secrets, https://www.opensecrets.org/lobby/clientsum.php?id=F17561&year=2011; "Salt Institute Supports Lawsuit Against NYC Salt Regulations," http://www.preparedfoods.com/articles/117418-salt-institute-supports-lawsuit-against-nyc-salt-regulations; Salt Institute v. Leavitt, http://www.ca4.uscourts.gov/opinions/Published/051097.P.pdf; Katz, *Influence Machine*; Mort Satin Facebook, https://www.facebook.com/mort.satin; Salt Guru Facebook, https://www.facebook.com/SaltGuru; Salt Guru Twitter, https://twitter.com/saltguru; YouTube, https://www.youtube.com/watch?v=ppZQpC26ivk; Salt Institute, https://www.facebook.com/ALittleSalt, https://twitter.com/WithALittleSalt.

31. *Calcium Chloride for Ice Control with Reference Data* (Washington, DC: Calcium Chloride Institute, 1954). The booklet was first published in 1949 and went through several editions. "Road Salt Saves Lives and Protects Commerce," http://www.saltinstitute.org/wp-content/uploads/2013/08/si_road_salt_fact_sheet.pdf; Balakrishnan, "Road Salt"; cited as "Personal Communication" in Hyman and Vary, *Best Management Practice for Environmental Issues Related to Highway and Street Maintenance.*

32. "North American Snow Conference—Historical Data—Cities and Dates," Folder 3, Box 191, APWA-SHSMO-KC.

33. Brian Clark Howard, "The Surprising History of Road Salt," *National Geographic* (February 2014), http://news.nationalgeographic.com/news/2014/02/140212-road-salt-shoratges-metling-ice-snow-science/; *Snowfighter's Handbook* (Alexandria, Salt Institute, 1973), 6–8.

34. A stronger chassis invented during World War I allowed the rise of the trucking industry in postwar America. McShane, *Down the Asphalt Path*, xiv; *Report on the Problem of Snow Removal in the City of Rochester*.

35. William D. Smith, "Snow Tire Sales May Reach Peak," *New York Times*, December 1, 1963, 227. Tire salesman quoted in Marshall Schuom, "In Winter, Snow Tires Are Still Champs," *New York Times*, January 29, 1978, 70.

36. American Public Works Association, Special Report no. 34, *Vehicular Corrosion Caused by Deicing Salts: Evaluation of the Effects of Regular v Inhibited Salt on Motor Vehicles* (September 1970), APWA-SHSMO-KC. Such concerns still exist, but Lori Roman, president of the Salt Institute, chided those who complained about salt on their cars and cited studies that showed the property damage increased in areas that did not use road salt. "The need to wash your car after a storm is a minor trade-off for the benefit for still having a car to wash," she said. Quoted in Steve Hendrix, "Welcome to Salt City: Where Cars, Sidewalks, and Shoes Bear Winter's Briny Crust," *Washington Post*, January 31, 2014, https://www .washingtonpost.com/local/welcome-to-salt-city-where-cars-sidewalks-and-shoes -bear-winters-briny-crust/2014/01/31/7a494a72-8a9c-11e3-916e-e01534b1e132 _story.html.

37. John W. Riley, "Highway Salt a Big Nuisance but It May Be Controlled," *Boston Globe*, December 24, 1961, 5; Craig Whitney, "Antisnow Salt Exacts a Price: Corrosion," *New York Times*, January 2, 1970, 26; Paul Valentine, "Snow Sends Area Back to the Salt Mines," *Washington Post*, February 18, 1979, C1; Transportation Research Board Highway, *Deicing Comparing Salt and Calcium Magnesium Acetate* (Washington, DC: National Research Council, 1991), see esp. chap. 3, "Effects of Road Salt on Vehicles and Infrastructure," 31–68. It seems no coincidence that after William E. Dickinson's retirement in 1987, the new public relations director of the Salt Institute was Lou Priebe, who formerly worked for National Automobile Dealers Association; see Warren Brown, "New Official at the Salt Institute Is Getting Peppered with Jokes," *Washington Post*, May 30, 1988, BF10. See also Dickinson's obituary, "William Edward Dickinson, Association Executive," *Washington Post*, October 15, 1994, B6.

38. In Buffalo Chevrolet ran full-page ads highlighting rocker panels that clean themselves of road salt and other corrosives; *Buffalo Courier-Express*, November 28, 1965, 11c. Buffalo-based retail chains such as AM&As touted boots that were resistant to road salt; see *Courier Express*, November 5, 1968, 26.

39. By the 1960s public works departments created instruction manuals, some as thick as phone books, on operating during ice and snowstorms. Personnel kept these by their side all winter long; see Leon M. Despres, "Why Doesn't the City Clear My Block?"; and Joseph Reichart, Superintendent of Streets, Kansas City, Missouri to Rod Fleming, President American Public Works Association,

"Declaring a Snow Emergency," Folder 22, APWA North American Snow Conference 1964, Box 71, "Snow and Ice," APWA-SHSMO-KC.

40. Lloyd, "Parking of Automobiles," 336–56. The Milwaukee Commissioner for Streets lamented in 1980 that "the present even/odd side street parking together with no restrictions of the weekend led to 'a game of Russian roulette for plows'"; "Street Use regulation for a Snow Control Program," *Public Works* (March 1962): 174; "Summary of Principal Materials on Snow and Ice from Our Files," Folder 22, Box 71, APWA-SHSMO-KC. Frank Lucia, Commissioner New York City Department of Sanitation, "Snow Removal and Ice Control in Urban Areas," Folder 2, Box 72, APWA-SHSMO-KC. Street-parked cars were the most challenging problem for public works personnel and their laments and ideas on how to fix these fill a large folder in the APWA archives; see "Parking," Folder 9, Box 72, APWA-SHSMO-KC. See also Monmonier, *Lake Effect*, 100–101; "Street Use Regulation for a Snow Control Program," *Public Works* (March 1962): 174; "Summary of Principal Materials on Snow and Ice from Our Files," Folder 22, Box 71, APWA-SHSMO-KC.

41. "Businessman Tells Government How to Do its Job," 197, Folder 1, Box 721, APWA-SHSMO-KC; American Public Works Association, Cohn, and North American Snow Conference, *Managing Snow Removal and Ice Control Programs*.

42. American Public Works Association, *Proceedings of the Northeast Conference on Urban Snow Removal*, Box 720, APWA-SHSMO-KC.

43. Passwell and Recker, *Problems of the Carless*, 1.

44. Ibid., 34.

3. The Blizzard of '77

1. Kenneth F. Dewey, "Lake-Effect Snow Fall in Buffalo and a Look at the Record-Breaking 1976–1977 Snowfall Season," http://nwafiles.nwas.org/digest/papers/1977/Vol02No3/1977v002no03-Dewey.pdf; Kneeland, *Buffalo Blizzard of 1977*.

2. Eichenlaub, *Weather and Climate of the Great Lakes*, 1; Alistair Cooke, "President Carter Inaugurated," *Letter from America January 1977*, http://www.bbc.co.uk/programmes/articles/3bGNCb1Yz4qMCp74tC3BdPg/president-carter-inaugurated; A. James Wagner, "The Severe Winter of 1976–1977: Precursors and Precedents," *National Weather Digest* (November 1977): 12–18, http://www.nwas.org/digest/papers/1977/Vol02No4/1977v002no04-Wagner.pdf; Christopher Moncton, "Coldest U.S. Winter in a Century," *What's Up with That*, March 26, 2014, https://wattsupwiththat.com/2014/03/26/coldest-u-s-winter-in-a-century/.

3. Federal Energy Administration, "The Natural Gas Shortage: A Preliminary Report," August 1975, Ron Nessen Papers, Gerald R. Ford Presidential

Library, http://www.fordlibrarymuseum.gov/library/document/0204/1511759.pdf. Carter scheduled weekly two-hour cabinet meetings to deal with the crisis; see Council of Economic Advisors, Folder: "Cabinet Meeting Minutes January 1977," Box 8, Records of the Office of Staff Secretary, Jimmy Carter Presidential Library; Timothy R. Smith, "James R. Schlesinger, CIA Chief and Cabinet Member, Dies," *Washington Post*, March 27, 2014, http://www.washingtonpost.com/national/james -r-schlesinger-cia-chief-and-cabinet-member-dies/2014/03/27/e4a8f01c-b5bb-11e3 -8020-b2d790b3c9e1_story.html; "Gas Use Called Alarming Schlesinger Warns Panel," *Boston Globe*, January 29, 1977, 1; "Luck Runs Out on Natural Gas," *Time*, January 31, 1977, 35–36; AP, "Winter Holds East and Midwest in Frigid Grip: Carter May Urge 4-day Work Week," *Boston Globe*, January 30, 1977, 1.

4. Robert F. McFadden, "Thousands Laid Off by Shortage; City Hall Declares an Emergency," *New York Times*, January 29, 1977, 1; "Snow Squalls Snarl Great Lakes Area," *Boston Globe*, February 1, 1977, 1; Ray Hill and Modesto Argenio, "Some Served Storm Victims; Others Stole," *Boston Globe*, February 2, 1977, 11; Jerry Allan, "Carey Invokes Emergency to Limit Gas Use," *Buffalo Evening News*, January 28, 1977, 1; Thomas O'Toole, "Gas Supply Ebbs in 12 States," *Washington Post*, January 30, 1977, http://www.washingtonpost.com/archive/politics/1977 /01/30/gas-supply-ebbs-in-12-states/c96aa9b5-7b56-44d4-9259-e5bf587884b6/; Dave Stout, "Business Slows across WNY as Gas Is Curtailed," *Buffalo Evening News*, January 28, 1977, 1; Bahr, *The Blizzard*, 31.

5. As we have seen in chapter 2, public works personnel complain more about abandoned cars than they do about the snow. See McKelvey, *Snow in the Cities*, 157; Goldman, *City on the Lake*, 152.

6. Frank Buell, "Mayor Signs July 1 Repeal of City Occupancy Tax," *Buffalo Evening News*, January 29, 1977, 2; Taylor, *Desegregation in Boston and Buffalo*; Bahr, *The Blizzard*, 26.

7. By 1976 Buffalo was besieged by malls. The Boulevard Mall opened outside of North Buffalo in 1962; the Seneca Mall opened outside of South Buffalo in 1969; and the Eastern Hills Mall, which opened in 1971, was northeast of the city. Due east of Buffalo was the Como Mall, built in 1973, and in 1977 the Thruway Plaza in Cheektowaga was enclosed to become the Thruway Mall. Buffalo businesses felt threatened by the rise of the suburban shopping mall, and they feared that a driving ban in the city would send shoppers elsewhere.

8. See Goldman, *City on the Edge*.

9. Whether Arthur Eve's encouragement for Makowski to challenge Sedita came from real affection for Stan the Man or perhaps from a feeling that Eve could control the mayor is unknown; see Anna Quindlen, "Snow Stories Flow as Buffalo Begins to Thaw," *New York Times*, February 25, 1977, B1 and B16. Makowski's rise is recounted in George Gates, "Makowski's Responsibilities Grow in Role of

Sedita's Heir Apparent," *Buffalo Evening News*, August 3, 1972, 1; George Borrelli, "Sedita Resigns on Doctor's Advice; Makowski Plans Sweeping Changes," *Buffalo Evening News*, February 8, 1973, 1.

10. The economic malaise of Buffalo is covered in Cowie, *Stayin' Alive*; Kraus, *Race Neighborhood and Community Power*, 2; Graebner, *Coming of Age in Buffalo*. The *New York Times Magazine* cover story is "Down and Out in Buffalo: In Anger and Sadness People in Buffalo Tell the Story of Unemployment," *New York Times Magazine*, February 9, 1975, http://query.nytimes.com/mem/archive/pdf?res =9500E6DF1431E034BC4153DFB466838E669EDE.

11. Robert F. McFadden, "Thousands Laid Off by Shortage," 1; "Snow Squalls Snarl Great Lakes Area," *Boston Globe*, February 1, 1977, 1; Hill and Argenio, "Some Served Storm Victims; Other Stole," 11; Stratton, *Disaster Relief*, 83. Makowski is quoted in Dale English, "State Snowplows Sent Here to Clear Streets," *Courier Express*, January 28, 1977, 1.

12. The National Weather Service defines a blizzard as winds over 35 miles per hour accompanied by blowing or drifting snow that cuts visibility down to less than a quarter of a mile. Schwartz and Schmidlin, "Climatology of Blizzards in the Conterminous United States, 1959–2000," *Journal of Climate* (July 2002); Lee Coppola, "Day-to-Day Story of Killer Blizzard of '77," *Buffalo Evening News*, February 12, 1977, B2. Very few people were aware of the impending blizzard, and 70 percent of those polled remembered no warning at all, although local weatherman Tom Jolls had predicted the storm two days earlier using AccuWeather. See Anthony Cardinale, "Study Shows Cost of '77 Blizzard to WNYers," *Buffalo Evening News*, January 27, 1978, 1. Tom Jolls's story is told in LaClair, "Snow Job in Buffalo," 13–15.

13. Stratton, *Disaster Relief*, 93; "Worst Ever Blizzard Wreaks Havoc, Kills Four," *Buffalo Evening News*, January 29, 1977, 1; Robert Bahr, *The Blizzard*.

14. "Worst Ever Blizzard Wreaks Havoc, Kills Four"; "Snow Squalls Snarl Great Lakes Area," *Boston Globe*, February 1, 1977, 1; Richard Korovsky, "Winter That Was Buffalo, 1976–1977," *Milwaukee Journal*, December 12, 1977, 34; Richard Roth, "Six Killed During a Blizzard Buffalo Will Never Forget," 23; McFadden, "Thousands Laid Off"; Kolker quoted in Vecsey, "6 Found Dead in Buffalo Blizzard."

15. "Snow Squalls Snarl Great Lakes Area," *Boston Globe*, February 1, 1977, 1; "How Buffalo Fought Its Toughest Winter," *Rural and Urban Roads* (June 1977): 38–40, 44, 46–48. Hundreds of square miles were under blizzard conditions. The entire region was besieged by snow from the small Canadian cities near the US border down to the Pennsylvania State border. The storm swept over unfrozen Lake Ontario, whose moisture turned into 100 inches of new snow for Jefferson County and Watertown, New York, see Kneeland, *The Buffalo Blizzard*

of 1977. For the Canadian perspective see Rossi, *White Death;* and Scanlon and Taylor, *Two Tales of Snowstorm.* Utility crew operations are reported in "E. Alfred Osborn to O. Mark Michele and Douglas Johnson," Internal Correspondence Niagara Mohawk, February 8, 1977 (personal communication).

16. "Buffalo Tries to Dig Out as New Snow Falls," *New York Times,* January 31, 1977, 25. Police officer quoted in "Storm of Looters Hits City Homes, Vehicles, Businesses," *Courier Express,* January 31, 1977, 1; Lee Copolla, "Day-to-Day Story"; Roth, "At Least Six Die as Storm Stuns Buffalo." Doctor quoted in "Buffalo: Camaraderie and Tragedy," *Time,* February 14, 1977, 19; Sally Fox, "Volunteers Deliver Food," *Courier Express,* January 31, 1977, 1; "Buffalo, Under First Sun in Week, Works to Dig out from Blizzard," 10. For the zoo story, see Bahr, *Blizzard at the Zoo.*

17. "Buffalo under First Sun," 10; New York State Assembly Ways and Means Committee, *Disaster and Recovery.* According to Ruth Stratton, the one employee was retained only so the county could continue to receive grants from the federal government; see Stratton, *Disaster Relief,* 33–35; Dale C. English, "State Snowplows Sent to Clear Streets," *Courier Express,* January 28, 1977, 1.

18. Ned Regan's biography remains unwritten, but his political career was the subject of newspaper articles throughout his lifetime; see "Edward V. Regan," *New York Times,* October 21, 1982, B10; Steven R. Weisman, "Many Turns of Fortune Led to the State Comptrollership: Edward Van Buren Regan," *New York Times,* November 9, 1978, B4; Robert McFadden, "Edward V. Regan, Longtime New York State Comptroller Dies at 84," *New York Times,* October 18, 2014, http://nyti.ms/1t1xe2x; Edward Regan, Author Interview (hereafter Ned Regan). For the response in the towns see Nathaniel Shepherd, "Town near Buffalo Buried by Snow, Struggles Out, *New York Times,* February 3, 1977, 25; Anthony Cardinale, "Study Shows Cost of '77 Blizzard to WNYers"; Regan quoted in Ruth Stratton, *Disaster Relief,* 86; and in Al Popiel, "Long Recovery Seen, Bureaucratic Snafus Irk County Executive," *Buffalo Evening News,* February 12, 1977, 1.

19. Carey received an outpouring of letters of gratitude for his handling of the storm. See Hugh Carey Papers Microfilm Edition, Reel 29, New York State Archives. For Carey's career, see Lachman and Polner, *The Man Who Saved New York.* Carey's initial response to the storm is described in "Buffalo Tries to Dig out as New Snow Falls," *New York Times,* January 31, 1977, 25. On his request for federal assistance see "Hugh Carey to Mr. Thomas Casey, January 28, 1977," Hugh Carey Papers Microfilm Edition, Reel 28.

20. Linda Greenhouse, "Any Emergency Can Be Perilous for a Governor," *New York Times,* February 6, 1977, C35; Erik Brady, "Carey Here, Asks Major Disaster Tag," *Courier Express,* January 31, 1977, 1; "Carey Lauds Area Spirit in Buffalo," *Courier Express,* January 31, 1977.

21. Hugh Carey, "Press Release February 14, 1977," Hugh Carey Papers, Microfilm Edition, Reel 28.

22. Ibid.

23. Brady, "Carey Here, Asks Major Disaster Tag," 1; "Carey Lauds Area Spirit in Buffalo," *Courier Express*, January 31, 1977, 1; Division of Military and Naval Affairs, *Annual Report 1977*, 31–33; Joseph Ritz, "More Guardsmen Called; Total on Duty Now Tops 500," *Courier Express*, February 1, 1977, 1; Vecsey, "6 Found Dead in Buffalo Blizzard"; Division of Military and Naval Affairs, *Annual Report 1977* (Albany 1978). Hugh Carey correspondence on the disaster is found in Hugh Carey, "Press Release, February 11, 1977"; "Thomas Corcoran to Hugh Carey February 7, 1977"; "Eckenbrecht to Hugh Carey, 27 March 1977"; "Robert D'Amoto to Hugh Carey, March 7, 1977"; "Stanley Makowski to Hugh Carey, March 21, 1977," Hugh Carey Papers Microfilm Edition. Disaster operations are revealed in H Division of Military and Naval Affairs, *Annual Report 1977* (Albany: n.p., 1978); Hugh Carey, Press Release, February 11, 1977, Hugh Carey Papers Microfilm Edition. Ray Harding was the leader of the Liberal Party of New York and had allied with Carey support his election in 1974. In later years Harding became a lobbyist who helped Carey's son Michael gain a top job on the Economic Development Corporation, but Harding lost power when he was charged with and pled guilty to a pay for play scandal with New York State Comptroller Alan Hevesi; see "Ray Harding, Sentenced to Prison for Pay for Play," *New York Daily News*, May 17, 2011, Sec A.

24. "Buffalo Tries to Dig Out as New Snow Falls," *New York Times*, January 31, 1977, 25; "Buffalo, Under First Sun in Week, Works to Dig out from Blizzard," *New York Times*, February 2, 1977, 1. After the crisis ended the mayor checked into a hospital and was treated for stress and depression; see George Gates, "Makowski Years: 'Heartaches Grew for a Mayor Who Cared So Much,'" *Buffalo Evening News*, May 23, 1977, 1.

25. Makowski is quoted in Stratton, *Disaster Relief*, 91.

26. Makowski had a thankless task, and he was playing out a nightmare scenario in which his decisions would make or break his political future. The Buffalo mayor knew all too well of the political consequences of John V. Lindsay's failure to cope with a snowstorm in 1969; see Cannato, *Ungovernable City*, 395–97. On the mayor's decision-making process see Bahr, *The Blizzard*, 156–57; Ruth Stratton typified Makowski as incompetent in *Disaster Relief*, 100; Tony Fuller, "Three Fights for Survival; Buffalo N.Y. Digging Out of the Ice Age," *Newsweek*, February 14, 1977, 26; Lee Coppola, "Renewed Driving Ban Still City Forecast Calls for Squalls, Cold," *Buffalo Evening News*, February 4, 1977, 1; Dale English, "Mayor's Decision to Lift Driving Ban Seems a Puzzler," *Courier Express*, February 4,

1977, 1; Lee Coppola, "Day-to-Day Story," B2; "Winter Aid Plan Hits a Problem," *The Guardian*, February 2, 1977, 2.

27. The behind the scenes response and quotes from Ray Harding and Chester Hardt are found in English, "Mayor's Decision to Lift Driving Ban Seems a Puzzler," 2; and in Dale C. English, "Confusion Reigns at Storm HQ," *Courier Express*, February 2, 1977, 1. More details are added by Lee Coppola, "Renewed Driving Ban Stalls City." For a description of Casey's discovery of the mayor's decision to lift the driving ban see Bahr, *The Blizzard*, 166. On the administrative weakness of local governments see Sylves, *Disaster Policy and Politics*, 13. The federal bureaucrat remains anonymous because the full quote he gave was, "If you print that I will deny saying it." See English, "Confusion Reigns."

28. The political consequences of inept response to disasters is found in Richard Sylves, *Disaster Policy and Politics*, 18 and 36. Lyndon Johnson was masterful at using disasters for his own political advantage as was his successor Richard Nixon; see Kneeland, *Playing Politics with Natural Disaster*. The politics of snowstorms is discussed in Rita Giordano, "Officials from Chicago to Buffalo Fear Snow-Removal Backlash: It Has Removed Some from Office They Said," *Philadelphia Inquirer*, January 11, 1996, A15; Sue O'Brien, "Politics of Snow Blizzards Can Bury Mayors," *Denver Post*, November 23, 1997, H1; Chan and Liz Robbins, "Mayors Grow Attuned to the Politics of Snow Removal," *New York Times*, February 11, 2010, A20; Jennifer Steinhauer, "Weathering the Storms of Voter Discontent," *New York Times*, December 31, 2010, A14. Academics studying this find that political actors can often escape blame but not always; see Arceneaux and Stein, "Who Is Held Responsible When Disaster Strikes?"

29. The storm was later dubbed "Lindsay's Snowstorm"; see Owen Moritz, "Winter of Discontent: Lindsay's Snowstorm, 1969," *Daily News*, October 22, 1998.

30. Korovsky, "Winter That Was: Buffalo, 1976–1977," 34.

31. Makowski's actions and quotes can be found in Bahr, *The Blizzard*, 158; see also Sally Fox, "Mayor Phones Carter, Gets Aide, No Encouragement," *Courier Express*, February 2, 1977, 1; David Bird, "Buffalo Is Heartened by Promise of US Aid," *New York Times*, February 6, 1977, L 47; Stratton, *Disaster Relief*, 87.

32. Stratton, *Disaster Relief*, 87. The federal government was represented in Buffalo by Tom Casey from the Federal Disaster Assistance Administration (FDAA), a forerunner of FEMA. There is no biography of Tom Casey; his career can be followed in newspaper accounts and reports and correspondence in archives across the United States. Casey had been working in the government's disaster bureaucracy since the 1964 Alaska earthquake; see Tom Casey to Bill Moyers, "Alaska Memo for the President," Disaster Declaration Files, Office of Emergency

Preparedness, RG 168, National Archives. It was Casey's job to determine whether the situation in Buffalo was an emergency or a disaster.

33. Public perception is significant because, as Arceneaux and Stein have found, voters rarely hold local officials accountable after natural disasters unless they perceive that the officials bungled their job. Makowski demonstrates this effect; see Arceneaux and Stein, "Who Is Held Responsible When Disaster Strikes?" Eve is quoted in Richard J. Roth, "Eve Calls Mayor 'Not Capable' of Running Buffalo," *Courier Express*, February 5, 1977, 2.

34. On Makowski's political rivals see Ray Herman, "Mrs. Starosciak May Run If Makowski Bows Out," *Courier Express*, Feb 10, 1977, 1; George Borelli, "63% in Survey Give Makowski a Negative Rating," *Buffalo Evening News*, February 21, 1977, 1.

35. Kraus, *Race, Neighborhoods, and Community Power*, 165–66.

36. Michael Hiltzik, "Makowski Is Slated for State Board Job," *Courier Express*, December 31, 1977, 2; David S. Witkerski, "Pull Out Today by Makowski Is Expected," *Courier Express*, May 23, 1977, 1; William Claiborne, "Buffalo Mayor's Race Becomes a Classic Contest," *Washington Post*, October 15, 1977, http://www.washingtonpost.com/archive/politics/1977/10/15/buffalo-mayors-race-becomes-a-classic-contest/b2cdaa1f-9619-4f50-b0bf-d0611288de93/; Terrence McElroy, "Lindner Plows Through an 'In and Out' Day," *Courier Express*, December 31, 1977, 2. Lindner was the only person Makowski ever fired. In a show of political spite by Jimmy Griffin, the new mayor reappointed Lindner to his old job; see Rizzo, *Through the Mayors' Eyes*. Reminiscences about Makowski are found in George Borelli, "Makowski Wins Tribute That Was Long Overdue," *Buffalo Evening News*, August 16, 1981, E5; Ray Herman, "Makowski's Grace Unfailing Instinct," *Courier Express*, August 6, 1981, 1 and 6; George Gates, "At City Hall He was Known as 'Stan the Man,'" *Buffalo Evening News*, August 9, 1981, C1; Mike Vogel, "Makowski Is Remembered as Honest Sensitive Leader," *Buffalo Evening News*, August 6, 1981, 1.

4. Buffalo's Disaster Declaration and Presidential Politics

1. Lee Dembart, "Carter Sees Cabinet: Activity Stalled in Northeast and Midwest with Roads Blocked by Blizzards," *New York Times*, January 30, 1977, 1; Myra MacPherson, "Federal Disaster Aid Tested by Fla. Freeze, NY Snow," *Washington Post*, February 8, 1977, A5.

2. Florida did not offer unemployment insurance to migrant workers, and it would be three months before a new crop was ready. Patricia Harris Roberts, the Secretary to HUD, noted that "information available to me is that the primary need is unemployment assistance for workers not otherwise covered by

State and Federal Programs"; Patricia Harris Roberts to President Carter, January 28, 1977, RG 311, 207.79 Folder "Declarations," Box 12, National Archives, College Park, MD.

3. Carter did declare emergencies for both Ohio and Pennsylvania.

4. The FDAA had no authority to declare a disaster for the gas shortage. Material from FEMA, the FDAA, or its predecessor agencies such as the Office of Emergency Planning can be spotty depending on whether the document has been declassified. Presidential papers are a rich source for unclassified material of a political nature. Memo: Rick Hutcheson to Jack Watson, February 3, 1977, "Coordination Committee on Energy and Weather Progress," Folder 9, Box 2, White House Staff Files, Jimmy Carter Presidential Library (hereafter WHSF, JCPL).

5. Born, "Reassessing the Decline of Presidential Coattails," 60–79.

6. Labor leaders are quoted in Tony Fuller, "Three Fights for Survival; Buffalo N.Y. Digging Out of the Ice Age," *Newsweek*, February 14, 1977, 26; on Carter as president see Jones, *Trustee Presidency*, 17–20; Kaufman and Kaufman, *Presidency of James Earl Carter, Jr.*; Horowitz, *Jimmy Carter and the Energy Crisis of the 1970s*.

7. Jones, *Trustee Presidency*, 78. At times, Carter was forced to build cross-party coalitions to achieve his goals, but this only complicated his relationship with the Democrats; see Reid, *Congressional Odyssey*. Out of frustration with Carter, Democratic Party leader Ted Kennedy challenged him for the 1980 Democratic nomination; see Drew, *Portrait of an Election*; Eizenstat, *President Carter*, 678.

8. Jones, *Trustee Presidency*, 1. Carter felt that after winning the election, politics was something he could put aside until his reelection; Eizenstat, *President Carter*, 569, 678.

9. Jones, *Trustee Presidency*, 11; Eizenstat, *President Carter*, 419.

10. Eizenstat, *President Carter*, 200. Moore and congressional relations are the focus of a *Washington Post* article by Judy Bachrach, "I Love Those People on the Hill," *Washington Post*, November 3, 1977, https://www.washingtonpost.com/archive/lifestyle/1977/11/03/i-love-those-people-on-the-hill/e38fd5fd-8a1e-4951-9f47-77dc3639c506.

11. Jones, *Trustee Presidency*, 84–86; Whipple, *Gatekeepers*, 79; Fallows, "The Passionless Presidency: The Trouble with Jimmy Carter's Administration," *The Atlantic* 243 (May 1979): 33–48, https://www.theatlantic.com/magazine/archive/1979/05/the-passionless-presidency/308516/; Eizenstat, *President Carter*, 694–95.

12. George Lardner, "Paralyzing Storm Stuns Midwest, East," *Washington Post*, January 29, 1977, A1; John Kifner, *New York Times*, January 29, 1977, 1; "Winter Holds East and Midwest in Frigid Grip," *Boston Globe*, January 30, 1977, 1.

13. Hutcheson to Jack Watson; United States Senate, Committee on Public Works, *Disaster Relief Act Amendments of 1974* (Washington, DC: US Government Printing Office, 1974); Memo: President Jimmy Carter to Patricia Harris Roberts, Secretary of Housing and Urban Development, January 29, 1977, "The accumulation of snow and ice resulting from a series of blizzards and snowstorms in the State of Pennsylvania was suffering severely in magnitude to warrant a declaration of emergency under Public Law 93-288?"; RG 311, Box 207, Folder "Declarations PA January 29, 1977," National Archives, College Park, MD; FEMA, "Emergency Declarations 1977, https://www.fema.gov/disasters/grid/year/1977.

14. Eizenstat, *President Carter*, 85.

15. As mentioned, presidential papers are a rich source for unclassified material of a political nature. In contrast, classified material is redacted or blanked out; see Memo: Rick Hutcheson to Jack Watson, February 3, 1977, "Coordination Committee on Energy and Weather Progress," Folder 9, Box 2, WHSF JCPL.

16. Between 1951 and 1974, the Executive Office of the President handled disasters through an agency known as the Office of Emergency Preparedness (OEP). Richard Nixon moved OEP to HUD and renamed it the Federal Disaster Assistance Administration.

17. Wilcox underlined the phrase in the original memo; see Memo: William Wilcox to President Carter, "FDAA Briefing 1/31/77," WHSF JCPL.

18. William Wilcox to President Carter; Kneeland, *Playing Politics with Natural Disaster.*

19. George Vecsey, "6 Found Dead in Buffalo Blizzard; Carter Extends US Assistance," *New York Times*, January 30, 1977, 1 and 27.

20. The politics of where to locate Casey's headquarters is discussed in Bahr, *The Blizzard*, 133.

21. Municipal and Erie County records of the disaster are limited. Newspapers, while containing their own bias, are useful for setting the scene. Vecsey, "6 Found Dead in Buffalo Blizzard," 1 and 27.

22. Memo: "Lynn Daft to Stuart Eizenstat, January 31, 1977," Folder DI2/S 32, Box DI, WHCF JCPL. Daft worked for Eizenstat as a domestic policy staffer.

23. The Army Corps released a report detailing their participation and offering one perspective on the disaster; see United States Army Corps of Engineers, *Operation Snow Go: The Blizzard of '77* (Washington, DC: US Army Corps of Engineers, 1977); MacPherson, "Federal Disaster Aid Tested," A5.

24. "How Buffalo Fought Its Toughest Winter," *Rural and Urban Roads* (June 1977): 39–40.

25. US Army Corps of Engineers, *Operation Snow-Go*, 27; Erno Rossi, *White Death*, 315–18.

26. Kneeland, *Buffalo Blizzard of '77*.

27. Army Corps of Engineers, *Operation Snow-Go*.

28. Pierakos is quoted in Korovsky, "Winter That Was: Buffalo, 1976–1977," 34.

29. Bahr, *The Blizzard*, 157.

30. David Bird, "In Buffalo, Digging out from Storm, Its Hardships, Humor, and Heroics," *New York Times*, February 7, 1977, 37.

31. William Kristol, "Big Tim," *New York Times*, June 16, 2008, http://www.nytimes.com/2008/06/16/opinion/16kristol.html. After taking over the Erie County machine, Joe Crangle replaced the saloon keepers and undertakers who used to run Buffalo politics with "bright, energetic and cocky young college and law school graduates"; quoted in Diana Dillaway, *Power Failure: Politics, Patronage, and the Economic Future of Buffalo, New York* (Amherst, NY: Prometheus Books, 2006), 46.

32. Using print and broadcast media to pressure public officials was a new but growing phenomenon in disaster policy and the forerunner of what disaster experts call the "CNN Syndrome," referring to intensive media coverage of disasters that greatly influenced political responsiveness. See NAPA, *Coping with Catastrophes: Building an Emergency Management System to Meet People's Needs in Natural and Manmade Disasters* (Washington, DC: National Academy of Public Administration, 1993), 18. Russert's career took off after the Buffalo disaster; see Chris Smith, "What Makes Russert Run?" *New York Times*, December 7, 1992, 48–53. Russert later worked for Mario Cuomo and after that for NBC News, where he became the host of *Meet the Press* from 1991 until his untimely death in 2008.

33. There is no biography of Crangle. His political biography is pieced together through comments by those who knew him and newspaper stories such as Martin Tolchin, "Crangle Is Selected to Lead Democrats," *New York Times*, December 29, 1971, 1; Martin Tolchin, "Crangle Is Expected to Play the Leader," *New York Times*, December 30, 1971, 1.

34. Eizenstat, *President Carter*, 391.

35. Russert, *Big Russ and Me*, 256; Timothy Crouse, "Daniel Patrick Moynihan: Ruling Class Hero," *Rolling Stone*, August 12, 1976, http://www.rollingstone.com/politics/news/ruling-class-hero-19760812; "Crangle to Announce Resignation," *New York Times*, November 22, 1974; "Crangle Wins Support in National Party Race," *Washington Post*, February 19, 1981; Shafer, *Quiet Revolution: Struggle for the Democratic Party and Shaping of Post-Reform*, 246–48. Ultimately, due to a political battle with Mario Cuomo, Crangle lost power in the 1980s. Cuomo called Crangle a "nonperson" and then worked to unseat him from power nationally, statewide, and locally; see Frank Lynn, "Cuomo Trying to Oust Crangle as Chairman in Erie County," *New York Times*, February 7, 1985.

36. Dr. Ruth Stratton, a Buffalo-area political science professor, studied the storm and concluded that Crangle's role was pivotal; see also George Borelli, "Carter Decision on Disaster Aid Linked to Crangle," *Buffalo Evening News*, February 5, 1977, A3.

37. "FDAA Briefing," WHSF JCPL.

38. Watson led the presidential transition team, led intergovernmental affairs, and was cabinet secretary and eventually Chief of Staff.

39. Memo: Jack Watson to the President, February 2, 1977, "Coordinating Committee on Energy and Weather," Folder 9, Box 2, WHCF Disasters, JCPL. Typically applications for assistance include the name and political party of affected congressional representatives and a list of letters of support from elected political leaders in the region; see Daniels and Clark-Daniels, "Vulnerability Reduction and Political Responsiveness," *"International Journal of Mass Emergencies and Disasters*, 225–53.

40. David Bird, "Airlifts Carry Aid to Snowy Buffalo," *New York Times*, February 3, 1977, 24.

41. Quoted in Fuller, "Three Fights for Survival; Buffalo, N.Y., Digging Out of the Ice Age," 26; Sally Fox, "Mayor Phones Carter, Gets Aide, No Encouragement," *Courier Express*, Feb 2, 1977, 1; David Bird, "Buffalo Is Heartened by Promise of US Aid," *New York Times*, February 6, 1977, L 47; Bahr, *The Blizzard*, 157.

42. Memo: Lynn Daft to Stuart Eizenstat, January 31, 1977, Folder DI2/S Box 32, WHCF JCPL.

43. Carter's economic views are considered in Kaufman, *Presidency of James Earl Carter Jr.*; Dumbrell, *The Carter Presidency: A Re-Evaluation*, 145.

44. "FDAA Briefing 1/31/77."

45. The politics behind disaster policy is explored in Abney and Hill, "Natural Disasters as a Political Variable"; Arceneaux and Stein, "Who Is Held Responsible When Disaster Strikes?" Rutherford Platt found evidence of "disaster gerrymandering" in which location of an event was significant for determining whether a president declared a major disaster or an emergency, especially during the Clinton administration; see Platt, *Disasters and Democracy*, 57–58. David K. Twigg studied how Hurricane Andrew in 1992 shaped subsequent elections in *The Politics of Disaster: Tracking the Impact of Hurricane Andrew*. Peter May found evidence that highly visible candidates benefited from their actions in the aftermath of a disaster. May, who studied presidential declarations of major disasters under Nixon, Ford, and Carter, found a statistically significant "election year effect" under Nixon; see May, *Recovering from Catastrophes*, 118 and 112. Daniels and Clark-Daniels found that presidents gained more from spending money after a disaster than spending money on mitigation before one occurred; see Daniels and

Clark-Daniels, "Vulnerability Reduction." Andrew Reeves studies how presidential disaster declarations assist in elections; see Reeves, "Political Disaster, 1142–51.

46. Memo: "Jody Powell to Stuart Eizenstat and Jack Watson January 28, 1977: Re Disaster Relief," Folder 9, Box 2, WHCF JCPL. Delay and confusion haunted Carter's presidency through the hostage crisis 1979–80.

47. Morris, "Hurricane Camille and the New Politics of Federal Disaster Relief, 1965–1970," 406–26; Kneeland, *Playing Politics with Natural Disaster.*

48. Disasters allow presidents to show their symbolic leadership and evince concern as head of the nation; see Daniels and Clark-Daniels, "Vulnerability Reduction," 228; "Carter Dons Long Johns Tours Area Hit by Cold," *Boston Globe,* January 31, 1977, 1 and 10.

49. Presidential tours of disaster areas became more formalized in the 1960s, and by 1977 the public expected a presidential visit to a disaster site. Ray Herman, "Carter's Son to Tour Area Storm Scene," *Courier Express,* February 4, 1977, 1.

50. David Bird, "Buffalo Snow Amazes Chip Carter, but He Makes No Promise of Aid," *New York Times,* February 5, 1977, 20.

51. Bird, "Buffalo Snow Amazes Chip Carter."

52. Lucian Warren, "The Unsinkable Midge Costanza Keeps Her Job under Fire," *Buffalo Evening News,* December 18, 1977, B3; John L. Mitchell, "A Breezy Midge Talks about Her Days with Jimmy Carter," *Buffalo Evening News,* February 16. 1985, C-7; Charles O. Jones, *The Trustee Presidency,* 93–99. Costanza is admired by feminists and members of the LGBTQ community; see Mattingly, *A Feminist in the White House.*

53. Bird, "Buffalo Heartened by Promise of U.S. Aid."

54. Javits's quote may have to be seen as wishful thinking, but it was more likely a political signal to the White House from the senior senator from New York. Bird, "Buffalo Snow Amazes Chip Carter."

55. It appears that Moynihan's staff prepared the memo as a legal pad with the report written in cursive; it is found in the Moynihan Papers at the Library of Congress, Folder 2 "Disaster Assistance, Buffalo, 1977, 1983," Box 2500, Daniel Patrick Moynihan Papers, Library of Congress.

56. "Senators Jacob Javits and Daniel Patrick Moynihan to President Carter, February 4, 1977," Hugh Carey Papers Microfilm Edition, Reel 29, New York State Archives.

57. Those who signed included AFL-CIO officials, Westinghouse Electric officials, Ed Rutkowski from Representative Kemp's office, officials from Bethlehem Steel, John Downing from the New York Department of Transportation, Tim Swift from Senator Moynihan's office, Peter Steeley from Senator Javits's office, Tim Russert of Senator Moynihan's staff, Arthur Eve of the New York Assembly, many town supervisors, and John Voss of New York State Electric and Gas.

58. Memo: Lynn Daft to Stuart Eizenstat, Bert Carp, Gail Harrison, "Buffalo New York Situation, February 4, 1977," Folder 12, Box D1, WHCF JCPL.

59. Memo: Lynn Daft to Stuart Eizenstat, "Subject Status Report from Federal Disaster Assistance," Folder 2/3/77 Box 5, Office of the Staff Secretary–Handwriting File JCPL.

60. Memo: "Jimmy Carter to Tim Kraft, January 25, 1977," Folder 1-25-77, Box 4, Office of the Staff Secretary–Handwriting File, JCPL. On family time see "Jimmy Carter Memo to Staff, February 2, 1977," Folder 2/277–2/5/77, Box 5, Office of Staff Secretary-Handwriting File, JCPL. For President Carter's okay of the New York delegation call, see Memo: "From Timothy Kraft to Jimmy Carter February 4, 5:15 pm," Folder 2 2/4/77, Box 4, Office of the Staff Secretary–Handwriting File, JCPL. Carter spoke to Moynihan at 6:29; see Jimmy Carter Presidential Diary, Folder 2/4/77, Box 2, Presidential Daily Diary, JCPL. For a study that demonstrates how senatorial power and partisanship lead to disaster relief see Olzhas Zhumadillayevich Zhorayev, "The Influence of Political Factors on the Allocation of Disaster Relief Payments," Thesis, Montana State Univ., 2008, 55.

61. Wahlert, "President Jimmy Carter as a Reluctant Decision Maker," 1–2.

62. Memo: Lynn Daft to Stu Eizenstat, Bert Carp, Gail Harrison, "Buffalo New York Situation."

63. Underlining in the original, probably by Jimmy Carter; see Memo: "To Carter, February 4, 5:15 pm," Folder 2/4/77, Box 4, Office of Staff Secretary–Handwriting File, JCPL. Disaster denials are signed by the bureaucrats involved in emergency management; approvals come from the president. Thus it was Thomas Dunne, the administrator for the Federal Disaster Assistance Administration, who wrote Milton Shapp to indicate Pennsylvania had been denied disaster status: "On the basis of our investigation we have neem unable to verify the need for additional federal assistance under the Disaster Relief Act of 1974"; Memo: Thomas Dunne to Milton Shapp, January 28, 1977, Folder: Declarations, RG 311 207.79, National Archives College Park, MD.

64. Memo: For the President through Stuart Eizenstat from Lynn Daft, "Subject: Reason for Recommending Approval Major Disaster Status for New York but Denial Pennsylvania," Folder 4/1/77–12/31/77, DI 2/32, Box 12, WHCF Disasters, JCPL.

65. Jimmy Carter, "Digest of Other White House Announcements," February 11, 1977, Gerhard Peters and John T. Woolley, *The American Presidency Project*, http://www.presidency.ucsb.edu/ws/?pid=7833; David Bird, "Buffalo Is Heartened by Promise of US Aid," 47.

66. Folder 5, "New York Emergency Declaration February 5, 1977," Box 3, WHCF JCPL.

67. Henry Nowak had tried to reach Carter that morning, but the call was not completed. Instead of calling Nowak back, Carter called Mayor Makowski; Presidential Diary, Folder 2/5/77, Box 2, JCPL.

68. Letter: "Stanley Makowski to Midge Costanza, February 9, 1977," Folder DI2/S 32, BOX DI WHCF-JCPL.

69. Letter: "Henry J. Nowak to Midge Costanza, February 7, 1977," Folder DI2/S 32, BOX DI WHCF-JCPL.

70. Letter: "Robert Maerten, Supervisor Town of Pendleton to Jimmy Carter February 7, 1977," Folder DI2/S 32, BOX DI, WHCF JCPL.

71. Letter: "Joe Crangle to Midge Costanza, February 9, 1977," Folder FG 6-1-1/Costanza a.m., BOX DI2/ST 32, WHCF JCPL.

72. Letter: "Del Rogers, Editor of La Tribuna, to President Carter, February 7, 1977"; Letter: "Milton Shapp to Mr. Arthur T. Doyle, Regional Director FDAA, February 9, 1977"; Letter: "Peggy Blakeslee to President Carter, February 10, 1977"; Letter: "Anthony Spagnola to President Carter, March 5, 1977." Carter forwarded these letters to Thomas Dunne or Frank J. Muckenhaupt, who replied that New York and New Jersey were different due to the high unemployment caused by the winter storm, whereas snow removal is considered a normal government expenditure. Folder Disaster Declarations Pa, January 29, 1977; FEMA RG Box 12, RG 311 207, FDAA National Archives, College Park, MD.

73. Bahr, The Blizzard, 177. Rosenthal suggests that Dunne overruled Casey; see Rosenthal, "Bargaining Analysis in Intergovernmental Relations," 5–44. Perhaps to soften the blow of being overruled, Lynn Daft sent a note of thanks to Tom Casey telling him the White House delegation was very impressed with him; Letter: "Lynn Daft to Thomas R. Casey, February 17, 1977," Folder: Buffalo, DI2/ST32 RG 311, National Archives, College Park, MD.

74. Letter: "Sinclairville Village Board to Senator Daniel Patrick Moynihan, April 7, 1977," Folder: Congressional Correspondence, Box 416, RG 311, FEMA.

75. David Lynch, "Foschio Assails U.S. Role in Storm Disaster Aid Plan," Courier Express, April 19, 1977, 4.

76. Memo: "Memorandum for Lynn Daft 'Potential Food Stamp and Unemployment Assistance Problems, February 16, 1977,'" Folder 3: Disaster Assistance General, Box 15 Domestic Policy Staff, Lynn Daft Files JCPL. Memo: "Margaret Costanza to Frank Moore, 'Return Trip to Buffalo—Request for Comment,' March 14, 1977," Folder 3: Disaster Assistance General, Box 15 Domestic Policy Staff, Lynn Daft Files JCPL. Frank Moore was Carter's Legislative Liaison.

77. Memos: Tom Swift to Senator Moynihan, March 4, 1977, "Buffalo Disaster Aid: Tom Swift to Senator Moynihan March 7, 1977," "Response to Your Question on Reducing Local Share of Snow Removal in Western New York,"

Folder "Disaster Assistance Buffalo, 1977, 1983," Box 2500, Moynihan Papers, Library of Congress; Memo: "Tom Dunne, Date Closing Disaster Field Office, Buffalo April 22, 1977," Folder July 1978, Box 5, WHCF Disaster, JCPL.

5. A Blizzard of Change

1. Memorandum for the President, from Stu Eizenstat, Recommendations for Major Disaster Declarations Maryland/Virginia, January 25, 1977, Office of Staff Secretary Presidential Files, Folder 1/26/77, Box 4; Memorandum for the President, from Stu Eizenstat and Lynn Daft, FDAA Status Report of Major Disaster/Emergency Declarations through February 16, 1977, February 28, 1977, Office of Staff Secretary Presidential Files, Folder 3/27/77, Box 9.

2. James Watson, Carter's Cabinet Secretary and Assistant to the President for Intergovernmental Affairs, joked that his title should have been "Assistant to the President for Natural Disasters: Catastrophes, Floods, Droughts, and Hurricanes." Interview with Jack H. Watson Sr., April 17–18, 1981, Carter Presidential Project, Miller Center, University of Virginia.

3. Casey quoted in Stratton, *Disaster Relief*, 92; on bureaucratic autonomy see Carpenter, *Forging of Bureaucratic Autonomy*; for the continuing tie between the FDAA and FEMA to the White House see Sylves, *Disaster Policy and Politics*, 108.

4. Eizenstat, *President Carter*, 78.

5. Sylves, *Disaster Policy and Politics*, 199–201.

6. Memo, "Jimmy Carter to 'Heads of Executive Department and Agencies,' August 25, 1977," Folder 2: 1/20/77–120/81, Box 1, White House Central Files, Jimmy Carter Presidential Library (hereafter WHCF JCPL).

7. Memo, "Jim McIntyre to Jimmy Carter, 'Memorandum for the President: Reorganization of Federal Emergency Preparedness, October 16, 1977,'" Folder: Administrative Information, White House Staff Files, Box 68, JCPL. McIntyre worked with Carter in Georgia, running the state office of planning and budget before joining the administration in Washington. Jimmy Carter, Gerhard Peters, and John T. Woolley, "Office of Management and Budget Nomination of James T. McIntyre, Jr., to be Deputy Director," February 16, 1977, The American Presidency Project, http://www.presidency.ucsb.edu/ws/?pid=7955.

8. Memo, "James T. McIntyre to the President, Mar 2, 1978," Folder 1, Federal Disaster Assistance, Box 4, WHCF JCPL.

9. Memo, "Greg Schneider to Distribution List, January 26, 1978," Folder 6, Form Letters, Box 1, WHCF JCPL.

10. National Governors Association, *State Comprehensive Emergency Management*, 76.

11. National Governors Association, *State Comprehensive Emergency Management*, 75. It is highly likely that the governor mentioned was Milton Shapp of Pennsylvania, who spent a great deal of his time on the aftermath of Hurricane Agnes.

12. National Governors Association, *State Comprehensive Emergency Management*, i–xiv. Perhaps they hoped that White House officials would be easier to put pressure on than career civil servants.

13. Memo, "Greg Schneider to Jack Watson Emergency Preparedness and Response Reorganization February 27, 1978," Folder: Final Report, Box 72, Greg Schneider Files, WHCF JCPL.

14. Greg Schneider, "'Memorandum for Jack Watson,' February 27, 1978," Folder Memorandum Outgoing, Box 72, Greg Schneider's Files, Jimmy Carter Presidential Library (hereafter JCPL); National Governors Association, *Final Report of the Emergency Preparedness Project*, ii–ix.

15. Memo: "McIntyre to President, May 25, 1978," Folder 1, Box 2, WHCF JCPL.

16. Lewis, *Politics of Presidential Appointment*, 149–53.

17. Ibid., 44.

18. Political consideration.

19. Humphrey's Executor v. the United States, No. 667, Oyez (295 US 602, 1935), https://www.oyez.org/cases/1900-1940/295us602; Lewis, *Politics of Presidential Appointment*, 7–8.

20. Lewis, *Politics of Presidential Appointment*, 147. The tragic consequences of this overpoliticization of FEMA can be seen in the ineptitude of the agency response to Hurricane Katrina in 2005.

21. Political scientist Hugh Heclo published an article detailing the problems of managing an independent agency at the same time Jimmy Carter's men were fashioning FEMA; see Heclo, "Political Executives and the Washington Bureaucracy," 395–424.

22. Memo: Nye Stevens to Katie Beardsley, December 29, 1978, Folder: Federal Emergency Management Agency, Box 29, First Ladies Office, JCPL.

23. Clark served only one term before being defeated in 1978. Carter appointed Clark Ambassador at Large; see "Clark, Richard Clarence (Dick)," *Biographical Directory of the United States Congress*, http://bioguide.congress.gov/scripts/biodisplay.pl?index=c000448.

24. Matt Schudel, "George M. Elsey, One of the Last Links to the FDR White House, Dies at 97," *Washington Post*, January 9, 2016, https://www.washingtonpost.com/national/george-m-elsey-one-of-the-last-links-to-the-fdr-white-house-dies-at-97/2016/01/09/02078ac8-b6fb-11e5-a842-0feb51d1d124_story.html.

25. "Mike O'Callaghan, 74, Nevada Governor," *New York Times*, March 8, 2004, http://www.nytimes.com/2004/03/08/us/mike-o-callaghan-74-nevada -governor.html.

26. "Wesley Posvar, 75, U. of Pittsburgh Chancellor," *New York Times*, August 2, 2001, http://www.nytimes.com/2001/08/02/us/wesley-posvar-75-u-of-pittsburgh -chancellor.html.

27. Memo: "From Arnold Miller and James T. McIntyre Subject: Director of the Federal Emergency Management," Folder: Federal Emergency Management Agency, Box 29, First Ladies Office, JCPL.

28. Memo: "Robert Lipshutz to Jimmy Carter Memorandum for the President, February 4, 1979," Folder Federal Emergency Management Agency 2/4/79, Box 16, White House Counsel, JCPL. Lipshutz was sensitive to politics; he was a Georgia attorney and early political supporter of Carter who assisted in Carter's run for governor and then served as campaign treasurer for the Carter presidential campaign. See Dennis Hevesi, "Robert Lipshutz, Carter Aide, Dies at 88," *New York Times*, November 10, 2010, http://www.nytimes.com/2010/11/11/us/politics /11lipshutz.html.

29. Nye Stevens to Katie Beardsley.

30. Wolfgang Saxon, "Gordon Vickery, 76, Founder of Model Paramedic Programs," *New York Times*, December 22, 1996, http://www.nytimes.com/1996/12/22 /us/gordon-vickery-76-founder-of-model-paramedic-programs.html; Jimmy Carter, "Federal Emergency Management Agency Nomination of John W. Macy, Jr., To Be Director," May 3, 1979, John T. Woolley and Gerhard Peters, The American Presidency Project, Santa Barbara, CA, http://www.presidency.ucsb.edu/ws/?pid =32273.

31. Carter, in a speech after Hurricane Katrina, suggested that he wanted three elements in FEMA: "One was that it would be headed by highly qualified professionals in dealing with disaster. Secondly, that they would be completely independent and not under another agency that would submerge it. And third, that it would be adequately funded." Jimmy Carter, "Federal Emergency Management Agency Nomination of John W. Macy, Jr., to Be Director," May 3, 1979, John T. Woolley and Gerhard Peters, The American Presidency Project, Santa Barbara, CA, http://www.presidency.ucsb.edu/ws/?pid=32273. Memo: Tim Kraft and Arnie Miller, Memorandum for the President, Response to Your Inquiry About Appointment of FEMA Associate Directors, June 22, 1979, Office of Staff Secretary, Presidential Files, Folder 6/22/1979, Box 122, JCPL.

32. Lewis, *Politics of Presidential Appointment*, 148–50. FEMA reflects Carter's ideas at the time, or as Patrick Roberts reminds us, "Policy change usually fixes reigning ideas into place rather than provides an occasion to rethink the premises of federal intervention"; Roberts, *Disasters and the American State*, 85.

33. Patrick S. Roberts discusses stovepiping in FEMA; see Roberts, *Disasters and the American State*, 79; Bovard, "FEMA Money, Come and Get It!," 25–31.

34. For Richard Nixon's policy, see Kneeland, *Playing Politics with Natural Disaster*.

35. Lewis, *Politics of Presidential Appointment*, 148; Federal Emergency Management Agency, "FEMA History," http://www.fema.gov/about/history.shtm.

36. Quoted in Roberts, *Disasters and the American State*, 79; originally in National Academy of Public Administration, *Coping with Catastrophe*, 16.

37. Jimmy Carter: "President's Commission on the Accident at Three Mile Island Remarks Announcing Actions in Response to the Commission's Report," December 7, 1979, Gerhard Peters and John T. Woolley, The American Presidency Project, http://www.presidency.ucsb.edu/ws/?pid=31788; Hollis, "A Tale of Two Federal Emergency Management Agencies," 1–14; Copeland, "The Cuban Boatlift of 1980: Strategies in Federal Crisis Management," 138–50; Newman, *Love Canal*; New York State Office of Public Health, *Love Canal*.

38. Moss, Schellhammer, and Berman, "The Stafford Act and Priorities for Reform," 2.

39. Sylves, *Disaster Policy and Politics*, 106; Roberts, *Disasters and the American State*, 85–86. State officials were delighted that the president's power to declare an emergency was increased because emergency declarations did not require governors to submit damage estimates as they would in the case of a disaster.

40. William Wilcox of the FDAA called it the "domino effect": "Memo from William Wilcox to Lynn Daft, Subject Domino Effect of Emergency Snow Declaration," January 31, 1979, WHCF, Disasters, Box 4, Folder 1. Carter's disaster category blurred the line between policy and politics, and many people questioned decision-making as to whether snow removal was a disaster, an emergency, or neither. Some critics of the snow disaster policy saw it as pork barrel politics; see Daniels and Clark-Daniels, "Vulnerability Reduction and Political Responsiveness"; Garret and Sobel, "The Political Economy of FEMA Disaster Payments"; Dymon and Platt, "U.S. Federal Disaster Declarations: A Geographical Analysis"; Mayer, "States: Stop Subsidizing FEMA Waste and Manage Your Own Disasters," 34.

41. Carter issued more emergency declarations than Reagan. Sylves, *Disaster Policy and Politics*, 106.

42. FEMA maintains a database of disaster and emergency declarations by category and year at https://www.fema.gov/disasters.

43. Earls, *Greater Boston's Blizzard of 1978*; "Top 10 Big, Bad Blizzards," *Time*, February 2, 2011, http://content.time.com/time/specials/packages/article/0,28804,2045627_2045629_2045672,00.html.

44. Changnon and Changnon, "Record Winter Storms in Illinois, 1977–1978."

45. Memo: "Memorandum for Bill Wilcox, from Lynn Daft October 22, 1979," Folder: Disasters Snowstorms and Snow Removal through Draft Impact Statements, Box 17, Lynn Daft Domestic Files, JCPL.

46. US Senate, Committee on Environment and Public Works, *Federal Response to the Rhode Island Blizzard*, 25.

47. Comptroller General, *Federal Snow Removal Reimbursement Policy*.

48. "William H. Wilcox, 84, Pushed for Change in City," *Philadelphia Inquirer*, June 7, 2004, B8. Wilcox elevated the capable Tom Casey to the position of deputy administrator; see "Casey Gets Appointment," *Star-Gazette*, October 30, 1978.

49. Sylves, *Disaster Policy and Politics*, 108.

50. Memo: "Memorandum for the President from Stu Eizenstat and Lynn Daft," Folder Lynn Daft Files, Box 6, JCPL.

51. Carpenter, *The Forging of Bureaucratic Autonomy*, 353.

52. Memo: "Bruce Kirshenbaum and Claire Hatfield to Jack Watson and Gene E., June 18. 1979," Folder 5, "Summary of GAO Staff Draft Report on Snow Removal Policy," WHCF JCPL.

53. Memo: "William H. Wilcox to Lynn Daft 'Domino Effect of Emergency Snow Declaration January 31, 1979,'" Folder 4, Box 4, Lynn Daft Files, JCPL.

54. The FDAA rejected snow thresholds as potentially illegal under the Disaster Relief Act of 1974. Federal policy may have unintentionally created a moral hazard whereby some localities reduced or determined not to increase readiness for winter storms in expectation of receiving federal money to assist when extreme weather did occur; see Shughart, "Disaster Relief as Bad Public Policy," 529–31. Congress responded to complaints from constituents and proposed an amendment to the law (H.R. 1320), which would have made states and localities eligible for reimbursements incurred from the time that the storm commenced; see Comptroller General, *Federal Snow Removal Reimbursement Policy*, 3–5.

55. US Senate, Committee on Environment and Public Works, *Federal Response to the Rhode Island Blizzard*, 99.

56. Comptroller General, *Federal Snow Removal Reimbursement Policy*, 27–31.

57. "Snow Fighting City Finds Its Own Catch-22," Folder 22, Snow and Ice Control, Box 71, American Public Works Association, State Historical Society Missouri–Kansas City (hereafter APWA-SHSMO-KC).

58. "Statement by William Wilcox Federal Disaster Assistance Administration," US Senate, Committee on Environment and Public Works, *Federal Response to the Rhode Island Blizzard*, 85–89; 94–101.

59. Ibid. Congress was already unhappy with disaster relief in general; see US Senate, *Disaster Relief Oversight*; US Senate, *Federal Disaster Relief Programs*.

60. "Statement by William Wilcox Federal Disaster Assistance Administration," US Senate, Committee on Environment and Public Works, *Federal Response to the Rhode Island Blizzard*, 136.

61. Memo: "Winter Preparedness Meeting," Folder 3, Box 4, WHCF Disaster JCPL.

62. Letter: "Norman Steilauf, FDAA, to Governor Hugh Carey, January 29, 1979," Hugh Carey Papers, Microfilm Edition, Reel 25, New York State Archives.

63. Frederickson, "Elmer B. Staats: Government Ethics in Practice," 214–40. Staats was later a member of the National Academy for Public Administration, which authored a scathing critique of federal emergency management in 1993; see National Academy of Public Administration, *Coping with Catastrophe*.

64. Walker, "Elmer Staats and Strategic Leadership in the Legislative Branch," 304–5; Mosher, *A Tale of Two Agencies*.

65. Comptroller General, *Federal Snow Removal Reimbursement Policy*, 32.

66. Ibid., ii.

67. Ibid.

68. Ibid., 20; Walker, "Elmer Staats," 292.

69. Memo: "Ray Schuler to Ray Harding, February 3, 1977. Summary Report of Snow Emergency," Hugh Carey Papers, Microfilm Edition, Reel 195, New York State Archives.

70. New York State Senate, *Natural Disasters*, 3.

71. John Moore, "State Conducts Snow Fighter's School on Location," *Public Works* (August 1979): 64–65, Folder Snow and Ice Control, Box 71, APWA-SHSMO-KC.

72. Kneeland, *Playing Politics with Natural Disaster*.

73. New York Division of Military and Naval Affairs, *Annual Report 1977*, 33–34.

74. Office of Disaster Preparedness, 30.

75. New York State Senate, *Natural Disasters*, 4.

76. The 1979 report constituted the third such senate investigation into state disaster preparedness since 1972; see New York State Senate, *Natural Disasters*.

77. New York State Senate, *Natural Disasters*, 12–17.

78. "Hugh Carey to the Senate, July 12, 1977," in New York State Senate, *Natural Disasters*, Appendix C.

79. New York Division of Military and Naval Affairs, *Annual Report 1983*, 19.

80. Stratton, *Disaster Relief*, 34–35.

6. "Grab a Six Pack"

1. Rita Giordano, "Officials from Chicago to Buffalo Fear Snow-Removal Backlash: It Has Removed Some from Office They Said," *Philadelphia Inquirer*, January 11, 1996, A15; Sue O'Brien, "Politics of Snow Blizzards Can Bury Mayors," *Denver Post*, November 23, 1997, H1; Chan and Liz Robbins, "Mayors Grow Attuned to the Politics of Snow Removal," *New York Times*, February 11, 2010, A20; Jennifer Steinhauer, "Weathering the Storms of Voter Discontent," *New York Times*, December 31, 2010, A14; Arceneaux and Stein, "Who Is Held Responsible When Disaster Strikes?"; Mergen, *Snow in America*, 72.

2. Waugh, *Living with Hazards*, 51.

3. Changnon, "Catastrophic Winter Storms," 133–34, Changnon estimates that the cost of winter storms has risen steadily since 1949 with the average loss per major storm of $174 million.

4. Grant Ujifusa, one of the coauthors of the *Almanac of Politics*, suggested that the public believes that a crisis reveals fundamental intention and character of a leader, quoted in O'Brien, "Politics of Snow," H1.

5. Waugh, *Living with Hazards*, 151; Wolfgang Saxon, "William McNichols, 87, Led Denver Boom in '70s," *New York Times*, May 31, 1997, 10, https://www.nytimes.com/1997/05/31/us/william-mcnichols-87-led-denver-boom-in-70-s.html; Whet Moser, "Snowpocalypse Then: How the Blizzard of 1979 Cost the Election for Michael Bilandic," *Chicago Magazine*, February 2, 2011, https://www.chicagomag.com/Chicago-Magazine/The-312/February-2011/Snowpocalypse-Then-How-the-Blizzard-of-1979-Cost-the-Election-for-Michael-Bilandic/.

6. Brian Heaton, "Internet of Things Helps Buffalo, Other Cities with Snow Removal," *Government Technology*, November 19, 2014, https://www.govtech.com/data/Internet-of-Things-Helps-Buffalo-Other-Cities-with-Snow-Removal.pdf.

7. Eileen Keerdoja, "After the Thaw," *Newsweek*, July 25, 1977, 7.

8. "Battling the Snowstorm in Buffalo," *Government Fleet*, January 16, 2015, https://www.government-fleet.com/155886/battling-the-snowstorm-in-buffalo.

9. Mary Ann Mandell, Folder 2, Snow conference 1986, Box 295, American Public Works Association Records, State Historical Society of Missouri–Kansas City (hereafter APWA-SHSMO-KC).

10. Camello, Folder 4, Snow Conference 1987, Box 295, APWA-SHSMO-KC; Constance Wilder "Dealing with the Public, the Media, and Neighborhood Groups, April 14, 1986," Folder 2, Snow Conference 1986, Box 295, APWA-SHSMO-KC. Most cities in the Snowbelt region invite reporters for a snowplow ride-along so they understand the challenges faced by plow drivers.

11. Thomas Low Comments, Folder 2, Snow Conference 1986, Box 295, APWA-SHSMO-KC.

12. Aaron Besecker, "Snow Fighters Are Primed and Ready," *Buffalo News*, November 18, 2011, https://buffalonews.com/news/snow-fighters-are-primed-and-ready-as-first-lake-effect-blast-hits-southern-tier-area/article_d6791f84-21f9-5c26-9dc0-625516108cc7.html; Heaton, "Internet of Things Helps Buffalo, Other Cities with Snow Removal."

13. Hughes, *A Century of Weather Service*, 178; Fleming, "Fixing the Weather and Climate," 175–95; Fleming, "Pathological History of Weather and Climate Modification," 3–25; Cochrane, *Urban Snow Hazard in the United States*, 12; Wyckoff, "Some Problems and Objectives in Weather Modification," 115, 123–24; Haas, "Social Aspects of Weather Modification," 647–57; Hosler, "Overt Weather Modification," 523–27; Changnon, "Paradox of Planned Weather Modification," 27–37; Howe, "'Legal Moguls,' Ski Areas, Weather Modification and the Law," 59–77; James Lawless, "New York Assembly Hearing on State Weather Modification Bill," National Oceanic and Atmospheric Administration Records, National Archives, College Park, MD; Joel Myers, President of AccuWeather, "Accurate Snow Forecast for Public Works Departments," 1979, Folder 31, Box 71, APWA-SHSMO-KC. AccuWeather claimed that private forecasters had higher accuracy in long-range forecasting than the NWS; Monmonier, *Lake Effect*, 108.

14. LaClair, "Snow Job in Buffalo"; Eichenlaub, *Weather and Climate of the Great Lakes Region*, 287–88; Call, "Rethinking Snowstorms as Snow Events," 1789.

15. Lorditch, "Advances in Weather Analysis and Forecasting," 22–27; Call, Grove, and Kocin, "Meteorological and Social Comparison of the New England Blizzards of 1978 and 2013," 1–10; Paul, "Predicting Lake Effect Snow Presents Quandaries."

16. Tom Hartley, "Weather Service's Impact Defined by Blizzard of '77," *Buffalo First*, January 14, 1999, 12.

17. Kerr, "Who Can Forecast the Worst Weather," 29; Henson, *Weather on the Air*, 18–19, 103–4.

18. Seventy-two percent of respondents to a poll on local newscasts indicated their primary interest was the weather forecast. See Henson, *Weather on the Air*, 20; "The Meteorologist in Your Life."

19. Extensive coverage of "the worst ever" winter storms after the fact is not new as a review of nineteenth- and early-twentieth-century Buffalo newspapers shows, but televised coverage of winter storms before they arrive began with the Storm of the Century in 1993; see Henson, *Weather on the Air*, 172–74.

20. Kerr, "Who Can Forecast the Worst Weather"; Trinkaus, "Television Station Weather-Person's Winter Storm Predictions," 65–66; Anthony Flint, "A Snow Job? Much Fanfare but Few Problems," *Boston Globe*, December 21, 1995, 1; "Meteorologist in Your Lifetime," 68–71; Potter, "Let It Snow," 68; Fry, *Constructing*

the Heartland; Vannini and Mccright, "Technologies of the Sky," 49–74; Lorditch, "Advances in Weather Analysis and Forecasting," 22–27; O'Rourke, "It Snows in Winter?" 48; "Must Winter Storms Have Their Own Names?" *Philadelphia Inquirer*, February 19, 2013, https://www.inquirer.com/philly/opinion/inquirer/20130219 _Inquirer_Editorial__Must_winter_storms_have_their_own_names_.html; Mark Jurkowitz, Paul Hitlin, Amy Mitchell, Laura Santhanam, Steve Adams, Monica Anderson, and Nancy Vogt, "The Changing TV News Landscape," Pew Research Center, http://stateofthemedia.org/2013/special-reports-landing-page/the-changing -tv-news-landscape/; Jason Samenow, "Weather Service Made Poor Decision in Over-playing Nor'easter Snow Predictions," *Washington Post*, March 15, 2017, https:// www.washingtonpost.com/news/capital-weather-gang/wp/2017/03/15/weather -service-made-poor-decision-in-overplaying-noreaster-snow-predictions/.

21. Maintenance Decision Support System, About, https://mdss.iteris.com/mdss /pfs/pages.pl?pg=about; Brad Plumer, "How America Got Addicted to Road Salt— and Why It's a Problem," *Vox*, January 25, 2015; CNBC, "Road Salt Winter's $2.3 Billion Game Changer"; *Snow Fighter's Handbook*.

22. Monmonier, *Lake Effect*, 106; New York State Department of Transportation, "Department of Transportation Announces New Tow Plows to Keep Roads Safe This Winter," December 22, 2015, https://www.dot.ny.gov/portal/page/portal /news/press-releases/2015/2015-12-22.

23. Plumer, "How America Got Addicted to Road Salt"; *Snow Fighter's Handbook*; Laura Fay et al., "Performance and Impacts of Current Deicing and Anti-icing Products: User Perspective Versus Experimental Data," https://www.academia .edu/26640441/Performance_and_Impacts_of_Current_Deicing_and_Anti-Icing _Products_User_Perspective_versus_Experimental_Data.

24. Kraus, *Race, Neighborhoods, and Community Power*, 168.

25. Gerber, *Making of American Pluralism*; George Gates, "Maverick Mayor-Elect Wears Brand of Early Years in City's First Ward," *Buffalo Evening News*, November 12, 1977, 1; Maurice Carroll, "County Executive's Race Spices Election in Buffalo," *New York Times*, October 29, 1979, B2; Jimmy Griffin, "In Buffalo, the Public and Private Focus Is on a Better Future," *New York Times*, December 14, 1982, A30; Howard Kurtz, "Buffalo Mayor Puts Teeth in Political Philosophy," *Washington Post*, April 18, 1983, A4.

26. Moore, *Buffalo Blizzard Book*, 255.

27. Ibid., 256.

28. Ibid., 261; Kraus, *Race, Neighborhoods, and Community Power*, 189; Moore, *Buffalo Blizzard Book*, 261.

29. Cichon, *Gimme Jimmy! Mayor James D. Griffin in His Own Words and Pictures*, 12–17; Kraus, *Race, Neighborhoods, and Community Power*, 189. The January 19–21 storm was massive, and winter weather touched on twenty-nine

states; see Changnon, "Catastrophic Winter Storms: An Escalating Problem," 133–34.

30. Moore, *Buffalo Blizzard Book*, 268.

31. Jolls, Meyer, and Van Meer, *Western New York Weather Guide*, 20–21; Moore, *Buffalo Blizzard Book*, 272.

32. Kraus, *Race, Neighborhoods, and Community Power*, 189.

33. Michael Desmond, "In Buffalo, the Worst of Times," *New York Times*, September 14, 1980, T3; "Guardsmen Help Buffalo Plow 35 Inches of Snow," *New York Times*, January 23, 1985, B4; Howard Kurtz, "Buffalo: Great Dreams, But Greater Needs," *Washington Post*, April 18, 1983, https://www.washington post.com/archive/politics/1983/04/18/buffalo-great-dreams-but-greater-needs /22b9c235-77b9-40ea-b8ea-40564f04daa3/; Maurice Carroll, "Buffalo's Mayor Griffin in Crowded Primary Fight," *New York Times*, August 24, 1985, 1, 26.

34. Sam Howe Verhovek, "Rivals' Contest Aids Buffalo's Mayor," *New York Times*, September 6, 1989, B4. In 1989 Griffin won 79 percent of votes cast; "Buffalo's Four Term Says He Won't Run for Reelection," *New York Times*, May 5, 1993, B6.

35. Korovsky, "Winter That Was," 34; McKelvey, *Snow in the Cities*, 181.

36. "Snowfall Brings Buffalo Region to a Standstill," *New York Times*, January 22, 1985, B4.

37. "County and Townships Form Mutual Aid and Snow Fight Plan," *Rural and Urban Roads*, June 1979, Folder 31, Box 71, APWA-SHSMO-KC.

38. Stratton, *Disaster Relief*, 34.

39. Ibid., 35.

40. State of New York Division of Military and Naval Affairs, *Annual Report 1985* (Albany, NY: DMNA, 1986), 27.

41. "Guardsmen Help Buffalo Plow 35 Inches of Snow"; Clifford D. May, "Buffalo Meets Record Snow with a Shrug," *New York Times*, December 30, 1985 (the tone of the article reinforced the idea that Buffalo is a snowbound region).

42. Quoted in Lewis, *Politics of Presidential Appointments*, 154. Under Witt, FEMA gained greater respect and autonomy.

43. Tomasky, *Bill Clinton*, 27–28.

44. FEMA, "Disasters," https://www.fema.gov/disasters. Some people assume that Clinton's largesse was calculated to bring electoral benefits; see Steve Twomey, "Disaster or Snow Job?" *Washington Post*, April 26, 1993, B1.

45. "Buffalo Election Finds Troubled City at Crossroads," *New York Times*, September 14, 1993, B5; Kim Balcerzak, "Mayor Masiello Enters 50 Plus," *Living Prime Time* (July 1995), http://www.livingprimetime.com/AllCovers/Jul1995 /mayor_masiello_enters_50_plus.htm; Kraus, *Race, Neighborhoods, and Community Power*, 207–8. A winter storm in 1999 was brief but quickly dealt with;

see "Snowstorm Brings Buffalo to a Halt," *New York Times*, January 5, 1999, B5; Anthony Masiello, "Operation Snow Removal Moves into Full Swing," *Buffalo News*, January 13, 1999, http://mayormas.tripod.com/jan13.htm; Giordano, "Officials from Chicago to Buffalo Fear Snow-Removal Backlash," A15; Ginger Thompson, "Even Buffalo, Citadel of Winter, Grows Weary of Relentless Snow," *New York Times*, January 16, 1999, 1.

46. Ward, "'Snow Problem' Buffalo Knows How to Deal with Winter," 26–33; Lisa A. Foderaro, "Removal Pro in a City of Snow: Blanket over Buffalo Keeps Cleanup Boss on His Toes," *New York Times*, February 21, 2003, B1; Call, "Rethinking Snowstorms as Snow Events," 1783–93.

47. Shaila K. Dewan, "Nature Lets Buffalo Know It's Not a Match for Winter," *New York Times*, November 22, 2000, B5; Ron Scherer, "Where Snowflakes Stay on Noses, Eyelashes," *Christian Science Monitor*, January 17, 2001; Call, "Snow Storms as Snow Events," 1786.

48. Don Singleton, "Buffalo Digging Out," *New York Daily News*, December 30, 2001, 22; Moore, *Buffalo Blizzard Book*, 294.

49. "State Shortfall Threatens Buffalo Cashflow," *New York Times*, April 30, 2003, B5; David Staba, "Layoffs Averted as Buffalo Gets Control Board," *New York Times*, June 21, 2003, B8; "An Act to Amend the Public Authorities Law and Tax Law, in Relation to Creating the Buffalo Fiscal Control Authority," July 2003, http://public.leginfo.state.ny.us/bstfrmcf.cgi; David Staba, "On Paper, Buffalo Sees Improvement; On the Streets, Many Disagree," *New York Times*, July 19, 2004, https://www.nytimes.com/2004/07/19/nyregion/on-paper-buffalo-sees -improvement-on-the-streets-many-disagree.html; David Staba, "Buffalo Mayor Won't Seek a Fourth Term in the Fall," *New York Times*, April 30, 2005, B7.

50. Byron Brown Biography: https://ny-buffalo.civicplus.com/495/Mayor -Browns-Biography.

51. Jonathan P. Hicks, "All Eyes on a Black Candidate in Buffalo's Mayor Race," *New York Times*, June 4, 2005, B2; Jonathan P. Hicks, "Race Plays Silent Role in Campaign for Mayor of Buffalo," *New York Times*, October 13, 2005, B6; David Staba, "Buffalo Elects First Black Mayor, Who Claims Mandate," *New York Times*, November 9, 2005, B10.

52. Brian Meyer, "Buffalo Turning Corner, Brown Says: Mayor Cites Development 'Surge,' Shares Vision in State of City Address," *Buffalo News*, February 21, 2007, 1; Danielle Taylor and Kellie May, "Meet the Mayor: Buffalo, New York's Byron Brown," *Parks and Recreation*, October 24, 2014, 22–23; Byron Brown, "Letter to the Editor: The Re-Imaging of Buffalo by Mayor Byron Brown," *The Record*, May 12, 2017.

53. "City Comptroller Calls on Mayor, Council to Resolve Bond Deadlock," *Buffalo News*, January 16, 2011.

54. Andrew Freedman, "Anatomy of a Forecast: 'Arborgeddon' Takes Buffalo by Surprise," *Weatherwise* (July/August 2007), 17–21; Matthew Spina, "October Storm Left Suburbs on Brink of Losing All Water: System Faced Greater Risk of Going Dry Than Thought," *McClatchy-Tribune Business News*, retrieved from https://search-proquest-com.ezproxy.naz.edu/docview/459598607?accountid =28167. For the process of converting trucks to plows see Ali Touhey, "Towns Tackle Snow Removal," WKBW TV, November 11, 2019, https://www.wkbw.com /news/local-news/towns-tackle-snow-removal.

55. "Editorial: This Storm Taught Lessons: Disaster Response Generally Was Good, but Fix the Flaws before Next Time," *Buffalo News*, October 27, 2006, https://buffalonews.com/news/this-storm-taught-lessons-disaster-response-generally -was-good-but-fix-the-flaws-before-next/article_cc5682fd-3254-5645-8c9d-e98d6 90f5c5f.html.

56. FEMA, Disaster Declarations, https://www.fema.gov/disasters.

57. Before 2006 Tom Reynolds was considered to be in a safe Republican district, having won his 2004 race against Jack Davis by twelve percentage points. In 2006 however, once again facing Davis, Reynolds was tied to a scandal involving congressman Mark Foley and a congressional page. How much Bush's declaration of disaster aided Reynolds is unknown. Still, after the disaster declaration, the incumbent won his 2006 reelection by just four percentage points. See Michael Beebe, Dan Herbeck, and T. J. Pignataro, "Major Disaster Status Expected," *Buffalo News*, October 22, 2006, https://buffalonews.com/2006/10/22/major-disaster -status-expected/.

58. Michael Beebe, "FEMA Teams Inspect Storm Damage: President Bush Urged to Speed Up Process for Dispensing Aid," *Buffalo News*, October 19, 2006, 1; Janis L. Magin and Maria Newman, "Magnitude 6.6 Earthquake Shakes Hawaii," *New York Times*, October 15, 2006, http://www.nytimes.com/2006/10/15 /us/15cnd-quake.html; George W. Bush, "Statement on Federal Emergency Assistance for New York," October 15, 2006, https://georgewbush-whitehouse.archives .gov/news/releases/2006/10/text/20061015.html; Louise Slaughter, "Press Release: Joint Statement on Approval of Major Disaster Declaration," October 24, 2006, https://louise.house.gov/media-center/press-releases/october-24-2006-joint-statement -approval-major-disaster-declaration; "Welcome Federal Storm Reimbursement Will Require an Accurate Accounting," *Buffalo News*, December 28, 2014, http:// www.buffalonews.com/opinion/buffalo-news-editorials/welcome-federal-storm -reimbursement-will-require-an-accurate-accounting-20141228; Patrick Lakamp, Mary Pasciak, and Susan Schulman, "FEMA Sent $9 Million after October Storm, Favoring Those with Flood Damage; But October Surprise Did Not Go to Areas Hardest Hit by the Storm," *McClatchy-Tribune Business News*, October 13, 2007, https://search.proquest.com/docview/463925946?accountid=28167; National

Weather Service, "Lake Effect Snow Event Archive: October 12, 2006, to October 13, 2006," https://www.weather.gov/buf/lesEventArchive2006-2007_a; Phil Fairbank, "Ugly Sign of October Storm to Disappear: FEMA Grant to Fund Tree Stump Removal," January 30, 2008, *McClatchy-Tribune Business News*, https://search-proquest-com.ezproxy.naz.edu/docview/462570802?accountid=28167.

59. "Press Release: Mayor Brown Reviews City Snow Fighting Equipment," December 5, 2018, https://www.buffalony.gov/CivicAlerts.aspx?AID=314; Jeff Preval, "State DOT, Buffalo Talk Snow Clearing Plans," December 5, 2017, WGRZ TV, https://www.wgrz.com/article/news/local/state-dot-buffalo-talk-snow-clearing-plans/71-497053495.

60. "Editorial: This Storm Taught Lessons: Disaster Response Generally Was Good"; Byron Brown, "Press Release: Mayor Brown Inspects City Snow Fighting Equipment," October 2006; Byron Brown, "City's New Plan Follows Internal Review of City Response to Recent Record Snowfalls," https://www.ci.buffalo.ny.us/Mayor/Home/Leadership/Archived_Press_Releases/2009Archives/January2009/SnowRemovalPlan; Emily Badger, "Zen and the Art of Snow Plow Maintenance," *Atlantic*, January 23, 2012, https://www.citylab.com/solutions/2012/01/zen-and-art-snow-plow-maintenance/1008/.

61. Buffalo Budgets are online at https://www.buffalony.gov/1109/2018-19-Adopted-Budget and at https://www.buffalony.gov/185/Archived-Budgets. These figures represent the operating budget only and do not include maintenance figures for vehicle upkeep or capital expenditures on new equipment; "Mayor Brown Unveils City Snow Fighting."

62. David Kuemmel and Rashad Hanbali, *Accident Analysis of Ice Control Operations* (1992), https://epublications.marquette.edu/transportation_trc-ice/1; American Highway Alliance, *The Economic Costs of Disruption from a Snowstorm: Study Prepared for the American Highway Alliance by IHS Global Insight* (2014), https://www.highways.org/wp-content/uploads/2014/02/economic-costs-of-snowstorms.pdf.

63. Mission Statement for the Buffalo Streets Department Snow Removal Operations.

64. Valentine, "Snows Send Area 'Back to the Salt Mines'"; Pamela G. Hilly, "Road Salt Supplies Short, Locked up in Ice," *New York Times*, February 11, 1978, 27; William E Dickinson, President Salt Institute, "Surviving without Sufficient Salt, 1980," Folder 41, North American Snow Conference Papers 1980, Box 38, APWA-SHSMO-KC.

65. "Enough Salt for Winter, Mine Officials Say," *New York Times*, November 25, 1994, B6; Katie Zezima, "Winter Storms Squeeze Supplies of Road Salt," *New York Times*, February 11, 2008, https://www.nytimes.com/2008/02/11/us/11salt.html.

66. Nate Schweber, "Road Crews Face Mounting Cost of Salt," *New York Times*, December 22, 2008, https://www.nytimes.com/2008/12/28/nyregion/long-island/28Rsalt.html; Corey Kilgannon and Marc Santora, "40,000 Tons of New Jersey Salt, Stuck in Maine," *New York Times*, February 18, 2014, http://nyti.ms/1eN5Ubf.

67. Anita Balakrishnan, "Road Salt: Winter's $2.3 Billion Game Changer," NBC News, http://www.nbcnews.com. In the wake of the 2008 economic recession, the State of Ohio accused Cargill and Morton of conspiracy and violating antitrust law. In 2012 the attorney general for Ohio, Mike DeWine, sued the companies claiming that they had created an agreement to divide Ohio between them with noncompete public bids. The suit was settled out of court. The companies admitted no wrongdoing but did pay the state of Ohio $11.5 million. Laura Bischoff, "Ohio Attorney General's Office Releases $11.5M to Local Governments in Settlement," *Dayton Daily News*, August 28, 2016, https://www.daytondailynews.com/news/office-releases-local-governments-settlement/MTsUVdQ9cCjG099PHfrPbP/; Katie Zezima, "Winter Storms Squeeze Supplies of Road Salt"; Nate Schweber, "Road Crews Face Mounting Cost of Salt"; Kilgannon and Santora, "40,000 Tons of New Jersey Salt, Stuck in Maine."

68. Plumer, "How America Got Addicted to Road Salt."

7. No Thruway

1. Aaron Besecker "Superintendent's Debate as County Prepares for Tuesday's Snow," *Buffalo News*, November 17, 2014, http://www.buffalonews.com/city-region/weather/superintendents-debate-as-county-prepares-for-tuesdays-snow-20141117.

2. Jeff Klein and Matt Higgins, "Heavy Snow Keeps Falling in Buffalo Area, Straining Nerves and Roofs," *New York Times*, November 20, 2014, https://www.nytimes.com/2014/11/21/nyregion/snowstorm-western-new-york.html.

3. "Across Erie County, Plows Are Challenged by Snow, Irritated by Abandoned Cars," *Buffalo News*, November 19, 2014, https://buffalonews.com/news/local/across-erie-county-plow-crews-are-challenged-by-snow-irritated-by-abandoned-cars/article_d9e92ad3-94fc-5166-b265-8a4ce77a154f.html.

4. Aaron Besecker and Robert McCarthy, "Day Two: Cuomo Says Situation 'Will Get Worse Before It Gets Better,'" November 19, 2014, https://buffalonews.com/news/local/day-two-cuomo-says-situation-will-get-worse-before-it-gets-better/article_4ef04bb0-bb4f-56ef-9194-0cc08e3d9ae5.html.

5. Jeff Z. Klein, "As Snow Subsides, Highways Reopen and Aid Crews Reach Western New York," *New York Times*, November 21, 2014, http://www.nytimes.com/2014/11/22/nyregion/buffalo-snowstorm-western-new-york.html.

6. Joseph Spector, "In Buffalo, a Snow Pile Remains from Winter," *Democrat and Chronicle*, July 28, 2015, http://www.democratandchronicle.com/story/vote-up/2015/07/28/-buffalo--snow-pile-remains--winter/30785995/.

7. Janet Ward, "Snow Problem: Buffalo Knows How to Deal with Winter," *American City and County*, April 1, 2000, https://www.americancityandcounty.com/1999/04/01/snow-problem-buffalo-knows-how-to-deal-with-winter/. In the children's book, when a blizzard threatens young Max's dream of meeting Byron Brown, a snowplow driver saves the day. Mark Goldman, *Max Meets the Mayor* (Buffalo: Criss-Cross Applesauce, 2014). Mayor Brown read the book during the COVID-19 pandemic; see post, May 5, 2020, https://www.facebook.com/ExploreAndMore/videos/2946038922145505.

8. "Michigan 'Fine Tunes' Winter Road Closures," *Rural and Urban Roads*, June 1979, 80–81, Box 720, APWA-SHSMO-KC.

9. Monmonier, *Lake Effect*, 115.

10. Stephen T. Watson and Maki Becker, "Officials Analyze Thruway Snow Woes," *Buffalo News*, December 5, 2010, 2010, http:/www.buffalonews.com/city/article274544; Maki Becker, "Closing Gates on Traffic Nightmares," *Buffalo News*, October 20, 2011, https://buffalonews.com/news/closing-gates-on-traffic-nightmares-memories-of-motorists-stranded-on-thruway-in-snowstorm-last-december/article_fdfbb604-521a-5d17-9281-07e6ab8b0d93.html.

11. Barbara O'Brien and Gene Warner, "'Massive Storm' Dumps Only a Few Inches of Snow," *Buffalo News*, February 2, 2011, https://buffalonews.com/news/storm-dumps-up-to-a-foot-of-snow-wind-a-problem-but-area-is-spared/article_f1c145e3-3d7d-5658-b317-555b5fb1d56f.html.

12. Jeff Z. Klein and Marc Santora, "Snow Piles Up in Buffalo Area, with More Expected, at Least 7 Die," *New York Times*, November 19, 2014, http://nyti.ms/1xoLrHE; Maki Becker and P. J. Pignataro, "A Wall of Snow: Monster Storm Dumps Historical Amount of Snow," *Buffalo News*, November 18. 2014, https://buffalonews.com/news/local/a-wall-of-snow-monster-storm-dumps-historic-amount-of-snow/article_29707526-b708-5203-b92d-148d1c994251.html.

13. Sara Dinatale, Laura D'Avolio, and Marc Santora, "'Extreme' Snowstorm Pummels Western New York," *New York Times*, November 19, 2014, http://nyti.ms/1xoLrHE.

14. "Man Found Dead in Snow Storm Tried to Get Help, but None Came, According to Family," WXXI News, November 21, 2014, http://wxxinews.org/post/man-found-dead-snow-storm-tried-get-help-none-came-according-family.

15. *Buffalo News Facebook*, November 24, 2014, https://www.facebook.com/TheBuffaloNews/posts/10152870987663151.

16. Klein, "Highways Reopen and More Cleanup Crews Arrive as Snow Abates in Buffalo Area."

17. Tom Precious, "Legislators Blast Thruway Authority over Refusal to Attend Meeting," *Buffalo News*, January 6, 2015, https://buffalonews.com/news/local /govt-and-politics/legislators-blast-thruway-authority-over-refusal-to-attend-meeting /article_ba517b3d-1d5d-5c54-8f8c-0d54aeb63abf.html.

18. Jimmy Vielkind, "Section of Thruway Still Closed in the Wake of Major Snowstorm," *Politico*, November 19, 2014, https://www.politico.com/states/new -york/albany/story/2014/11/section-of-thruway-still-closed-in-wake-of-major-snow storm-017585.

19. Eric Holthaus, "Politicians, Please Stop Blaming Meteorologists for Inept Storm Response," *Future Tense*, November 24, 2014, http://www.slate.com/blogs /future_tense/2014/11/24/andrew_cuomo_criticized_national_weather_service_for _buffalo_forecast_but.html.

20. Gary Holmes, "Department of Transportation Announces New Tow Plows to Keep Roads Safe This Winter," December 22, 2015, https://www.dot.ny.gov /news/press-releases/2015/2015-12-22; Nick Musgrave, "N.Y. Expands Emergency Response for Disasters," *Democrat and Chronicle*, August 17, 2015, http://www .democratandchronicle.com/story/news/local/2015/08/17/ny-expands-emergency -response-disasters/31893947/.

21. Robert J. McCarthy and T. J. Pignataro, "Snow Emergency Builds on Lessons of November," *Buffalo News*, January 10, 2015, http://www.buffalo news.com/city-region/winter/snow-emergency-builds-on-lessons-of-november -20150109; Maki Becker and T. J. Pignataro, "State Readies Help for Expected Lake Effect Storm," *Buffalo News*, January 8, 2015, http://www.buffalonews .com/city-region/winter/state-readies-help-for-expected-lake-effect-storm-2015 0108.

22. Will Cleveland, "Update: New York State Lifts Ban on Tractor-Trailers and Buses," *Democrat and Chronicle*, January 29, 2019, https://www.democratand chronicle.com/story/news/2019/01/29/rochester-weather-thruway-bans-buses -tractor-trailers-thruway-and-other-interstates/2713905002/.

23. Niraj Chokshi, "Out of the Office: More People Are Working Remotely, Survey Finds," *New York Times*, February 15, 2017, https://www.nytimes.com /2017/02/15/us/remote-workers-work-from-home.html; "The Rise of E-Commerce in the United States," *Statista*, June 21, 2019, https://www.statista.com/chart/14011 /e-commerce-share-of-total-retail-sales/. Remote work increased to two-thirds of the US workforce during the COVID-19 pandemic; see "Is the Five Day Office Week Over?" *New York Times*, July 2, 2020, https://www.nytimes.com/2020/07/02/up shot/is-the-five-day-office-week-over.html.

24. Evelyn Keene, "A Ban Proposed," *Boston Globe*, January 9, 1972, A3; A. S. Plotkin, "Road Salt Cuts Worked, Further Cuts Won't State Says," *Boston Globe*, August 12, 1976, 3.

25. Harry A. Smith, "Environmental Effects of Snow Removal and Ice Control Programs," *Highway Research News* (Winter 1971), n.p.; Roger E. Hanes, L. W. Zelazny, and R. E. Blaser, *Effects of Deicing Salts on Water Quality and Biota: Literature Review and Recommended Research* (Washington, DC: Highway Research Board, 1970); Donald M. Murray and Marie Eiermann, *A Search for New Technology for Pavement Snow and Ice Control* (Washington, DC: Environmental Protection Agency, 1972). The EPA Study is discussed in "Two New Studies Fuel Debate on Road Salt," *Boston Globe*, January 9, 1977, 47.

26. The film is described in David Bird, "Pollution Linked to Road Salting," *New York Times*, April 22, 1973, 37. The Institute for Safety Analysis conducted the study for the Salt Institute; see "Two New Studies Fuel Debate on Road Salt."

27. "Salt on Roads Use Continues Despite Alarms," *New York Times*, December 15, 1980, A18.

28. David Jay, "Minimizing the Environmental Impact of the Disposal of Snow from Urban Areas," June 11–12, 1984, Folder 12, Snow Disposal, Box 157, APWA-SHSMO-KC; Jay Lindsay, "Dump Snow in Rivers? Harborsides? There's a Downside," NBC News, February 4, 2011, http://www.nbcnews.com/id/41427190/ns/us_news-environment/t/dump-snow-rivers-harbors-theres-downside/#.V4UBZfkrK00.

29. Robert Ward, "Salt Woes Called Burlington's Own Fault," *Boston Globe*, January 11, 1972, 10; Salt Institute, *Salt Storage Handbook: Practical Recommendations for Storing and Handling Deicing Salt* (1968, 1980, 1986, 1987, 1997, 2006, 2013); Salt Institute, *Snowfighter's Handbook: Safe and Sustainable Snowfighting*, 1967, 1977, 1991, 1999, 2007, 2013.

30. Salt Institute, *Salt Storage Handbook*; Salt Institute, *Snowfighter's Handbook*; *Road Salt and the Environment*, 2014; Kristine Bradford, "The Deicing Debate: Will It Ever Be Put on Ice?" *WellSpring*, January 1994, http://cseo.mtu.edu/community/publications/wellspring/deicingdebate.html; Steve Hendrix, "Welcome to Salt City, Where Cars, Sidewalks, and Shoes Bear Winter's Briny Crust," *Washington Post*, January 31, 2014, https://www.washingtonpost.com/local/welcome-to-salt-city-where-cars-sidewalks-and-shoes-bear-winters-briny-crust/2014/01/31/7a494a72-8a9c-11e3-916e-e01534b1e132_story.html.

31. Dudley Clendinen, "Of Snows and Cars of Yesteryear," *New York Times*, January 30, 1983, 16; Paul Stirzek, "The Effect of Banning the Use of Salt for Snow and Ice, Tulsa, 1985–1986," Folder 7, Annual Snow Conference 1991, Box 295, APWA-SHSMO-KC; "Salt Use Continues Despite Alarms." The 1986 Conference is covered in Eugene Carlson, "To Salt or Not to Salt: That Is the Snow-Belt States' Question," *Wall Street Journal*, April 22, 1986, 31.

32. Cary Institute, *Report on Road Salt*, 2010; Joseph Stromberg, "What Happens to All the Salt We Dump on the Roads?" *Smithsonian*, January 6, 2014,

http://www.smithsonianmag.com/science-nature/what-happens-to-all-the-salt-we
-dump-on-the-roads-180948079; "Supply Crunch for Road Salt," *Wall Street Journal*, December 28, 2014; Ben Guarino, "Salt from Icy Roads Is Contaminating
North American Lakes," *Washington Post*, April 10, 2017, https://www.washington
post.com/news/speaking-of-science/wp/2017/04/10/salt-keeps-icy-roads-safe-its
-also-putting-north-americas-freshwater-lakes-at-risk; Sara Labashosky, "The Salty
Truth: Revealing the Need for Stricter Road Salt Application and Storage Regulations in the United States," *Villanova Environmental Law Journal* 26, no. 1
(2015), http://digitalcommons.law.villanova.edu/elj/vol26/iss1/3; Jennifer Marie
Hurley, "Can Road Salt and Other Pollutants Disrupt Our Circadian Rhythms?"
Echo Watch, https://www.ecowatch.com/road-salt-pollution-2522450009.html.

33. Robert B. Jackson and Esteban G. Jobbagy, "From Icy Roads to Salty
Streams," *Proceedings of the National Academy of Sciences* 102, no. 41 (October
2005): 14487–88; Steve Orr, "Road Salt Showing Up in Local Bays and Creeks,"
Democrat and Chronicle, March 19, 2016, https://www.democratandchronicle
.com/story/news/2016/03/19/road-salt-and-environment/81809308/.

34. New York State uses 189,000 tons of road salt to keep roads open. Over
11,000 tons were used in Ontario County where the case was brought; see Steve Orr,
"Did Road Salt Used on Thruway Kill an Ontario County Dairy Herd," *Democrat
and Chronicle*, January 9, 2020, https://www.democratandchronicle.com/story
/news/2020/01/09/ny-dairy-farmers-argue-road-salt-used-thruway-killed-their-herd
/2835676001/.

35. Nell Greenfieldboyce, "After a Century, a Voice for the US Salt Industry
Goes Quiet," *NPR*, March 30, 2019, https://www.npr.org/transcripts/707747077.

36. Dennis and Urry, *After the Car*; Seiler, "The End of Automobility," 389–91;
Manderscheid, "The Movement Problem, the Car and Future Mobility Regimes,"
604–26; Norton, *Fighting Traffic*; Emily Badger, "The Myth of the American Love
Affair with Cars," *Washington Post*, January 27, 2015, https://www.washington
post.com/news/wonk/wp/2015/01/27/debunking-the-myth-of-the-american-love
-affair-with-cars/.

37. Garceau, Atkinson-Palumbo, and Garrick, "Peak Travel in the United
States"; Emily Badger, "The American Decline in Driving Actually Began Way Earlier Than You Think," *Washington Post*, January 16, 2015, https://www.washington
post.com/news/wonk/wp/2015/01/16/the-american-decline-in-driving-actually
-began-way-earlier-than-you-think.

38. Marc Fisher, "America's Once Magical Now Mundane Love Affair with
Cars," *Washington Post*, September 2, 2015, https://www.washingtonpost.com/sf
/style/2015/09/02/americas-fading-car-culture/.

39. David Schaper, "Like Millennials, Elder Americans Steering Away from
Driving," *NPR*, February 11, 2016, http://www.npr.org/2016/02/11/466178523

/likemillennialsmoreolderamericanssteeringawayfromdriving; Avery Hartmans and Nathan McAlone, "The Story of How Travis Kalanick Built Uber into the Most Feared and Valuable Startup in the World," *Business Insider*, August 1, 2016, http://www.businessinsider.com/ubers-history/; Dan Neil, "Could Self Driving Cars Spell the End of Ownership," *Wall Street Journal*, December 1, 2015, https://www.wsj.com/articles/could-self-driving-cars-spell-the-end-of-ownership-1448986572.

40. Rossant and Baker, *Hop, Skip, Go*, xi–xii; Emily Badger, "The Streets Were Never Free: Congestion Pricing Makes That Plain," *New York Times*, April 4, 2019, https://www.nytimes.com/2019/04/04/upshot/the-streets-were-never-free-congestion-pricing-finally-makes-that-plain.html; Andrew Tangel, "Cities Target Elevated Level of Pedestrian Deaths," *Wall Street Journal*, December 19, 2014, https://www.wsj.com/articles/cities-target-elevated-levels-of-pedestrian-deaths-14 19027750; Norton, "Four Paradigms: Traffic Safety in the Twentieth-Century United States," 319–34. The ultimate move may be to ban cars entirely from city centers, an idea that is developing in Europe; see Graeme Paton, "York to Ban Cars from City Centre within Three Years," *London Times*, December 31, 2019, https://www.thetimes.co.uk/article/york-wants-private-cars-banned-from-city-centre-within-three-years-8ktmrb6kp.

41. Conley and Jensen, "Parks Not Parkways," 399–423.

42. David Harrison, "Highways Give Way to Homes as Cities Rebuild," *Wall Street Journal*, December 1, 2019, https://www.wsj.com/articles/highways-give-way-to-homes-as-cities-rebuild-11575208801; Keith Schneider, "Taking Out a Highway That Hemmed Rochester In," *New York Times*, November 1, 2016, https://www.nytimes.com/2016/11/02/business/old-highway-paves-road-for-recovery-in-rochester.html; City of Rochester, "Inner Loop East Project," http://www.cityofrochester.gov/InnerLoopEast/.

43. The silence of the Automobile Club of Western New York is worth noting. See Mark Sommer, "Winning Skyway Redesign Calls for Tearing Down Part of the Bridge," *Buffalo News*, September 17, 2019, https://buffalonews.com/2019/09/17/skyway-contest-winner-calls-for-tearing-down-part-of-the-bridge/; Mark Sommer, "Skyway Plan's Impact on Drive Time? 'About 5 Minutes,'" *Buffalo News*, September 19, 2019, https://buffalonews.com/2019/09/19/longer-southtowns-commute-without-skyway-how-about-5-minutes/; Mark Sommer, "'The Skyway Is Coming Down': Higgins Touts Plan That Costs Less, Boosts East Side," *Buffalo News*, October 8, 2019, https://buffalonews.com/2019/10/08/higgins-suggests-plan-to-relieve-skyway-traffic-boost-east-side/; Mark Sommer, "Cuomo Hits Reset on 198, Pushing Plan in New Direction," *Buffalo News*, September 11, 2019, https://buffalonews.com/2019/09/11/planning-for-scajaquada-corridor-takes-new-direction/.

44. Jonathan D. Epstein, "Parking Spaces Become More Elusive as Downtown Booms," *Buffalo News*, November 23, 2018, https://buffalonews.com/2018/11/23/brother-can-you-spare-a-parking-space/.

45. Ian Austen, "City of the Future? Humans, Not Technology, Are the Challenge in Toronto," *New York Times*, December 29, 2017, https://nyti.ms/2pYYWCV.

46. New York, Chicago, Boston, and Washington have all relied heavily on subways to move large numbers of people around. Still, until recently, these systems were often neglected, but this has changed. Even Los Angeles, infamous for its automotive culture, has announced plans to invest $120 billion to recreate its mass transit system. David Hosansky, "Traffic Congestion," *C.Q. Researcher* 28, no. 4 (January 26, 2018): 73–96, http://library.cqpress.com/cqresearcher/cqresrre2018012600; Jonathan Nahler, "The Case for the Subway," *New York Times*, January 3, 2018, https://www.nytimes.com/2018/01/03/magazine/subway-new-york-city-public-transportation-wealth-inequality.html.

47. "'Bomb Cyclone': Rare Snow in South as North Braces for Bitter Cold," *New York Times*, January 3, 2018, https://www.nytimes.com/2018/01/03/us/cold-weather-winter-storm.html. Stanley Changnon's research on this has indicated climate change is expanding the zone of winter; see Changnon, "Catastrophic Winter Storms." Holly Moeller responds to climate skeptics like Senator James Inhofe of Oklahoma; see Holly Moeller, "Winter in the Anthropocene: Why Snowstorms Don't Disprove Climate Change," *Millennium Alliance for Humanity and the Biosphere*, March 17, 2015, https://mahb.stanford.edu/blog/winter-in-the-anthropocene/.

Epilogue

1. Dennis and Urry, *After the Car*; Seiler, "End of Automobility"; Manderscheid, "Movement Problem."

2. Richard Usiak, "Buffalo, N.Y.: Miami of the North," UPI Archives, https://www.upi.com/Archives/1983/02/16/Buffalo-NY-Miami-of-the-North/5902603410441/; Ward, "Snow Problem."

3. *Niagara Gazette*, January 28, 2017, A1.

4. Bodnar, "Public Memory in an American City"; Gray and Oliver, "Memory of Catastrophe," 10; Nora, "Between Memory and History," 7–24. An excellent introduction to collective memory is Olick, Vinitzky-Serous, and Levy, *Collective Memory Reader*, 3–11. Some scholars have rejected the phrase "collective memory" because it suggests that public recollection is analogous to individual memory. Instead, they prefer the term "collective remembrance" to focus on the public display

of mind. See Winter and Sivan, *War and Remembrance in the Twentieth Century*, 1–7; Gray and Oliver, *Memory of Catastrophe*, 2–7; Lipsitz, *Time Passages*.

5. The classic study of deindustrialization is Bluestone and Harrison, *Deindustrialization of America*.

6. Howard Kurtz, "Buffalo: Great Dreams, but Bigger Needs," *Washington Post*, April 18, 1983, A4; Kraus, *Race Neighborhoods and Community*.

7. Kevin Sack, "From Rust Belt to Money Belt in Buffalo," *New York Times*, July 20, 1990, B1.

8. "They're 'Talking Proud' in Buffalo: A City Tries to Shuffle Off That Old Put Down Feeling," *Washington Post*, December 26, 1980, A2; Leslie Eaton, "A Fine Place to Live, and Leave; A Shrinking Population Shapes Buffalo's Psyche," *New York Times*, April 9, 2000, 1 and 32; *Turner Classic Movies*, "Shuffle Off to Buffalo," *42nd Street* (1933), http://www.tcm.com/mediaroom/video/770635/42nd -Street-Movie-Ciip-Shuffle-Off-To-Buffalo.html.

9. Kevin Sack, "From the Rust Belt to the Money Belt in Buffalo," *New York Times*, July 20, 1990, B1.

10. Steven Springer, "Bragging in Buffalo," *Los Angeles Times*, January 23, 1993, 1.

11. Sara Sdovich, "Hail to Thee, Oh Buffalo," *Washington Post*, February 13, 1983, C1.

12. Jeff Simon, Give Buffalo a Sitcom That Reflects Our City," *Buffalo News*, March 21, 2007, 1; *Best Friends* Plot Summary, Internet Movie Data Base, https://www.imdb.com/title/tt0083641/plotsummary.

13. After the 1990s jokes about the Buffalo Bills, who lost four Super Bowls in a row, became nearly as ubiquitous. See Chris Sinacola, "The World Is Wise in Buffalo; Dante Would Admire Politics and Football," *Worcester Telegram and Gazette*, November 6, 2002, B1.

14. "Buffalo Talking Proud," https://www.youtube.com/watch?v=46Ive-dR XVo.

15. Denise Jewell Gee, "Hey World, We're More Than Weather," *Buffalo News*, November 23, 2014.

16. Sharon Linstdet "The Perfect Snowstorm Recalled: Survivors Relive the Blizzard of '77," *Buffalo News*, January 29, 1977, A1; John Affleck, "Buffalo Parties 20 Years after Blizzard," *Albany Times Union*, January 26, 1997, A1; John Sillick, "Blizzard of '77 Evokes Memories of Survival," *Buffalo News*, January 26, 1997, B2; John F. Bonfatti, "King of the Storms: A Quarter-Century Ago, A Blizzard Yet Unequaled," *Buffalo News*, January 19, 2002, A1; Brandon Stickney, "Blizzard of '77 Brought Out the Best in Us," *Lockport Union-Sun Journal*, January 29, 2012, A1.

17. Bodnar, "Public Memory in an American City."

18. Gray and Oliver, "The Memory of Catastrophe," 10.

19. Healy and Malhotra, "Myopic Voters and Natural Disaster Policy," 387–406. Glen Kuecker found that after a disaster beset a small Mexican town locals preferred a narrative that celebrated an oil well fire as their part in the broader modernization process of Mexico rather than remember it as the result of elites who cared less about safety and more about profit. See Kuecker, "'The Greatest and the Worst': Dominant and Subaltern Memories of the Dos Bocas Well Fire of 1908," in Gray and Oliver, *The Memory of Catastrophe*, 65–78.

20. Wolfgang quoted in Jeffrey Schmalz, "In Buffalo, A Gala Ball Recalls Blizzard of '77," *New York Times*, February 27, 1984, B1; Affleck, "Buffalo Parties 20 Years after Blizzard"; Steve Cichon, "The Blizzard of '77 Brought out Fellowship in People of Buffalo," BuffaloStories.Com, February 1, 2017, http://blog.buffalo stories.com/the-blizzard-of-77-brought-out-fellowship-in-people-of-buffalo/.

21. Jimmy Carter, "Message from the President to the People of Buffalo," February 9, 1977. The idea of communities coming together is critical to the creation of public memory or a quasi-official history of disaster events, which is developed by elites to deflect criticism or calls for policy change. Some sociologists have seen a community come together after disaster; see, for example, Solnit, *Paradise Built in Hell*. Timothy Kneeland's *Buffalo Blizzard of 1977*, written for the nostalgia-driven Arcadia Publishing, devoted an entire section of the book to how the community came together to assist one another during the blizzard.

22. WGRZ Staff, " Remembering the Blizzard of '77," http://www.wgrz.com /article/news/local/remembering-the-blizzard-of-77/71-393850323.

23. Rossi, *White Death*. On his website, the author calls his book "A Canadian American survival classic"; http://www.whitedeath.com/whitedeath/index.html.

24. Erno Rossi, BuffaloBooks.com, http://www.wnybooks.com/rossi.html.

25. Rossi's website, *White Death*, devoted to the storm, is where he sells his book and a DVD of images of the event: http://www.whitedeath.com/white death/index.html. A typical news story calls Rossi the "blizzard expert"; see Mike Randall, "He Wrote the Book on the Blizzard," WKBK, broadcast January 28, 2017, available on YouTube, https://www.wkbw.com/news/he-wrote-the-book-about -the-blizzard-of-77.

26. Erno's fans are fiercely loyal; see https://www.facebook.com/groups/407 60468369/.

27. Bahr, *The Blizzard*; Bahr, *Blizzard at the Zoo*. For Bahr's background, see *The Writer's Directory*, edited by Katherine H. Nemeh, vol. 1, 32nd ed. (Detroit: St. James Press, 2013), 133; "Robert Bahr Obituary," http://obits.al.com/obituaries /mobile/obituary.aspx?page=lifestory&pid=188201474.

28. Stratton, *Disaster Relief.* Stratton was a political science professor at Daemen College in Buffalo who died early in her career.

29. Nora, "Between Memory and History: *Les Lieux de Memoire*," 7–24.

30. An unconscious reflection of this may be the title of Don Glynn's story on the fortieth anniversary of the Blizzard: "Blizzard of '77: Frozen in Memory."

Bibliography

Abney, Glenn F., and Larry B. Hill. "Natural Disasters as a Political Variable: The Effect of a Hurricane on an Urban Election." *American Political Science Review* 60, no. 4 (December 1966): 974–81.

Ahlstrom, Harold J. *The Last Decade of Buffalo Trolleys*. Williamsville, NY: Bee Publications, 1973.

American Public Works Association, Morris M. Cohn, Rodney R. Fleming, and North American Snow Conference. *Managing Snow Removal and Ice Control Programs: A Practical Guide to the How, When, Where and Why of Effective Public Work Practices; A Collation of Papers Presented at the Annual North American Snow Conferences 1969–1973*. American Public Works Association Special Report, No. 42. Chicago: n.p., 1974.

Arceneux, Kevin, and Robert M. Stein. "Who Is Held Responsible When Disaster Strikes? The Attribution for Responsibility for a Natural Disaster in an Urban Election." *Journal of Urban Affairs* 28, no. 1 (2006): 43–53.

Bahr, Robert. *The Blizzard*. Englewood Cliffs, NJ: Prentice Hall, 1980.

———. *Blizzard at the Zoo*. New York: Lothrop, Lee and Shepard Books, 1982.

Barthes, Roland. "The New Citroen." In *Mythologies*. Trans. Annette Lavers. New York: Hill & Wang, 1972.

Beekman, Scott. *NASCAR Nation: A History of Stock Car Racing in the United States*. Santa Barbara: Praeger, 2010.

Bentham, Garrett C. *The International Railway Company Strike of 1922 in Buffalo New York: A Thesis in History*. PhD diss., State Univ. College at Buffalo, 2008.

Bodnar, John. "Public Memory in an American City: Commemoration in Cleveland." In John R. Gillis, *Commemorations: The Politics of National Identity*. Princeton: Princeton Univ. Press, 1994.

Bohm, Steffen, Campbell Jones, Chris Land, and Matthew Paterson, eds. *Against Automobility*. Malden, MA: Blackwell, 2006.

Born, Richard. "Reassessing the Decline of Presidential Coattails: U.S. House Elections from 1952–80." *Journal of Politics* 46, no. 1 (February 1984): 60–79.

Boustan, Leah Platt. "Was Postwar Suburbanization 'White Flight'? Evidence from the Black Migration." *Quarterly Journal of Economics* 125, no. 1 (February 2010): 417–43.

Bovard, James. "FEMA Money, Come and Get It!" *American Spectator* 9, no. 9 (September 1996): 25–31.

Brouillette, John R., and James L. Ross. *Organizational Response to the Great Chicago Snowstorm of 1967*, Research Note #14. Columbus, Ohio: Disaster Research Center, 1967.

Buffalo and Erie County Historical Society. "The Pierce-Arrow Motor Company." *Niagara Frontier* 25, no. 3 (1978): 57–84.

Burnham, John C. "The Gasoline Tax and the Automobile Revolution." *Mississippi Valley Historical Review* 48, no. 3 (December 1961): 435–59.

Call, David A. "Rethinking Snowstorms as Snow Events: A Regional Case Study from Upstate New York." *Bulletin of the American Meteorological Society* 86, no. 12 (December 2005): 1783–94.

Call, David A., Katelyn E. Grove, and Paul J. Kocin. "A Meteorological and Social Comparison of the New England Blizzards of 1978 and 2013." *Journal of Operational Meteorology* 3, no. 1 (2015): 1–10.

Cannato, Vincent. *Ungovernable City: John Lindsay and His Struggle to Save New York*. New York: Basic Books, 2002.

Caro, Robert A. *The Power Broker: Robert Moses and the Fall of New York*. 1974; reprint ed., New York: History Book Club, 2006.

Carpenter, Daniel P. *The Forging of Bureaucratic Autonomy: Reputations, Networks, and Policy Innovations in Executive Agencies, 1862–1928*. Princeton: Princeton Univ. Press, 2001.

Changnon, Stanley A. "Catastrophic Winter Storms: An Escalating Problem." *Climatic Change* 84, (2007): 131–39.

———. "The Paradox of Planned Weather Modification." *Bulletin of the American Meteorology Association* 56, no. 1 (January 1975): 27–37.

Changnon, Stanley A., Jr., and David Changnon. "Record Winter Storms in Illinois, 1977–1978." *Illinois State Water Survey*. Urbana, IL: n.p., 1978.

Changnon, Stanley, and David Changnon. "Lessons from the Unusual Impacts of an Abnormal Winter in the USA." *Meteorological Applications* 12, no. 3 (2005): 187–91.

Cichon, Steve. *Gimme Jimmy! Mayor James D. Griffin in His Own Words and Pictures.* Buffalo, NY: Buffalo Stories, 2013.

Cochran, Thomas C. *The American Business System: A Historical Perspective, 1900–1955.* Cambridge, MA: Harvard Univ. Press, 1957.

Cochrane, Harold C. *Urban Snow Hazard in the United States: A Research Assessment.* Boulder: Institute of Behavioral Science, Univ. of Colorado, 1975.

Committee on Transportation and Infrastructure. *Hearings Snow Disasters for Local State and Federal Governments in the National Capital Region.* Washington, DC: US Government Printing Office, 2010.

Common Council. *Manual of the Common Council City of Buffalo for 1896.* Buffalo, NY: Wenborne-Sumner Co., 1897.

Comptroller General. *Federal Snow Removal Reimbursement Policy: Improvements Needed.* Washington, DC: General Accounting Office, 1979.

Conley, Jim, and Ole B. Jensen. "'Parks Not Parkways': Contesting Automobility in a Small Canadian City." *Canadian Journal of Sociology* 41, no. 3 (2016): 399–423.

Conley, Jim, and Arlene Tigar McLaren. *Car Troubles: Critical Studies of Automobility and Auto-Mobility.* London: Ashgate, 2009.

Copeland, Ronald. "The Cuban Boatlift of 1980: Strategies in Federal Crisis Management." *Annals of the American Academy of Political & Social Science* 467, no. 1 (May 1983): 138–53.

Cowie, Jefferson R. *Stayin' Alive: The 1970s and the Last Days of the Working Class.* New York: New Press, 2010.

Crouse, Timothy. "Daniel Patrick Moynihan: Working Class Hero." *Rolling Stone,* August 12, 1976. https://www.rollingstone.com/politics/politics-news/daniel-patrick-moynihan-ruling-class-hero-228185/.

Daniels, R. Steven, and Carolyn L. Clark-Daniels. "Vulnerability Reduction and Political Responsiveness: Explaining Executive Decisions in U.S. Disaster Policy during the Ford and Carter Administrations." *International Journal of Mass Emergencies and Disasters* 20, no. 2 (August 2002): 225–53.

Dennis, K., and John Urry. *After the Car.* Cambridge, MA: Polity Press, 2009.

Dillaway, Diana. *Power Failure: Politics, Patronage, and the Economic Future of Buffalo, New York.* Amherst, NY: Prometheus Books, 2006.

Dispenza, Marguerite. *From Elite Social Club to Motoring Service Organization: The Automobile Club of Buffalo, 1900–1920.* PhD diss., State Univ. of New York at Buffalo, 1994.

Dovers, Stephen, and Karen Hussey. *Environment and Sustainability: A Policy Handbook.* Alexandria, Australia: Federation Press, 2013.

Drew, Elizabeth. *Portrait of an Election: The 1980 Presidential Campaign.* New York: Simon & Schuster, 1981.

Dumbrell, John. *The Carter Presidency: A Re-Evaluation.* Manchester, UK: Manchester Univ. Press, 1995.

Dymon, Ute J., and Rutherford H. Platt. "U.S. Federal Disaster Declarations: A Geographical Analysis." In Rutherford H. Platt, ed., *Disasters and Democracy: The Politics of Extreme Natural Events.* Washington, DC: Island Press, 1999.

Earls, Alan R. *Greater Boston's Blizzard of 1978.* Charleston, SC: Arcadia Publishing, 2008.

Edholm, C. L. "New York's Army of Snow Fighters." *Scientific American* 115, no. 25 (December 1916): 547.

Eichenlaub, Val. *Weather and Climate of the Great Lakes.* South Bend, IN: Univ. of Notre Dame, 1991.

Eizenstat, Stuart E. *President Carter: The White House Years.* New York: Thomas Dunne Books, 2018.

Eyerman, R., and R. Löfgren. "Romancing the Road: Road Movies and Images of Mobility." *Theory, Culture and Society* 12 (1995): 53–79.

Fay, Laura, Kevin Volkening, Chase Gallaway, and Xianming Shi. "Performance and Impacts of Current Deicing and Anti-icing Products: User Perspective versus Experimental Data." 2007. https://www.academia.edu/26640441/Performance_and_Impacts_of_Current_Deicing_and_Anti-Icing_Products_User_Perspective_versus_Experimental_Data.

Feldman, James, and Lynne Heasley. "Recentering North American Environmental History: Pedagogy and Scholarship in the Great Lakes Region." *Environmental History* 12, no. 4 (October 2007): 951–58.

Fetherston, John T. "Discussion of Street Cleaning." *Proceedings of the Academy of Political Science in New York* 5, no. 3 (1915): 187–91.

Fleming, James Rodger. "Fixing the Weather and Climate: Military and Civilian Schemes for Cloud Seeding and Climate Engineering." In Lisa Rosner, ed., *The Technological Fix: How People Use Technology to Create and Solve Problems*. New York: Routledge, 2004, 175–200.

———. "The Pathological History of Weather and Climate Modification: Three Cycles of Promise and Hype." *Historical Studies in the Physical and Biological Sciences* 37, no. 1 (2006): 3–25.

Fleming, Rodney. "Snow-Fighting's New Techniques." *The American City* (November 1965): 83–85, 110, 112.

Flink, James J. "Three Stages of Automobile Consciousness." *American Quarterly* 24, no. 4 (October 1972): 451–73.

Frederickson, George H. "Elmer B. Staats: Government Ethics in Practice." In Terry L. Cooper and N. Dale Wright, eds., *Exemplary Public Administrators: Character and Leadership in Government*. San Francisco: Jossey Bass, 1992.

Freedman, Andrew. "Anatomy of a Forecast: 'Arborgeddon' Takes Buffalo by Surprise." *Weatherwise* 60, no. 4 (January 2007): 16–21.

Fry, Katherine. *Constructing the Heartland: Television News and Natural Disaster*. Cresskill, NJ: Hampton Press, 2003.

Garceau, Timothy J., Carol Atkinson-Palumbo, and Norman Garrick. "Peak Travel in the United States: Two-Decade Long Phenomenon at the State Level." *Transportation Research Record: Journal of the Transportation Research Board* 2531 (2019): 36–44.

Garrett, T. A., and R. S. Sobel. "The Political Economy of FEMA Disaster Payments." In C. K. Rowley and F. Schneider, eds., *The Encyclopedia of Public Choice*. Boston: Springer, 2004.

Geels, Frank W., Rene Kemp, Geoff Dudley, and Glenn Lyons, eds. *Automobility in Transition: A Socio-Technical Study of Sustainability in Transport*. New York: Routledge, 2012.

Gerber, David. *The Making of American Pluralism: Buffalo, New York, 1825–1860*. Springfield: Univ. of Illinois Press, 1989.

Goldman, Mark. *City on the Edge: Buffalo NY 1900 to Present*. Buffalo: Prometheus Books, 2007.

———. *City on the Lake: The Challenge of Change in Buffalo, New York*. Amherst, NY: Prometheus Books, 1990.

Graebner, William. *Coming of Age in Buffalo: Youth, and Authority in the Postwar Era*. Philadelphia: Temple Univ. Press, 1990.

Gray, Peter, and Kendrick Oliver. *The Memory of Catastrophe*. Manchester, UK: Manchester Univ. Press, 2004.

Guterbock, Thomas M. "The Effect of Snow on Urban Density Patterns in the United States." *Environment and Behavior* 22, no. 3 (1990): 358–86.

Haas, J. Eugene. "Social Aspects of Weather Modification." *Bulletin of the American Meteorological Society* 54, no. 7 (July 1973): 647–57.

Hanes, Roger E., L. W. Zelazny, and R. E. Blaser. *Effects of Deicing Salts on Water Quality and Biota: Literature Review and Recommended Research*. Washington, DC: Highway Research Board, 1970.

Healy, Andrew, and Neil Malhotra. "Myopic Voters and Natural Disaster Policy." *American Political Science Review* 103, no. 3 (2009): 387–406.

Heaton, Brian. "Internet of Things Helps Buffalo, Other Cities with Snow Removal." *Government Technology*, November 19, 2014. https://www.govtech.com/data/Internet-of-Things-Helps-Buffalo-Other-Cities-with-Snow-Removal.html.

Heclo, Hugh. "Political Executives and the Washington Bureaucracy." *Political Science Quarterly* 92, no. 3 (Autumn 1977): 395–424.

Henderson, Jason. "Secessionist Automobility: Racism, Anti-Urbanism, and the Politics of Automobility in Atlanta, Georgia." *International Journal of Urban and Regional Research* 30, no. 2 (June 2006): 293–307.

Henson, Robert. *Weather on the Air: A History of Broadcast Meteorology*. Boston: American Meteorological Association, 2010.

Hollis, Amanda Lee. "A Tale of Two Federal Emergency Management Agencies." *Forum* 3, no. 3 (2005): 1–14.

Horowitz, Daniel J. *Jimmy Carter and the Energy Crisis of the 1970s: The Crisis of Confidence Speech of July 15, 1979*. New York: Bedford St. Martin's Press, 2004.

Hosansky, David. "Traffic Congestion." *CQ Researcher* 28, no. 4 (January 26, 2018): 73–96.

Hosler, C. L. "Overt Weather Modification." *Review of Geophysics* 12, no. 3 (1974): 523–27.

Howe, J. D. "Legal Moguls, Ski Areas, Weather Modification and the Law." *University of Pittsburgh Law Review* 33 (1971–72): 59–77.

Hughes, Patrick. *A Century of Weather Service: A History of the Birth and Growth of the National Weather Service, 1870–1970*. New York: Gordon and Breach Science Publishing, 1970.

Hunt, Hal W. "Winning the Battle with Snow." *Scientific American* 170, no. 1 (January 1944): 19–21.

International Railway Company. *Comprehensive Transit Plan for Buffalo.* Buffalo, NY: International Railway Company, 1932.

Jackson, Robert B., and Esteban G. Jobbagy. "From Icy Roads to Salty Streams." *Proceedings of the National Academy of Sciences* 102, no. 41 (October 2005): 14487–88.

Jain, Sarah S. Lochlann. "Violent Submission: Gendered Automobility." *Cultural Critique* 61 (Fall 2005): 186–214.

Jenks, J. W. "The Michigan Salt Association." *Political Science Quarterly* 3, no. 1 (March 1888): 78–98.

Jolls, Tom, Brian Meyer, and Joseph Van Meer. *Western New York Weather Guide: A Century of Sun, Snow, and Rain.* Buffalo, NY: Western New York Wares, 1996.

Jones, Charles O. *The Trustee Presidency: Jimmy Carter and the United States Congress.* Baton Rouge: Louisiana State Univ. Press, 1988.

Katz, Alyssa. *The Influence Machine: The US Chamber of Commerce and the Corporate Capture of American Life.* New York: Spiegel & Grau, 2015.

Kaufman Burton I., and Scott Kaufman. *The Presidency of James Earl Carter, Jr.* 2nd rev. ed. Lawrence: Univ. Press of Kansas, 2006.

Kerr, Richard A. "Who Can Forecast the Worst Weather." *Science* 250, no. 4977 (October 5, 1990): 29–31.

Kneeland, Timothy W. *Buffalo Blizzard of 1977.* Charleston, SC: Arcadia Publishing, 2017.

———. *Playing Politics with Natural Disaster: Hurricane Agnes, the 1972 Election, and the Origins of FEMA.* Ithaca, NY: Cornell Univ. Press, 2019.

Kostof, Spiro. *America by Design.* New York: Oxford Univ. Press, 1987.

Kowsky, Francis R. "Municipal Parks and City Planning: Frederick Law Olmsted's Buffalo Park and Parkway System." *Journal of the Society of Architectural Historians* 46, no. 1 (March 1987): 49–64.

Kraus, Neil. *Race Neighborhood and Community Power: Buffalo Politics, 1934–1997.* Albany: SUNY Press, 2000.

Kurlansky, Mark. *Salt: A World History.* New York: Walker Books, 2002.

Labashosky, Sara. "The Salty Truth: Revealing the Need for Stricter Road Salt Application and Storage Regulations in the United States."

Villanova Environmental Law Journal 26, no. 1 (2015). http://digital commons.law.villanova.edu/elj/vol26/iss1/3.

Lachman, Seymour, and Robert Polner. *The Man Who Saved New York: Hugh Carey and the Great Fiscal Crisis of 1975.* Albany: SUNY Press, 2010.

LaClair, Richard. "Snow Job in Buffalo: Weather as News." *Community College Journal* 5, no. 3 (1977): 13–15.

Leary, Thomas, and Elizabeth Sholes. *Buffalo's Waterfront.* Charleston, SC: Arcadia Publishing, 1997.

Lewis, David E. *The Politics of Presidential Appointment: Political Control and Bureaucratic Performance.* Princeton: Princeton Univ. Press, 2008.

Lipsitz, George. *Time Passages: Collective Memory and American Popular Culture.* 1990; reprint ed., Minneapolis: Univ. of Minnesota Press, 2001.

Lloyd, William H. "The Parking of Automobiles." *University of Pennsylvania Law Review* 77, no. 3 (January 1929): 336–56.

Longville, Alfred. "New York's Snow-Fighting Tractor Plows." *Scientific American* 124, no. 5 (January 1921): 85.

Lorditch, Emilie. "Advances in Weather Analysis and Forecasting." *Weatherwise* 69, no. 1 (January/February 2009): 22–27.

Manderscheid, Katharina. "The Movement Problem, the Car and Future Mobility Regimes: Automobility as Dispositif and Mode of Regulation." *Mobilities* 9, no. 4 (2014): 604–26.

Mattingly, Doreen. *A Feminist in the White House: Midge Costanza, the Carter Years, and America's Culture Wars.* New York: Oxford Univ. Press, 2016.

May, Peter. *Recovering from Catastrophes: Federal Disaster Relief Policy and Politics.* Westport, CT: Prager, 1985.

Mayer, Matt. "States: Stop Subsidizing FEMA Waste and Manage Your Own Disasters." *Backgrounder*, no. 2323 (September 29, 2009): 1–9.

McDonogh, Gary. "Coming of Age." In Robert Gregg, Gary W. McDonogh, and Cindy H. Wong, eds., *Encyclopedia of Contemporary American Culture.* New York: Routledge, 2001.

McKelvey, Blake. *Snow in the Cities: A History of America's Urban Response to Snow.* Rochester, NY: Univ. of Rochester, 1995.

———. "Snowstorms and Snow Fighting: The Rochester Experience." *Rochester History* 27, no. 1 (1965): 1–24.

McShane, Clay. *Down the Asphalt Path: The Automobile and the American City*. Columbia History of Urban Life. New York: Columbia Univ. Press, 1994.

———. "Transforming the Use of Urban Space: A Look at the Revolution in Street Pavements, 1880–1924." *Journal of Urban History* 5, no. 3 (May 1979): 279–307.

Melosi, Martin. "The Automobile Shapes the City: With Some Examples from Boston." *Public Works History* 97 (Summer 2010): 5–9.

Merchant, Carolyn. *The Death of Nature: Women, Ecology, and the Scientific Revolution*. Reprint ed. San Francisco: HarperCollins, 1990.

Mergen, Bernard. *Snow in America*. Washington, DC: Smithsonian Institute Press, 1997.

"The Meteorologist in Your Life." *Weatherwise* 48, no. 3: 68–70.

Monmonier, Mark. *Lake Effect: Tales of Large Lakes, Arctic Winds, and Recurrent Snows*. Syracuse: Syracuse Univ. Press, 2012.

Moore, Paul K. *The Buffalo Blizzard Book: The Snowy Saga of the City of "Good Neighbors" as Reported in Its Newspapers, 1811–2011*. Auburn Hills, MI: Data Reproduction, 2011.

Morris, Andrew. "Hurricane Camille and the New Politics of Federal Disaster Relief, 1965–1970." *Journal of Policy History* 26, no. 3 (Summer 2014): 406–26.

Morrison, Sara. "Conquering Winter: Snow Removal from Boston's Streets from the Colonial Period to the Present." *Historical Journal of Massachusetts* 45, no. 1 (Winter 2007): 2–19.

Mosher, Frederick C. *A Tale of Two Agencies: A Comparative Analysis of the General Accounting Office and the Office of Management and Budget*. Baton Rouge: Louisiana State Univ. Press, 1984.

Moss, Mitchell, Charles Schellhammer, and David A. Berman. "The Stafford Act and Priorities for Reform." *Journal of Homeland Security and Emergency Management* 6, no. 1 (2009): 1–21.

Murray, Donald M., and Marie Eiermann. *A Search for New Technology for Pavement Snow and Ice Control*. Washington, DC: Environmental Protection Agency, 1972.

National Academy of Public Administration. *Coping with Catastrophes. Building an Emergency Management System to Meet People's Needs in Natural and Manmade Disasters.* Washington, DC: National Academy of Public Administration, 1993.

National Governors Association Center for Policy Research. *State Comprehensive Emergency Management: Final Report of the Emergency Preparedness Project.* Washington, DC: Defense Civil Preparedness Agency, 1979.

Natural Disasters: The Oft-Repeated Failures a Report of the New York State Senate Ad Hoc Committee on Natural Disasters. Albany: New York State Senate, 1979.

Newman, Richard S. *Love Canal: A Toxic History from Colonial Times to the Present.* New York: Oxford Univ. Press, 2016.

New York Assembly Ways and Means Committee. *Disaster and Recovery: Toward a New State System.* Albany, NY: State Legislature, 1975.

New York Division of Military and Naval Affairs. *Annual Report 1977.* Albany, NY: n.p., 1977.

———. *Annual Report 1983.* Albany, NY: n.p., 1984.

New York State Office of Public Health. *Love Canal: Public Health Time Bomb.* Albany, NY: New York State Department of Health, 1978.

New York State Senate. *Natural Disasters: The Oft-Repeated Failures a Report of the New York State Senate Ad Hoc Committee on Natural Disasters.* Albany: New York State Senate, 1979.

Nora, Pierre. "Between Memory and History: *Les Lieux de Memoire.*" *Representations* 26 (Spring 1989): 7–24.

Norton, Peter D. *Fighting Traffic: The Dawn of the Motor Age in the American City.* Cambridge, MA: MIT Press, 2008.

———. "Four Paradigms: Traffic Safety in the Twentieth-Century United States." *Technology and Culture* 56, no. 2 (2015): 319–34.

———. "Street Rivals: Jaywalking and the Invention of the Motor Age Street." *Technology and Culture* 48, no. 2 (April 2007): 331–59.

O'Rourke, Morgan. "It Snows in Winter?" *Risk Management* 58, no. 1 (January/February 2011): 48.

Passwell, Robert E., and Wilfred W. Recker. *Problems of the Carless.* Washington, DC: Department of Transportation, 1976, 1.

Patterson, James T. *Restless Giant: The United States from Watergate to Bush v Gore.* New York: Oxford Univ. Press, 2005.

Platt, Rutherford H. *Disasters and Democracy: The Politics of Extreme Natural Events*. 2nd ed. Washington, DC: Island Press, 1999.

Potter, Deborah. "Let It Snow: Just Lay Off the Incredibly Hyped 'Storm Trackers' Coverage and Give It to Us Straight." *American Journalism Review* 24, no. 9 (2002): 68.

Price, Alfred D. "Urban Renewal: The Case of Buffalo, NY." *Review of Black Political Economy* 19, no. 3 (Winter/Spring 1991): 125–59.

Ralston, Marc. *Pierce-Arrow*. San Diego: A. S. Barnes Co., 1980.

Reeves, Andrew. "Political Disaster: Unilateral Powers, Electoral Incentives, and Presidential Disaster Declarations." *Journal of Politics* 73, no. 4 (2011): 1142–51.

Reid, T. R. *Congressional Odyssey: The Saga of a Senate Bill*. New York: Henry Holt, 1980.

Report on the Problem of Snow Removal in the City of Rochester. Rochester, NY: n.p., 1917.

Rizzo, Michael F. *Through the Mayors' Eyes: Buffalo New York, 1832–2005*. New York: Lulu.com, 2009.

Roberts, Patrick S. *Disasters and the American State: How Politicians, Bureaucrats, and the Public Prepare for the Unexpected*. New York: Cambridge Univ. Press, 2013.

Rooney, John F., Jr. "The Urban Snow Hazard in the United States: An Appraisal of Disruption." *Geographical Review* 57, no. 4 (October 1967): 538–59.

Rosenthal, Donald B. "Bargaining Analysis in Intergovernmental Relations." *Publius: The Journal of Federalism* 10, no. 3 (Summer 1980): 5–44.

Rossant, John, and Stephen Baker. *Hop, Skip, Go: How the Mobility Revolution is Transforming Our Lives*. New York: Harper Business, 2019.

Rossi, Erno. *White Death: The Blizzard of '77*. N.p.: Seventy-Seven Publishing, 2006.

Russert, Tim. *Big Russ and Me: Father and Son; Lessons of Life*. New York: Miramax Books, 2004.

Salt Institute. *Salt Storage Handbook: Practical Recommendations for Storing and Handling Deicing Salt*. 1968, 1980, 1986, 1987, 1997, 2006, 2013.

———. *Snowfighter's Handbook: Safe and Sustainable Snowfighting*. 1967, 1977, 1991, 1999, 2007, 2013.

Sass, Herbert. *Stewart Manufacturers of Motor Trucks, 1912–1942*. Buffalo: Herbert Sass, 1987.

Scanlon, Joseph, and Brian Taylor. *Two Tales of Snowstorm: How the Blizzard of January 1977 Affected the Niagara Region*. Ottawa: Emergency Communications Research Unit, Carleton University, 1977.

Scholzman, Kay Lehman, and John Tierney. "More of the Same: Washington Pressure Group Activity in a Decade of Change." *Journal of Politics* 45, no. 2 (May 1983): 351–77.

Schrag, Zachary M. "'The Bus Is Young and Honest': Transportation Politics, Technical Choice, and the Motorization of Manhattan Surface Transit, 1919–1936." *Technology and Culture* 41, no. 1 (January 2000): 51–79.

Schulz, David. "Benefits of the Interstates Undeniable." *Public Works History* 91 (Fall 2006): 4.

Schwartz, Robert M., and Thomas W. Schmidlin. "Climatology of Blizzards in the Conterminous United States, 1959–2000." *Journal of Climate* 15, no. 13 (July 2002): 1765–72.

Seely, Bruce E. "The Interstate System: A Golden Anniversary." *Public Works History* 91 (Fall 2006): 2.

Seiler, Cotton. "The End of Automobility." *History and Technology* 26, no. 4 (December 2010): 389–91.

———. *Republic of Drivers: A Cultural History of Automobility in America*. Chicago: Univ. of Chicago Press, 2008.

Shafer, Byron E. *Quiet Revolution: Struggle for the Democratic Party and Shaping of Post-Reform*. New York: Russell Sage Foundation, 1983.

Shea, Eileen L. *A History of the NOAA: Being a Complication of Facts and Figures Regarding the Life and Times of the Original Whole Earth Agency*. Washington, DC: National Oceanic and Atmospheric Administration, 1987.

Sheller, Mimi, and John Urry. "The City and the Car." *International Journal of Urban and Regional Research* 24, no. 4 (December 2000): 737–57.

Shughart, William F. "Disaster Relief as Bad Public Policy." *The Independent Review* 15, no. 4 (2011): 529–31.

Smoak, Shelby. "Framing the Automobile in Twentieth-Century American Literature: A Spatial Approach." Unpublished PhD diss., Univ. of North Carolina, 2007.

Solnit, Rebecca. *A Paradise Built in Hell: The Extraordinary Communities That Arise in Disaster.* New York: Penguin Books, 2010.

Steinberg, Ted. *Acts of God: The Unnatural History of Natural Disasters in America.* 2nd ed. New York: Oxford Univ. Press, 2006.

Stratton, Ruth M. *Disaster Relief: The Politics of Intergovernmental Relations.* Lanham, MD: Univ. Press of America, 1988.

Subcommittee on Water Resources and the Environment of the Committee on Transportation and Infrastructure, House of Representatives. *H.R. 3348, The Snow Removal Policy Act of 1996.* Washington, DC: US Government Printing Office, 1997.

Sylves, Richard. *Disaster Policy and Politics: Emergency Management and Homeland Security.* 3rd ed. Washington, DC: CQ Press, 2020.

Taylor, Steven J. L. *Desegregation in Boston and Buffalo: The Influence of Local Leaders.* SUNY Series in African American Studies. Albany, NY: SUNY Press, 1998.

Olick, Jeffrey, Vered Vinitzky-Serous, and Daniel Levy, eds. *The Collective Memory Reader.* New York: Oxford Univ. Press, 2011.

Tomasky, Michael. *Bill Clinton.* The American Presidency Series: The 42nd President, 1993–2001. New York: Times Books, 2017.

Transportation Research Board. *Deicing Comparing Salt and Calcium Magnesium Acetate.* Washington, DC: National Research Council, 1991.

Trinkaus, John. "Television Station Weather Person's Winter Storm Predictions: An Informal Look." *Perceptual and Motor Skills* 79 (August 1994): 65–66.

Twigg, David K. *The Politics of Disaster: Tracking the Impact of Hurricane Andrew.* Gainesville: Univ. Press of Florida, 2012.

Urry, John. "Inhabiting the Car." Department of Sociology, Lancaster University, Lancaster LA1 4YN, UK, http://www.comp.lancs.ac.uk/sociology/papers/Urry-Inhabiting-the-Car.pdf.

US Army Corps of Engineers. *Operation Snow-Go: Post Storm Report Nine Counties in New York.* Buffalo, NY: US Army Corps of Engineers, 1977.

US House of Representatives Committee on Public Works and Transportation. *Federal Disaster Relief Programs: Hearings before the Subcommittee on Investigation and Review of the Committee on Public Works and Transportation, House of Representatives, April 1978.* Washington, DC: US Government Printing Office, 1978.

US Senate, Committee on Public Works. *Disaster Relief Act Amendment of 1974*. Washington, DC: US Government Printing Office, 1974.

US Senate, Committee on Environment and Public Works. *Disaster Relief Oversight: Hearings before the Subcommittee on Regional Community Development of the Committee on Environment and Public Works of the U.S. Senate, June 14 & 22, 1977*. Washington, DC: US Government Printing Office, 1977.

US Senate, Committee on Government Affairs. *Government Preparedness for Weather Emergencies for Winter 1977–1978: Hearings before the Subcommittee on Intergovernmental Relations of the Committee on Government Affairs United States Senate, September 19, 20, 21, October 15, November 2, 1977*. Washington, DC: US Government Printing Office, 1977.

US Senate, Committee on Environment and Public Works. *Federal Response to the Rhode Island Blizzard Emergency: Hearings before the Subcommittee on Regional and Community Development of the Committee on Environment and Public Works, March 7, 1978*. Washington, DC: US Government Printing Office, 1978.

Vanderbilt, Tom. *Traffic: Why We Drive the Way We Drive (and What We Can Do About It)*. New York: Alfred Knopf, 2008.

Vannini, Phillip, and Aaron M. Mccright. "Technologies of the Sky: A Socio-semiotic and Critical Analysis of Televised Weather Discourse." *Critical Discourse Studies* 4, no. 1 (2007): 49–74.

Wagner, A. James. "The Severe Winter of 1976–1977: Precursors and Precedents." *National Weather Digest* (November 1977): 12–18. http://nwafiles.nwas.org/digest/papers/1977/Vol02No4/1977v002no04-Wagner.pdf.

Wahlert, Matthew H. "President Jimmy Carter as a Reluctant Decision Maker." *White House Studies* 12, no. 1 (January 2012): 1–16.

Walker, Wallace Earl. "Elmer Staats and Strategic Leadership in the Legislative Branch." In Jameson W. Dog and Erwin C. Hargrove, eds., *Leadership and Innovation: A Biographical Perspective on Entrepreneurs in Government*. Baltimore: Johns Hopkins Univ. Press, 1987.

Ward, Janet. "'Snow Problem' Buffalo Knows How to Deal with Winter." *American City and County* (April 1999): 30.

Warner, Sam Bass. *Streetcar Suburbs: The Process of Growth in Boston, 1870–1900*. 2nd ed. Cambridge: Harvard Univ. Press, 1978.

Waugh, William L. *Living with Hazards, Dealing with Disasters: An Introduction to Emergency Management.* Armonk, NY: M. E. Sharpe, 2000.

Whipple, Chris. *The Gatekeepers: How the White House Chiefs of Staff Define Every Presidency.* New York: Crown, 2017.

Wickstrom, Becky. "History and Consequences of the Interstate." *Public Works History* 92 (Spring 2007): 3.

Winter, Jay, and Emmanuel Sivan. *War and Remembrance in the Twentieth Century.* New York: Oxford Univ. Press, 2000.

Worster, Donald. "Appendix: Doing Environmental History." In Donald Worster, ed., *The Ends of the Earth: Perspectives on Modern Environmental History.* New York: Cambridge Univ. Press, 1988.

Wyckoff, Peter H. "Some Problems and Objectives in Weather Modification." In Howard J. Taubenfeld, ed., *Controlling the Weather: A Study in Law and Regulatory Processes.* New York: Cambridge Univ. Press, 1970.

Yergin, Daniel. *The Prize: The Epic Quest for Oil, Money and Power.* New York: Free Press, 1991.

Zhorayev, Olzhas Zhumadillayevich. "The Influence of Political Factors on the Allocation of Disaster Relief Payments." Dissertation, Montana State Univ., 2008.

Index

Page numbers appearing in italics refer to illustrations.

Dr. Timothy W. Kneeland is professor of history and political science at Nazareth College in Rochester, New York. He is the author of *Pushbutton Psychiatry: A Cultural History of Electroshock in America* (2002; 2008), *Democrats and Republicans on Social Issues* (2016), *The Buffalo Blizzard of 1977* (2017), and *Playing Politics with Natural Disaster: Hurricane Agnes, the 1972 Election, and the Origins of FEMA* (2020). He has authored numerous chapter-length studies and encyclopedia articles on the history of science and medicine, American politics, and natural disasters. In addition to teaching and writing, Dr. Kneeland provides political analysis for local media in Upstate New York.

CPSIA information can be obtained
at www.ICGtesting.com
Printed in the USA
LVHW091804140421
684500LV00001B/8